BY MEANS OF THE URIM & THUMMIM

Restoring Translation to the Restoration

James W. Lucas
Jonathan E. Neville

By Means of the Urim & Thummim: Restoring Translation to the Restoration
Copyright © 2023 by James W. Lucas and Jonathan E. Neville
All rights reserved.
First Edition
2-25-23

This is a work of nonfiction. The authors have made every effort to be accurate and complete and welcomes comments, suggestions, and corrections, which can be emailed to **lostzarahemla@gmail.com**.

All opinions expressed in this work are the responsibility of the authors alone.
ISBN-13: 978-1-937735-43-2
ISBN-10: 1-937735-43-5

Published by Museum of the Book of Mormon Press
An imprint of Digital Legend Press & Publishing, Inc.
Salt Lake City UT

For permissions and/or to obtain copies visit www.digitalegend.com, email info@digitalegend.com or call 801-810-7718.

Front cover: "Study It Out" by William Rasoanaivo of Mauritius. The painting depicts the translation process. As Joseph turns the leaf of the plates, he is studying out in his mind the best way to express in English the meaning of the literal translation of the characters provided by the Urim and Thummim, which he will then dictate to Oliver Cowdery.

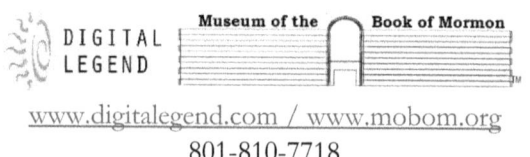

www.digitalegend.com / www.mobom.org
801-810-7718

Also, that there were **two stones in silver bows**—and these stones, fastened to a breastplate, constituted what is **called the Urim and Thummim—deposited with the plates**; and the possession and use of these stones were what constituted "seers" in ancient or former times; and that **God had prepared them for the purpose of translating the book.**

Joseph Smith-History 1:35

Question 4th. How, and where did you obtain the Book of Mormon?

Answer. **Moroni, the person who deposited the plates, from whence the Book of Mormon was translated,** in a hill in Manchester, Ontario County, New York, being dead, and raised again therefrom, appeared unto me and told me where they were and gave me directions how to obtain them. **I obtained them and the Urim and Thummim with them, by the means of which I translated the plates and thus came the Book of Mormon.**

Joseph Smith, 1835 (*Elders' Journal* I.3:42 ¶20–43 ¶1)

With the records was found a curious instrument which the ancients called "Urim and Thummim," which consisted of two transparent stones set in the rim of a bow fastened to a breastplate. **Through the medium of the Urim and Thummim I translated the record by the gift, and power of God.**

Joseph Smith 1842 (*Times and Seasons* III.9:707 ¶5–6)

TABLE OF CONTENTS

INTRODUCTION i
PREFACE: Losing the Urim and Thummim iii
1. Current Status of the Question 1
   A. Origins of the Translation Narrative 5
   B. Origins of the Composition Narrative 10
   C. Origins of Transcription and the SITH Narratives 12
   D. An Odd Configuration of Sides 21
   E. Evaluating the Three Approaches – the Language 24
   F. Evaluating the Three Approaches – the People 27
2. Transcription and the SITH Narrative 32
   A. The Stone-in-the-Hat (SITH) 32
   B. The "Last Testimony of Sister Emma" 38
   C. Edward Stevenson's report of Martin Harris in Utah 56
   D. David Whitmer - leading source for the SITH narrative 69
   E. Was the seer stone also called a Urim and Thummim? 77
   F. The Demonstration and Pop-Out Hypotheses 80
   G. Early Modern English 88
3. Assessing SITH 93
   A. The Shamanist Explanations 93
   B. Why not both the interpreters and the seer stone? 95
   C. Whither SITH? 98
   D. Applying Neutral Scholarly Criteria 102
   E. Summary – Issues Transcription Cannot Resolve 104
4. Composition 111
   A. Similarities As Evidence of Composition and Translation 114
   B. Translation More Persuasive Than Composition 118
   C. Are 19th Century Concepts Evidence? 130
   D. Summary – What Level of Proof? 140
5. Translation 142
   A. The Nature of the Book of Mormon 142
   B. The Nature of the Translation 144
   C. Of Seer Stones and Interpreters, Then and Now 152

D. Joseph Smith – Young Seeker to Prophet/Translator 159
6. How the Book of Mormon Was Translated – A Theory 176
   A. The Plates 177
   B. The Interpreters 178
   C. The Interpretation 187
   D. Verification 192
   E. Both Loose and Tight Control 194
   F. The Nature of the Book of Mormon's Translation 195
7. Why Does This Matter? 197
   A. Privileging the SITH accounts undermines
   Joseph Smith's credibility 199
   B. The Book of Mormon is quantitatively different
   than any other revelation 201
   C. The Book of Mormon is materially different
   than any other revelation 202
   D. The plates and interpreters ground the Book of Mormon
   in the real world. 203
   E. The Book of Mormon's physical and historical
   reality is central to its mission 205
   F. The Book of Mormon as fulfillment of
   Christian aspirations 207
REFERENCES CITED 209
Appendix A. Three Explanations for the Book of Mormon 235
Appendix B. Joseph and Oliver on the Translation (+ Lucy) 237
Appendix C. Translation and the Critics 259
INDEX 272

TABLES

Table 1 - the late war comparison 1 119
Table 2 - the late war comparison 2 120
Table 3 - intertextuality 121
Table 4 - Book of Mormon origin theories 236

INTRODUCTION

Thanks to modern technology, we are close to "the time ... when the knowledge of a Savior [has] spread throughout every nation, kindred, tongue, and people." (Mosiah 3:20) The Bible and the Book of Mormon, together, are teaching the world about the Savior.

Everyone knows the Bible was compiled from ancient manuscripts. People familiar with the Book of Mormon know that Joseph Smith, Jr., dictated the text to scribes (mainly Oliver Cowdery).

But that does not tell us where the Book of Mormon came from. People want to know, what was the *source* for the words Joseph dictated?

Joseph and Oliver claimed Joseph translated ancient plates given to him by Moroni, a resurrected ancient American prophet. Critics have long rejected Joseph's explanation that he translated the plates, but today, even believers do not agree where the text came from.

What did Joseph mean when he said he *translated* the text? Some believers think Joseph dictated an actual translation; i.e., using the Nephite interpreters which came with the plates, he rendered the characters on the plates into the English language he knew. Others think he dictated a revelation and did not even use the plates, except perhaps as a sort of talisman. They think the words were given to him supernaturally, either in vision or as a text appearing on a stone he found in a well.

Meanwhile, unbelievers think Joseph composed the text, either alone or with others. Maybe he performed the narrative, effectively ad-libbing from an outline. Or maybe he memorized it. Or maybe the words came from a supernatural force that was not divine.

Generally, all sceptics and the latter group of modern LDS scholars agree that, whatever he was doing, Joseph was looking at a stone in a hat rather than at the plates.

Supporters of each theory cite historical evidence, accompanied by their respective assumptions, inferences, and interpretations. However, we think previous efforts to assess the evidence have overlooked key factors.

In this short book, we analyze the various interpretations of the evidence. Then, we offer new approaches to the evidence, explore previously overlooked evidence and, drawing on modern translation scholarship and technology, propose a new model for the translation process which corroborates and supports what Joseph and Oliver said from the beginning. We think this model offers a refreshing new look, for both believers and sceptics, at the Book of Mormon.

These claims that the Book of Mormon was produced from very physical means - translated from ancient metal plates using even more ancient interpretation devices - set the Book apart from the many other spiritual writings given directly to the mind of their authors.

We hope that readers new to the Book of Mormon will find our book to be accessible, because it goes to the heart of this original and primary claim of Mormonism, a religious movement now almost two centuries old which has attained a worldwide reach. To this end, we have tried in the Preface and Chapter 1 to give a reader new to the subject enough background to follow the argument in this book as readily as will readers already familiar with the Book of Mormon.

NOTE on affiliation. Shortly after the publication of the Book of Mormon, Smith and his followers formed a new church, the Church of Christ. Numerous religious groups trace their origins to this church. Today by far the largest of these is the Church of Jesus Christ of Latter-day Saints with headquarters in Salt Lake City, Utah, in the United States. For convenience we will refer to this group as the "LDS Church." The authors are both adherents of this group.

PREFACE: Losing the Urim and Thummim

The Book of Mormon was dictated in the late 1820s by a young American in his early twenties named Joseph Smith, Jr. He dictated it to a number of scribes, the principal of whom was another young man named Oliver Cowdery. In 1830 it was published in the town of Palmyra in northwestern New York state with the financial support of an older man named Martin Harris, a prosperous local farmer who had also scribed for Smith in the early stages of the dictation.

Most of the book presents itself as a thousand-year history of a civilization founded by a group of Israelites who fled from Jerusalem circa 600 BCE. Mormon was a prophet, historian and soldier who lived at the end of the civilization, roughly circa 400 CE. He abridged ancient records to document the triumphs and tragedies of his people, including their visitation by a resurrected Jesus. Mormon's son Moroni deposited the plates, along with a special translation instrument, in a stone box he constructed on a hill in western New York. The hill, which Moroni called Cumorah, was not far from where Smith's family would settle in the early 1800s.

When asked, "How, and where did you obtain the book of Mormon?" Smith explained:

> Moroni, the person who deposited the plates, from whence the book of Mormon was translated, in a hill in Manchester, Ontario County, New York, being dead; and raised again therefrom, appeared unto me, and told me where they were, and gave me directions how to obtain them. I obtained them, and the Urim and Thummim with them, by the means of which, I translated the plates; and thus came the Book of Mormon.[1]

---

[1] Joseph Smith, Jr., *Elders' Journal* (Far West, MO: July 1838) at https://www.josephsmithpapers.org/paper-summary/elders-journal-july-1838/10.

In 1842, to provide "correct information," Smith reiterated his explanation that:

> With the records was found a curious instrument which the ancients called "Urim and Thummim," which consisted of two transparent stones set in the rim of a bow fastened to a breastplate. Through the medium of the Urim and Thummim I translated the record by the gift, and power of God.[2]

For over a century and a half, most believers accepted Smith's translation narrative. Concurrently, critics have challenged that narrative by pointing to 19th century language and concepts in the text as evidence of 19th century origins.

Recently, this debate has been complicated by LDS scholars who have agreed with critics in rejecting Smith's translation narrative in favor of historical sources who describe Smith dictating words that appeared on a stone he put in the bottom of a hat, or that he received some visionary experience while his face was buried in the hat with the stone in it. In either case, the plates and the Urim and Thummim interpreters played no role except possibly serving in some way as catalysts to Smith's inspiration (or imagination).

This "stone-in-the-hat" (SITH) narrative now dominates current scholarship on the Book of Mormon, both faithful and critical. A book on the "translation" of the Book of Mormon published by two professors at Brigham Young University (BYU) in February 2023, compares current models for the production of the Book of Mormon - but only those that accept the SITH narrative.[3] A survey article published at the end of 2021 in *BYU Studies* similarly took the SITH narrative for granted; the article did not even list as a possibility Smith's

---

[2] Joseph Smith, Jr., "Church History," *Times and Seasons* (1 March 1842) vol. 3, no. 9, quote at p. 707, available at https://www.josephsmithpapers.org/paper-summary/church-history-1-march-1842/2.

[3] Gerrit J. Dirkmaat and Michael Hubbard MacKay, *Let's Talk About the Translation of the Book of Mormon* (Salt Lake City, UT: Deseret Book, 2023), pp. 62-102.

claim that he translated from the plates using the Urim and Thummim interpreters.[4] And a 2022 book by another set of BYU professors purporting to be a survey of current literature on the Book of Mormon does not contain a single mention of the Urim and Thummim.[5]

Thus, the stone box in the Hill Cumorah might as well have been empty for all the significance modern LDS scholarship accords to its contents in the production of the Book of Mormon we have today.[6]

Critics have claimed victory, arguing that Smith's original translation narrative has been shown to be false and that the LDS Church "hid the truth" about the Book of Mormon's origins.

In this book, we attempt to unravel these competing narratives. Chapter 1 overviews these narratives: translation, composition and transcription, and their origins and sources. It then describes research into the 19th century sources of the language of the English version of the Book of Mormon, which supports Joseph's claim as translator. It concludes by discussing how to approach evaluating evidence from historical sources.

Chapter 2 analyzes the stone-in-the-hat (SITH) transcription sources and arguments, and finds them, however well-intentioned, to be vague, inconsistent and unreliable. Some appear to be coordinated hearsay, intended to refute the then-predominant secular explanation that Smith dictated from a modified manuscript originally written by

---

[4] Grant Hardy, "The Book of Mormon Translation Process," *BYU Studies* (2021) Vol 60, no. 3 (2021), pp. 203 – 211.

[5] Daniel Becerra, Amy Easton-Flake, Nicholas J. Frederick and Joseph M. Spencer, *Book of Mormon Studies: An Introduction and Guide* by (Provo, UT: Brigham Young University Religious Studies Center and Salt Lake City, UT: Deseret Book, 2022).

[6] As will be discussed in this book, the sources for this SITH narrative are often contradictory. Some do say that the initial translation used the Urim and Thummim. However, as all of those pages were lost by Martin Harris, the models still assume the use of the stone in the hat for the Book of Mormon that was finally published in 1830, and which is accepted by millions of followers of the Restoration as the Word of God.

Solomon Spalding. We propose that the SITH accounts originated from one or more instances when Smith used the stone in the hat as a demonstration to allay his followers' curiosity (because he was forbidden to expose the plates and interpreters).

Chapter 3 reviews variations on the SITH narrative from believing scholars which remove the Book of Mormon even further from the ancient sources it claims. We then discuss where all the various SITH narratives take us and leave us, and summarize the issues which transcription explanations fail to resolve.

In Chapter 4 we examine the 19th century language and other influences in the Book of Mormon which are used to argue that the Book of Mormon is a product of Smith's imagination. We argue that this evidence actually corroborates Smith's claim of being an actively engaged translator, contrary to claims he either (i) composed the text or (ii) simply transcribed an English text previously produced by an unknown supernatural source.

In Chapter 5 we analyze the implications of Smith as an actively engaged translator. Drawing upon modern translation technology and scholarship (particularly the work of the dean of modern Bible translation, Eugene Nida), we analyze the nature of translation as it would apply to the Book of Mormon, addressing such issues as 19th century language, the Book's use of the King James Bible, and what light current science and technology can shed on the Urim and Thummim interpreters. We challenge the traditional understanding of Smith as an ignorant "blank slate," arguing instead that, beginning with his long childhood convalescence from major surgery on his leg, Smith became a religious seeker and acquired an "intimate acquaintance" with Christian authors as well as with the Bible, well qualified to undertake the task of rendering the meanings of the text on the plates into language and concepts accessible to Smith's contemporaries.[7]

---

[7] Joseph Smith Jr., *History circa Summer 1832*, quote at p. 2, at https://www.josephsmithpapers.org/paper-summary/history-circa-summer-1832/1

Based on our book's analysis, in Chapter 6 we then propose a new model of the translation process that both (i) explains why the Book of Mormon text is the way we have it and (ii) corroborates Smith's claim that he translated (as that term is commonly understood) the Book of Mormon from the plates using the interpreters with specified divine assistance.

Finally, in Chapter 7, we argue that the SITH transcription narrative, by contradicting Joseph's own explanations, undermines the authenticity of the Book of Mormon—a book whose message is critical to the modern world.

We acknowledge the invaluable assistance of the staffs and facilities of the New York Public Library and Brigham Young University and of the historical libraries and collections of the Community of Christ and the Church of Jesus Christ of Latter-day Saints. We also thank Susan Easton Black, Richard Bushman and Richard Rust, who reviewed various parts of our manuscript. However, all views expressed here are our sole responsibility.

We propose this addition to the existing spectrum of working hypotheses because we think it best reconciles the available evidence, recognizing that rational, informed people can reach different conclusions based on the same evidence. We hope that our arguments here will be understood as efforts to increase everyone's understanding of where the Book of Mormon comes from.

1. Current Status of the Question

He [Count Tolstoy] asked me about the Mormons, some of whose books had interested him. He thought two-thirds of their religion deception, but said that on the whole he preferred a religion which professed to have dug its sacred books out of the earth to one which pretended that they were let down from heaven.

Andrew D. White, quoting Count Leo Tolstoy[8]

Two hundred years after Moroni's first visit to Joseph Smith on the autumn equinox of 1823, questions about the origins of the Book of Mormon persist. If it is a solely human invention, how did an ill-educated young farmer come up with a book of more than 500 pages with a complex and intricate thousand-year secular and religious history? If one accepts that there is something other-worldly about its origins, by what process was it generated?

Joseph Smith gave an account of gold plates and a strange translation instrument called "interpreters" (also referred to as "spectacles" or the "Urim and Thummim") deposited with the plates in a stone box by the ancient American warrior/prophet Moroni centuries before Joseph's time. Joseph and his primary scribe, Oliver Cowdery, claimed that the Book of Mormon was a translation of engravings on these gold plates, accomplished with the assistance of this translation instrument and by the gift and power of God.

Until recently, leaders of the Church of Jesus Christ of Latter-day Saints reiterated what Joseph Smith and Oliver Cowdery claimed. The

---

[8] Andrew D. White, "Walks and Talks with Tolstoy," *McClure's Magazine*, volume 16 (April 1901), p. 511 (available at https://babel.hathitrust.org/cgi/pt?id=uc1.b000540672&view=1up&seq=535&skin=2021) and *Autobiography* (New York: The Century Co., 1905), Volume II, p. 87.

1

Church of Jesus Christ of Latter-day Saints (herein referred to as the LDS Church to distinguish it from other churches that accept the Book of Mormon) has canonized this account as scripture in Joseph Smith – History in the Pearl of Great Price, one of the four Standard Works of the LDS Church, considered to be as authoritative as the Bible, Book of Mormon and Doctrine and Covenants.

Soon after the book was published, critics claimed Joseph or someone else composed it. For the rest of the 19th century, the predominant explanation among nonbelievers for the Book of Mormon was the Spalding theory—the claim that Joseph dictated the text from a manuscript written by Solomon Spalding and edited by Sidney Rigdon and/or others.

Lately, Joseph's translation narrative has also been challenged by a revived transcription narrative which originally received wide distribution in 1834 in the first major anti-LDS book, *Mormonism Unvailed*.[9] Based on statements by David Whitmer, Emma Smith, and others, the transcription narrative has Joseph dictating words that appeared, supernaturally, on a seer stone he put into a hat while the plates remained covered by a cloth, either nearby or at some distance.

Critics of the Restoration use the stone-in-the-hat challenge to Joseph Smith's account of the origins of the Book of Mormon to argue that the LDS Church has "lied" about its origins, undermining confidence in the Book's historical authenticity.[10] While there will

---

[9] Eber B. Howe, *Mormonism Unvailed, or, A Faithful Account of That Singular Imposition and Delusion, From its Rise to the Present Time* (Painesville: Printed and published by the author, 1834), available at https://archive.org/details/mormonismunvaile00howe

[10] Although precise statistics are hard to come by, podcaster John Dehlin claims that tens of thousands have left the LDS Church because of doubts about Church history and the Book of Mormon. For example, in 2007 Dehlin interviewed historian Richard Bushman. In a brief segment of the two-hour long interview, Bushman discussed some of the sources which suggest a different narrative for the process of the Book of Mormon's production Dehlin refers to that interview as one of his "Top

always be a core of believers whose spiritual witness of the Book of Mormon is so strong that these questions do not affect them, those within the LDS faith community who have questions, and those not of the LDS faith community who are or may become sincerely interested, deserve plausible explanations that corroborate the traditional teachings.

Alternative explanations for the Book of Mormon persist because there is no indisputable evidence. The plates and the "interpreters" instrument are not available for examination. Believers say they were returned to the divine messengers who delivered them. Nonbelievers say they never existed.[11]

One possible evidence of authenticity—the geographical setting—remains inconclusive. There has been no definitive identification of any geographical location connected with the Book of Mormon other than the Hill Cumorah near Palmyra, New York, where Joseph found the plates and related objects. Early Church leaders identified the site as the Cumorah of Mormon 6:6. Believers disagree among themselves about the reliability of that identification.[12]

25" interviews. https://www.mormonstories.org/episodes/top-25-most-important-episodes/. A review of 956 of Dehlin's podcasts found that Bushman or his book were referred to by Dehlin in 18% of those podcasts (based on private research, copies in possession of the authors). Dehlin argues that the LDS Church has lied about the origins of the Book of Mormon, citing the *Ensign* and the Gospel Topics Essays among other sources. See https://www.mormonstories.org/truth-claims/the-books/the-book-of-mormon/book-of-mormon-authorship-translation-timeline/.

[11] A comprehensive survey of descriptions of the translation instruments is Craig James Ostler, "Book of Mormon Translation Instrument Descriptions: Interpreters, Urim & Thummim and Seer Stones," (April 2020) available at https://www.bookofmormonevidence.org/streaming/videos/bom/dr-craig-j-ostler-book-of-mormon-translation-instrument-descriptions-interpreters-urim-thummim-and-seer-stones/.

[12] The primary historical source for the New York Cumorah is Oliver Cowdery's Letter VII, which Joseph had copied into his own history. See http://

Richard Bushman commented on the current framing of the issues regarding the production of the Book of Mormon.

> Modern Mormons read the Book of Mormon well aware of how critics think of the book... Perhaps the surest evidence of this condition is the frequently heard comment from educated Mormons that Joseph Smith could not have written the Book of Mormon. The affirmation implies that readers are constantly asking themselves: Did Joseph Smith write the book himself? The question is inescapable. Thus it is that modern readers go through the text thinking with two minds: the religious teachings of the prophets are processed with one mind, and the question about Joseph Smith's authorship is entertained in another.... Some [passages] may look very much like an insertion by the nineteenth-century Joseph.[13]

To compound questions about authorship, believing readers are now vexed with conflicting information about how it was produced – translated from the plates, or transcribed from the stone? Explanations of the origin of the Book of Mormon fall within one or more of three approaches: translation, composition and transcription. We will review the origins of these explanations in chronological order.

---

www.josephsmithpapers.org/paper-summary/history-1834-1836/90. Most LDS scholars have adopted the Mesoamerican/two-Cumorahs theory originally laid out by RLDS scholar L.E. Hills in 1917. See David Palmer, *In Search of Cumorah: New Evidences for the Book of Mormon from Ancient Mexico* (Bountiful, UT: Horizon Publishers, 1981, 2005) and John L. Sorenson, *Mormon's Codex: An Ancient American Book* (Salt Lake City, UT: Deseret Book, 2013). Neville offers a defense of the New York Cumorah in *Between These Hills: A Case for the New York Cumorah* (Salt Lake City, UT: Digital Legend, 2021).

[13] Richard Lyman Bushman, "Reading From the Gold Plates," in Blair G. Van Dyke, Brian D. Birch and Boyd J. Petersen (eds) *The Expanded Canon: Perspectives on Mormonism & Sacred Texts* (Salt Lake City, UT: Greg Kofford Books, 2018), p. 86.

A. Origins of the Translation Narrative

We start with the explanation given by Joseph Smith. Joseph used the word *translate* to describe his interface with the Book of Mormon. In the Preface to the first (1830) edition, Joseph wrote "I would inform you that I translated, by the gift and power of God, and caused to be written" the 116 pages that Martin Harris lost, and that rather than retranslate that part of the record, the Lord told him "thou shalt translate from the plates of Nephi … until ye come to that which ye have translated, which ye have retained."[14] Although the 1830 edition listed Joseph Smith, Junior, as "Author and Proprietor," (which was required even for translations to secure copyright) beginning with the 1837 edition, the Title Page reads "translated by Joseph Smith, Jun."

The term *translation* was well understood in Joseph's day as a process of interpreting one language and rendering it in another. The title page of every King James Bible declares it was "Translated out of the Original Tongues." Translation was a common experience, especially on the frontiers where local Native American tribes still spoke their native tongues, and in the northeastern United States (including New York) where Americans interacted with French Canadians.

Oliver Cowdery explained the process to Native Americans telling them that the record "was written in the language of the forefathers of the [Native Americans]; therefore this young man, being a pale face, could not understand it; but the angel told him and showed him, and gave him knowledge of the language, and how to interpret the Book. So he interpreted it into the language of the pale faces."[15]

---

[14] Doctrine and Covenants 10:41. The copyright page designates Joseph Smith as "Author and Proprietor," a term required by copyright law even for translated works.

[15] Parley P. Pratt, *The Autobiography of Parley Parker Pratt* (Chicago, IL: Law, King & Law, 1888), quote at p. 59, available at https://archive.org/details/autobiographyofp00prat/page/58/mode/2up

Webster's 1828 American Dictionary of the English Language defined translation this way:

> ... to render into another language; to express the sense of one language in the words of another. The Old Testament was translated into the Greek language more than two hundred years before Christ. The Scriptures are now translated into most of the languages of Europe and Asia.[16]

Some object to understanding Joseph as a traditional translator because they assume (i) that his own unlearned English lexicon could not produce such a text even in translation, and (ii) that he could not have known the source language (Nephite). (Hence the need for the "interpreters" instrument.)

Unlike the transcription and composition narratives, the translation narrative follows Joseph's official accounts. Moroni told Joseph it was his privilege "to obtain and translate the same by the means of the Urim and Thummim, which were deposited for that purpose with the record."[17] (In this book we will generally use the original Book of Mormon term "interpreters" to avoid confusion due to recent obfuscation of the term "Urim and Thummim."[18])

---

[16] http://webstersdictionary1828.com/Dictionary/ translate

[17] Oliver Cowdery, Letter IV, https://www.josephsmithpapers.org/paper-summary/history-1834-1836/69.

[18] Some historians who promote the "stone-in-the-hat" account over the canonical account argue that the term "Urim and Thummim" was also applied to the seer stone. See https://www.churchofjesuschrist.org/study/manual/gospel-topics-essays/book-of-mormon-translation?lang=eng. Michael Hubbard MacKay and Gerrit J. Dirkmaat, *From Darkness unto Light: Joseph Smith's Translation and Publication of the Book of Mormon* (Salt Lake City, UT: Deseret Book Company and Provo, UT: Brigham Young University Religious Studies Center, 2015), pp. 63 – 64, 129, and Gerrit J. Dirkmaat and Michael Hubbard MacKay, *Let's Talk About the Translation of the Book of Mormon* (Salt Lake City, UT: Deseret Book, 2023), pp. 81-84. However, there are only a few late ambiguous references from years after the conclusion of the

Current Status of the Question

In 1842 the *Times and Seasons* published a narrative of Joseph's early experiences with the beginnings of the Restoration, which was canonized with the rest of the Pearl of Great Price in 1880. Here Joseph describes the origins of the Book of Mormon.[19]

> **33** He called me by name and said unto me that he was a messenger sent from the presence of God to me, and that his name was Moroni; that God had a work for me to do; and that my name should be had for good and evil among all nations, kindreds, and tongues, or that it should be both good and evil spoken of among all people.
>
> **34** He said there was a book deposited, written upon gold plates, giving an account of the former inhabitants of this continent, and the source from whence they sprang. He also said that the fulness of the everlasting Gospel was contained in it, as delivered by the Savior to the ancient inhabitants;
>
> **35** Also, that there were two stones in silver bows—and these stones, fastened to a breastplate, constituted what is called the Urim and Thummim — deposited with the plates; and the possession and use of these stones were what constituted "seers" in ancient or former times; and that God had prepared them for the purpose of translating the book. ...
>
> **42** Again, he told me, that when I got those plates of which he had spoken—for the time that they should be obtained was not yet fulfilled—I should not show them to any person; neither the breastplate with the Urim and Thummim; only to those to whom I should be commanded to show them; if I did I should be destroyed. While he was conversing with me about the plates, the vision was

---

translation. As will be discussed in Chapter 2(E), most witnesses, including those cited to support the SITH narrative such as David Whitmer and Emma Smith, always clearly distinguished between the two items.

[19] From Joseph Smith—History in the 1981 LDS edition of the Pearl of Great Price, adapted from "History of Joseph Smith," *Times and Seasons*, 15 April 1842, https://www.josephsmithpapers.org/paper-summary/times-and-seasons-15-april-1842/3.

opened to my mind that I could see the place where the plates were deposited, and that so clearly and distinctly that I knew the place again when I visited it.

Before dictating any translation, Joseph copied characters off the plates and translated them "by means of the Urim and Thummim."

62 By this timely aid was I enabled to reach the place of my destination in Pennsylvania; and immediately after my arrival there I commenced copying the characters off the plates. I copied a considerable number of them, and by means of the Urim and Thummim I translated some of them, which I did between the time I arrived at the house of my wife's father, in the month of December, and the February following.

In some way this instrument provided Joseph with the basic meaning of the Nephite engravings which he then rendered into English words, phrases and concepts comprehensible to him and his contemporaries, just as would any translator. (In Chapters 5 and 6 we will discuss how these may have functioned for Joseph.) The key point here: Joseph interacted with the characters on the plates. He did not merely read words that appeared supernaturally on the instrument.

In 1834, Oliver Cowdery published an account of his experiences in the *Messenger and Advocate*.[20] Joseph's scribes copied Oliver's account into Joseph's *History 1834-1835* as part of his life story.[21] It was reprinted multiple times with Joseph's permission or at his direction.[22]

---

[20] *Latter Day Saints' Messenger and Advocate*, Vol. 1, No. 1, October 1834, available at https://contentdm.lib.byu.edu/digital/collection/NCMP1820-1846/id/7160

[21] Joseph Smith, Jr., *History 1834 – 1836*, p. 86, at http://www.josephsmithpapers.org/paper-summary/history-1834-1836/90

[22] See the *Gospel Reflector*, https://archive.org/details/GospelReflector1841/page/n161 ; *The Millennial Star*, Oct. 1840, p. 152 https://contentdm.lib.byu.edu/digital/collection/MStar/id/70,; the *Times and Seasons*, May 1, 1841, p. 377 http://www.latterdaytruth.org/pdf/100147.pdf; a special pamphlet published in Liverpool

Current Status of the Question

This account is excerpted in the note to Joseph Smith – History 1:71 in the current LDS edition of the Pearl of Great Price. There Oliver recounts that:

> These were days never to be forgotten—to sit under the sound of a voice dictated by the inspiration of heaven, awakened the utmost gratitude of this bosom! Day after day I continued, uninterrupted, to write from his mouth, as he translated with the Urim and Thummim, or, as the Nephites would have said, Interpreters,' the history or record called 'The Book of Mormon.'[23]

History 1834-1835 relates another account Joseph gave, this time on November 9, 1835, during a discussion with a visitor.

> He [Moroni] also informed me that the Urim & Thummim was hid up with the record, and that God would give me power to translate it with the assistance of this instrument; he then gradually vanished out of my sight or the vision closed.[24]

Joseph Smith and Oliver Cowdery were the principal participants in producing the Book of Mormon as published in 1830. They repeatedly testified about the translation with the interpreters, and never once referred to the use of a stone in a hat or any other method of translation to understand what was written on the gold plates.

Apart from explaining that he copied and translated the characters before dictating any translation, Joseph did not leave a detailed description of the translation process. However, other contemporary revelations provide additional critical insight into the process.

---

in early 1844, https://archive.org/details/lettersbyoliverc00oliv ; and *The Prophet*, Jun 29, 1844, https://catalog.churchofjesuschrist.org/assets/b6ca5a6b-374b-4fbc-ad25-c66b91e43820/0/2

[23] Oliver Cowdery, *Messenger and Advocate*, vol. 1 (October 1834), p. 14, available at https://archive.bookofmormoncentral.org/content/dear-brother-letter-i.

[24] Joseph Smith, Jr., *History 1834 – 1836*, p. 121, available at https://www.josephsmithpapers.org/paper-summary/history-1834-1836/125

Although Oliver had been authorized to also translate (Doctrine and Covenants 6:25), his efforts were unsuccessful. The Lord explained in what is now Doctrine and Covenants Section 9 that:

> **7** Behold, you have not understood; you have supposed that I would give it unto you, when you took no thought save it was to ask me.
>
> **8** But, behold, I say unto you, that you must study it out in your mind; then you must ask me if it be right, and if it is right I will cause that your bosom shall burn within you; therefore, you shall feel that it is right.

Although now fittingly used as general advice on receiving personal revelation on all matters, this revelation originally explained how the process of translation using the interpreters was to work. The process entailed some form of intellectual effort by the translator to first "study it out in [his] mind." Our suggested description of the translation process in Chapter 6 will examine what this intellectual effort may have consisted of.

B. Origins of the Composition Narrative

The idea that Joseph and/or others composed the text encompasses the traditional secular explanations of the Book of Mormon's origins, which began to appear soon after its first publication. If it was not written by God or ancient Americans, it had to come from some human source in upstate New York in the 1820s.

As initially set forth in the 1834 book *Mormonism Unvailed*, the widely accepted explanation among unbelievers held that the Book of Mormon was based on a historical romance written by a man named Solomon Spalding (1761-1816), which was subsequently acquired by Sidney Rigdon, who then "Christianized" the text and secretly delivered it to Joseph Smith.

Current Status of the Question

This theory, which depended on Joseph dictating from behind a screen, curtain or "vail," fell out of favor after a manuscript by Spalding was discovered in Hawaii in 1884 and turned out to be unrelated to the Book of Mormon.[25] The Spalding theory further diminished in acceptance when Fawn Brodie denounced it in her best-selling 1945 psycho-biography of Joseph, *No Man Knows My History*.[26]

Although some continue to advocate the Spalding theory, the evidence they cite is speculative. Today most composition explanations follow Brodie in arguing that Joseph was brighter than he may have seemed at first glance, and invented the Book of Mormon story himself.

Versions of this approach in recent years have argued that Joseph's composing efforts were supplemented by his acquaintance with any one or more of a number of books available in his locale at the time the Book of Mormon was produced.

Composition advocates have pointed to books such as *The Late War* and *View of the Hebrews* as major influences on the Book of Mormon, albeit not so directly plagiarized as was supposedly the case with Spalding's book. They argue that Joseph had access to hundreds[27] or thousands[28] of books in the vicinity of his home.

---

[25] Supporters of the Spalding theory point out that witnesses denied the Hawaii manuscript was the one they had been familiar with. See Wayne L. Cowdrey, Howard A. Davis and Arthur Vanick, "'Manuscript Found' and the Moroni Myth: The Importance of Being Honest, A Reply to the Matthew Roper-BYU/FARMS review of 'Who Really Wrote The Book of Mormon?—The Spalding Enigma'," pp. 26-33 available at https://www.whatismormonism.com/SPALDING_ENIGMA_ROPER_REBUTTAL.pdf.

[26] Fawn McKay Brodie, *No Man Knows My History: The Life of Joseph Smith the Mormon Prophet* (New York: Alfred A. Knopf, 1945), pp. 419-433.

[27] Noel A. Carmack discusses floating bookstores on the Erie canal and the Palmyra bookstore and print shop. Noel A. Carmack "Joseph Smith, Captain Kidd Lore, and Treasure-Seeking," *Dialogue: A Journal of Mormon Thought*, Vol. 46, no. 3 (Fall 2013), p. 108, available at https://www.dialoguejournal.com/wp-content/uploads/sbi/articles/Dialogue_V46N03_412b.pdf

[28] D. Michael Quinn, *Early Mormonism and The Magic World View* (Salt Lake City, UT: Signature Books, 1998, 2nd edition), p. 179.

The composition theory includes such variations as plagiarism, collaboration, mental illness, genius, and "automatic writing." [29] Another recent variation of composition is the proposal by William L. Davis that Joseph used a method "of oral composition that involved the use of private notes and the semi-extemporaneous amplification of skeletal narrative outlines."[30]

C. Origins of Transcription and the SITH Narratives

In contrast to the translation and composition narratives, transcription narratives argue that Joseph Smith had minimal or no intellectual input into the production of the Book of Mormon. Instead, he read the English text as it appeared to him essentially word-for-word, supernaturally, on a stone he placed in a hat. Alternatively, he dictated words he received through direct inspiration from God without referring to any kind of physical object, whether the plates, the interpreters, or the stone. In this view, Joseph and his scribes were simply a team of transcribers of an English text produced by some other source. Joseph's only contribution was to access and verbalize this supernaturally predetermined text so his scribe could write it down.

Most transcription explanations look to accounts of Joseph dictating the text not from the plates but rather by looking at a seer stone at the bottom of a hat (for brevity hereinafter referred to as SITH, for *stone-in-the-hat*). This SITH narrative is based on many sources, and these sources are not fabrications. Indeed, the earliest newspaper reports of the Book of Mormon refer to Joseph putting the "spectacles"

---

[29] Brian C. Hales, "Automatic Writing and the Book of Mormon: An Update," *Dialogue*, Vol. 52, No. 2, (Summer 2019), available at https://www.dialoguejournal.com/wp-content/uploads/sbi/articles/Dialogue_V52N02_1.pdf.

[30] William L. Davis, *Visions in a Seer Stone: Joseph Smith and the Making of the Book of Mormon* (Chapel Hill, NC: University of North Carolina Press, 2020), p. 184.

into a hat to produce his "gold bible."[31]

By 1834 when the first anti-Mormon book, E. B. Howe's *Mormonism Unvailed*, was published, the SITH and the canonical translation narratives were both well known.[32] It was also clear that they were contradictory alternatives, and Howe accurately presented them as such.

Figures such as Martin Harris, Emma Smith, and David Whitmer are cited as sources of SITH accounts. These will be considered in detail in Chapter 2. However, before delving into the depths of the historical record, many readers may have a preliminary question – what's up with "seer stones" in the first place?

To understand this, we must understand something of the world in which Joseph Smith, his family and neighbors lived. While that world was deeply Christian and also affected by Enlightenment rationalism, it still retained a strong bond to older folk beliefs and practices. Nearly two centuries later we still remember these traditions.

---

[31] These early references mentioned "spectacles" in the hat instead of a "stone," which suggests the accounts were based on hearsay instead of eyewitnesses because "spectacles" was a term used to describe the Nephite interpreters (the Urim and Thummim), but no one was allowed to see the interpreters until after the translation was complete. See Note 1 to Joseph Smith, Jr., "Letter to Oliver Cowdery," (October 22, 1829), available at https://www.josephsmithpapers.org/paper-summary/letter-to-oliver-cowdery-22-october-1829/1 as well as *Palmyra Freeman* available at https://contentdm.lib.byu.edu/digital/collection/BOMP/id/4381 and "Golden Bible," *The Gem: A Semi-Monthly Literary and Miscellaneous Journal* (Rochester, NY: 5 Sept. 1829), p. 70, available at https://contentdm.lib.byu.edu/digital/collection/BOMP/id/161. Note though that almost all early accounts speak of two stones and/or the spectacles rather than a single stone, which describes the interpreters rather than the lone seer stone. See Craig Ostler, "Book of Mormon Translation Instrument Descriptions" and MaryAnn Clements, "Before the Urim & Thummim: Pre-1833 Newspaper Accounts of the Book of Mormon Translation," (January 26, 2023) available at https://wheatandtares.org/2023/01/26/before-the-urim-thummim-pre-1833-newspaper-accounts-of-book-of-mormon-translation/.

[32] Howe, *Mormonism Unvailed*. See specifically p. 18, available at https://play.google.com/books/reader?id=KXJNAAAAYAAJ&printsec=frontcover&pg=GBS.PA18.

And if anyone doubts their enormous and enduring appeal in our times, we would simply ask if you have ever heard of a boy named Harry Potter.

Like many in his time and place, the young Joseph Smith had a stone (which he found while digging a well) which he believed would help him see things beyond normal sight. The stone, which is now in the LDS Church's archives, is oval-shaped, very smooth and striated with light and brown streaks, leading witnesses to describe it as chocolate-colored.[33] In Joseph's locale such stones were especially popular for seeking buried treasure, and Joseph was employed in such endeavors (see Joseph Smith—History 1:56).

For Joseph the stone was a sort of "lucky charm" or, in more recent parlance, a "pet rock," and he often carried it about with him until eventually giving it to Oliver Cowdery. This was the stone which the SITH witnesses claimed to have seen Joseph use to translate without the plates or interpreters. We will address these claims in Chapter 2.

The important point here is that having such a stone was not unusual in Joseph's social environment.[34] What is unusual is what was to become of the story of the stone.

Almost all of the SITH accounts came from people who either broke with Joseph during his lifetime, or did not follow the LDS Church's westward emigration under Brigham Young. As noted earlier, the LDS Church adhered to Joseph's translation narrative, which it made a part of its canon (Standard Works) in 1880 with the rest of the

---

[33] Photographs of the stone can be seen here: https://www.churchofjesuschrist.org/church/news/book-of-mormon-printers-manuscript-photos-of-seer-stone-featured-in-new-book?lang=eng

[34] Alan Taylor, "The Early Republic's Supernatural Economy: Treasure Seeking in the American Northeast, 1780-1830," *American Quarterly*, Vol. 38, No. 1 (Spring 1986), pp. 6-34 available at http://inside.sfuhs.org/dept/history/US_History_reader/Chapter3/The%20Early%20Republics%20Supernatural%20Economy%20Treasure%20Seeking%20in%20the%20American%20Northeast,%201780%201830.pdf

Current Status of the Question

Pearl of Great Price. While the SITH accounts were noted in LDS Church histories, they were not given preferential placement, and it is likely that most LDS Church members were unfamiliar with them.³⁵ Instead most Church histories and artwork emphasized the canonical translation account found in the Pearl of Great Price.³⁶

This was to change in the latter part of the 20th century. The LDS Church began an effort to explore its history more thoroughly, led by faithful professional historians such as Leonard Arrington, and more

---

³⁵ Compare for example the approaches in the writings of B. H. Roberts and Joseph Fielding Smith. As we will discuss further below, David Whitmer stated the translation of the Book of Mormon after Martin Harris lost the first pages was carried out entirely with the seer stone and Oliver Cowdery said that it was done using the interpreters. B. H. Roberts dodged this fundamental conflict and reported both accounts as compatible. We will get into the specifics in the next chapter, but the point for now is that Roberts did provide the most common SITH accounts. See B. H. Roberts, *Defense of the Faith and the Saints* (Salt Lake City, UT: Deseret News, 1907) volume 1, pp. 255 – 262, available starting at http://www.solomonspalding.com/docs2/1907RobA.htm#p255a. Joseph Fielding Smith acknowledged the existence of the SITH accounts (without detailing them), but dismissed them as hearsay because he could not see why the Lord would have prepared the interpreters and preserved them since the time of the Jaredites only to have Joseph replace them with "something evidently inferior under these circumstances. It may have been so, but it is so easy for a story of this kind to be circulated due to the fact that the Prophet did possess a seer stone, which he may have used for some other purposes." Joseph Fielding Smith, *Doctrines of Salvation* (Bruce R. McConkie compiler, Salt Lake City, UT: Bookcraft, 1956), volume 3, p. 226 available at https://archive.org/details/Doctrines-of-Salvation-volume-3-joseph-fielding-smith/page/n133/mode/2up.

³⁶ A sample of these traditional depictions of the translation can be seen in the discussion of the CES Letter in Appendix C. Like the author of the CES Letter, Gerrit Dirkmaat and Michael MacKay, two of the leading SITH advocates, blame this traditional LDS artwork for depriving Latter-day Saints of knowledge of the SITH narrative (*Let's Talk About the Translation* at p. 80-81). Neither CES Letter author Jeremy Runnels nor Dirkmaat and MacKay acknowledge that traditional LDS artists were only following Joseph and Oliver's authoritative translation accounts, even though they typically avoided depicting the interpreters (as Dirkmaat and MacKay note).

recently Richard Bushman.[37] This was fortunate, or even inspired, for soon little-known facts about church history which had previously only been accessible on dusty library shelves or anti-Mormon books (where they were inevitably presented in the most negative way possible) would be broadcast across the internet.

Unfortunately, this renewed interest in Church history was soon exploited by a con man named Mark Hofmann. Acting under the guise of being a faithful LDS document collector, he was actually an apostate who skillfully forged documents designed to embarrass and undermine the LDS Church. One of his most notorious jobs was known as the "salamander letter," in which the angel Moroni was portrayed as a magical salamander and the discovery of the Book of Mormon as immersed in white magic practices.

This excited huge interest in the folk magic beliefs of the social environment of the early Latter-day Saints. Hofmann operated successfully throughout the mid-1980s until his murder of two people in an attempt to cover his crimes exposed his forgery career.[38]

---

[37] An excellent collection of essays by Arrington describing these developments and his own historical research is Leonard J. Arrington, *Reflections of a Mormon Historian: Leonard J. Arrington on the New Mormon History*, Reid L. Neilson and Ronald W. Walker (eds) (Norman, OK: The Arthur H. Clark Company, 2006).

[38] The connection between Hofmann and the increasing interest in folk magic and early Mormonism which lead in turn to the rise of the SITH narrative is made by SITH proponents Brant Gardner in *The Gift and Power: Translating the Book of Mormon* (Salt Lake City, UT: Greg Kofford Books, 2011), pp. 11 – 15 and Roger Nicholson in "The Spectacles, the Stone, the Hat, and the Book: A Twenty-first Century Believer's View of the Book of Mormon Translation" in *Interpreter: A Journal of Latter-day Saint Faith and Scholarship* 5 (2013), pp. 181-182 available at https://journal.interpreterfoundation.org/the-spectacles-the-stone-the-hat-and-the-book-a-twenty-first-century-believers-view-of-the-book-of-mormon-translation/#rf30-2896. The Hofmann story has resulted in many books and media presentations. A recently updated and considered work which best explores the story's religious aspects is Richard E. Turley, Jr., *Victims: the LDS Church and the Mark Hofmann case* (Champaign, IL: University of Illinois Press, 1992; Salt Lake City, UT: Digital Legends 2nd edition, 2021).

One historian who seized the opportunities offered by both this new approach to LDS history, and the interest in early Mormonism's possible folk magic connections engendered by Hofmann's salamander letter and similar forgeries, was a BYU professor named D. Michael Quinn. Quinn (who passed away in 2021) was a prodigious and indefatigable researcher who pushed into many previously little explored areas of LDS history.

One of his pioneering works, published in 1987 at the height of the brouhaha created by Hofmann's salamander letter, was *Early Mormonism and the Magic World View*.[39] In it he studied in detail the folk belief traditions of Joseph's society, and argued that they strongly influenced the early Restoration.

Not all scholars accepted Quinn's argument. Eminent LDS historian Richard Lloyd Anderson observed that Quinn's work was characterized by "over-generalizing by claiming that young Joseph Smith believed all parts of a 'magic world view' because it existed in his culture or is found in his vicinities. But such cultural typing goes against the Joseph Smith sources that show that he was a dissenter, a creative, individualistic religious reformer, who gave God credit for guiding his career," not the superstitious beliefs of his time and place.[40]

And Quinn's zeal in exposing new corners of history often led him to accept any evidence that supported his thesis uncritically at face value while ignoring contrary evidence.[41] An example of Quinn's questionable methodology can be seen in his treatment of the SITH

---

[39] D. Michael Quinn, *Early Mormonism and The Magic World View* (Salt Lake City, UT: Signature Books, 1987, 2nd edition 1998).

[40] Richard Lloyd Anderson, "A Scholar as a Witness: A Conversation with Richard Lloyd Anderson, Interview by Kay and Joseph F. Darowski," *Mormon Historical Studies* 7 (Spring Fall 2006), quote at p. 78, available at https://ensignpeakfoundation.org/mormon-historical-studies-spring-fall-2006-vol-7-no-1-2.

[41] For an extensive critique of Quinn's methodology in *Early Mormonism and The Magic World View*, see William J. Hamblin, "That Old Black Magic," in *Review of Books on the Book of Mormon 1989–2011*: Vol. 12 (2000): No. 2, available at: https://scholarsarchive.byu.edu/msr/vol12/iss2/17.

accounts. Since they supported his overall theory, he accepted them whole cloth. Yet, at the same time he never cited Joseph and Oliver's explicit statements that it was the Nephite interpreters which were used for the translation.

Quinn did acknowledge the reports that the interpreters were with the plates in the Hill Cumorah, but treated them as just another kind of folk magic seer stone, and blended his discussion of them into that of other seer stones without according them any distinct status even though, unlike other seer stones, the interpreters came from God.[42]

Despite the well-known questions about Quinn's research, both LDS and non-LDS historians quickly gravitated towards his perspective.[43] Within years, inspired by Quinn's book, at least one young historian was writing a graduate thesis on folk magic and seer stones and asking to see any in the LDS Church's possession.[44] Soon even more senior historians were rejecting Joseph and Oliver's testimonies in favor of giving priority to the SITH narrative.[45] In 2013 the LDS Church released a Gospel Topics essay promoting the SITH narrative and in 2015 the LDS Church released photos of a seer stone

---

[42] Quinn, *Early Mormonism and The Magic World View*, (1998), pp. 169 – 175.

[43] In fact, many historians continued to refer to the Hofmann letters even after they were exposed as forgeries. This is discussed in Terryl L. Givens, *By the Hand of Mormon: The American Scripture that Launched a New World Religion* (New York: Oxford University Press, 2002), pp. 168 – 169.

[44] Mark Ashurst-McGee, "Foreword" in Michael Hubbard MacKay and Nicholas J. Frederick, *Joseph Smith's Seer Stones* (Salt Lake City, UT: Deseret Book Company and Provo, UT: Brigham Young University Religious Studies Center, 2016), p. xi.

[45] In *Book of Mormon Studies: An Introduction and Guide* by Daniel Becerra, Amy Easton-Flake, Nicholas J. Frederick and Joseph M. Spencer (Provo, UT: Brigham Young University Religious Studies Center and Salt Lake City, UT: Deseret Book, 2022) the authors state that "historians intrigued by increased clarity about the Prophet's youthful folk-magic associations developed a relative scholarly consensus about the mechanics of translation and the use of seer stones" (quote at p. 35). See further discussion and references in Chapter 3(C).

of Joseph's which it held.⁴⁶

Today, Latter-day Saints are told by LDS academics that they should make a "paradigm shift" to accept the SITH accounts instead of what Joseph and Oliver taught in the Pearl of Great Price and elsewhere. They are expected to change their religious beliefs to accommodate a new "theology of seer stones."⁴⁷

Not all Latter-day Saints have been willing to heed the academics' call to reject the canonical translation narrative. In 2019, L. Hannah Stoddard and James F. Stoddard III published a book called *Seer Stone v. Urim & Thummim* challenging the SITH transcription narrative.⁴⁸ The Stoddards' position is absolute and uncompromising. They reject any suggestion that the Smith family were attuned to the folk traditions of their time and place as equivalent to saying that the Restoration was birthed in satanic sorcery and occult practices.

They do present well researched evidence that the only real firsthand witnesses, Joseph and Oliver, consistently attributed the translation to the use of the interpreters and never mentioned the use

---

⁴⁶ See https://www.churchofjesuschrist.org/study/manual/gospel-topics-essays/book-of-mormon-translation?lang=eng&_r=1 and https://www.churchofjesuschrist.org/church/news/book-of-mormon-printers-manuscript-photos-of-seer-stone-featured-in-new-book?lang=eng. Critiques of the Gospel Topics essay on the Book of Mormon's translation include Jonathan E. Neville, "Analysis: The Gospel Topics Essay on Book of Mormon Translation" (September 1, 2022) available at http://www.ldshistoricalnarratives.com/2022/09/analysis-gospel-topics-essay-on-book-of.html, Neville, *A Man That Can Translate*, pp. 315 – 356, and John-Charles Duffy, "The 'Book of Mormon Translation' Essay in Historical Context," in Matthew L. Harris and Newell G. Bringhurst (eds), *The LDS Gospel Topics Series: A Scholarly Engagement* (Salt Lake City, UT: Signature Books, 2020), pp. 97 – 130.

⁴⁷ MacKay and Frederick, *Joseph Smith's Seer Stones*, pp. xv – xxiii, 125 - 138. We apologize for being retrograde, but thought one of the main points of the Restoration was that new doctrine would be revealed through prophets, seers and revelators, not academic scribblers.

⁴⁸ L. Hannah Stoddard and James F. Stoddard III, *Seer Stone v. Urim & Thummim: Book of Mormon Translation on Trial* (Salem, UT: Joseph Smith Foundation, 2019).

of a seer stone, a conclusion with which we fully agree. However, there are some problematic aspects to their argument.

First, if the seer stone is a token of satanism, they do not explain why Joseph had one in the first place. Even Joseph Fielding Smith agreed that Joseph carried a seer stone around with him.[49] And Joseph's successors in the LDS Church considered the stone valuable enough to preserve after it came into the Church's possession. (An alternate viewpoint sees belief in folk magic practices as keeping Joseph and other early Saints open to the possibility of the supernatural, and resistant to the hard materialism which had arisen since the previous century as an aspect of the Enlightenment.[50])

Another difficulty with the book is that, while it thoroughly debunks David Whitmer's SITH claims, it does not address other significant SITH accounts such as those attributed to Emma Smith and Martin Harris. (These will be discussed in Chapter 2(B) and (C) of this book.) Also, the Stoddards propose that the SITH narrative arose during a period of apostasy in Kirtland, but they ignore the 1829 newspaper accounts of the spectacles in the hat, presumably related by Martin Harris.

We also question the Stoddards' harsh judgements on the SITH witnesses and the scholars who study them. In Chapter 2 we will show that many of the SITH witnesses may have been motivated by a misguided but sincere desire to defend the Book of Mormon against the Spalding theory. As for the SITH oriented scholars, their book decries in no uncertain terms the "progressive" and "revisionist" scholarship which has promoted the SITH narrative.[51] LDS academic elites in turn have ignored the Stoddards' book, probably dismissing

---

[49] Smith, *Doctrines of Salvation*, volume 3, p. 226 available at https://archive.org/details/Doctrines-of-Salvation-volume-3-joseph-fielding-smith/page/n133/mode/2up.

[50] Richard L. Bushman, *Joseph Smith and the Beginnings of Mormonism* (Urbana, IL: University of Illinois Press, 1984), pp. 6-8, 71-80.

[51] See Stoddard and Stoddard, *Seer Stone v. Urim & Thummim*, pp. 192 – 226.

them as fringe voices. We would hope instead that greater dialogue regarding the canonical narrative will be possible.

(We should also note here that in 2020 author Neville's book *A Man That Can Translate: Joseph Smith and the Nephite Interpreters* was published.[52] *By Means of the Urim and Thummim* extends and expands on that work.)

As outsiders to the world of professional LDS academia, we can only speculate as to how or why the SITH narrative has come to so dominate in that group. One factor may be a generalized desire for more "openness" in Mormon history, which could encompass more acknowledgement of the existence of the SITH accounts. Certainly, the SITH accounts cannot be simply ignored, but nor need they be adopted at face value. Based on the literature to date, since the rise of the SITH narrative in the 1980s we have found (i) little to no critical evaluation of the historical reliability of the SITH accounts and (ii) little to no effort to defend or understand the canonical translation narrative. This short book will attempt at least partially to address these gaps in the study of the Book of Mormon's origins.

D. An Odd Configuration of Sides

The discussion of the Book of Mormon's origins had created a surprising consensus among both critics and LDS scholars (many of whom are employed by the LDS Church and/or BYU). They collectively reject Joseph's claim of having translated the Book of Mormon from the gold plates using the interpreters, and agree that he instead dictated it with his face buried in a hat.

This has been pure gold (to use an expression) for the critics. They claim the scholars' approach is tantamount to an admission that the LDS Church has lied about the Book of Mormon's origins. The critics

---

[52] Jonathan Neville, *A Man That Can Translate: Joseph Smith and the Nephite Interpreters* (Salt Lake City, UT: Digital Legend, 2020, 2nd edition).

ridicule the SITH narrative with *South Park*-style cartoon images of Joseph Smith looking silly talking into a hat. If the text of the Book of Mormon was not translated from the plates, but rather put into Joseph's head either by reading off a seer stone at the bottom of a hat, or through some kind of direct inspiration (which only came while his face was buried in a hat), the Book of Mormon's origins are indistinguishable from what they would look like if Joseph was just making it all up while his face was in his hat.

Perhaps even more odd is what becomes of Joseph himself in contemporary discussions. Having surrendered the plates and the interpreters as irrelevant to the production of the Book of Mormon, LDS scholars are now also diminishing Joseph for apologetic reasons. The traditional translation narrative recognized that the Book of Mormon was subject to the translator's understanding and limitations.[53] However, by presenting Joseph as nothing more than a reading automaton reciting some supernatural translator's English, LDS scholars have emphasized an image of Joseph as a near-illiterate

---

[53] The interpretation "was expressed in such language as the Prophet could command, in such phraseology as he was master of and common to the locality and time where he lived … . This view of the translation of the Nephite record accounts for the fact that the Book of Mormon, though the translation of an ancient record, is, nonetheless, given in the English idiom of the period and locality in which the Prophet lived; and in the faulty English, moreover, both as to composition, phraseology and grammar, of a person of Joseph Smith's limited education; and also accounts for the sameness of phraseology and literary style which runs through the whole volume. … While every detail and shade of thought [was] preserved," Joseph "had to give expression to those facts and ideas in such language as he could command, and that was faulty English." B. H. Roberts, *New Witness for God* (Salt Lake City, UT: Deseret News, 1909) volume 2, pp. 116, 121, available at https://babel.hathitrust.org/cgi/pt?id=uc1.31210001369782&view=1up&seq=144&skin=2021 and https://babel.hathitrust.org/cgi/pt?id=uc1.31210001369782&view=1up&seq=149&skin=2021.

who could not possibly have contributed anything to the Book.[54]

In contrast, composition advocates' literature is full of arguments for Joseph's intellect, talents and awareness of the world around him. Indeed, many friendly non-LDS scholars, such as Harold Bloom and John Christopher Thomas, have written respectfully of Joseph's work.[55] So, we have the peculiar scene of those who profess to believe Joseph to be God's first modern prophet actively disparaging his intelligence and disclaiming any possibility of his substantive involvement with his largest contribution to the Restoration, while those who reject his prophetic ministry praise the man's intellect, learning and abilities.[56]

We believe the LDS scholars who advance these arguments have put themselves (and Latter-day Saints who follow their views) into an impossible corner, where any evidence that Joseph was actually a bright fellow, as well as evidence of 19th century language or concepts in the Book of Mormon, all become hard arguments against its authenticity.

---

[54] See, for example, Michael Hubbard MacKay, "The Secular Binary of Joseph Smith's Translations," *Dialogue*, Vol. 54, No. 3, (Fall 2021): 1-40 (available at https://www.dialoguejournal.com/articles/the-secular-binary-of-joseph-smiths-translations/#pdf-wrap) where BYU religion professor MacKay argues, with much postmodernist jargon, that Joseph was in "a scenario in which he could not personally compare the gold plates with the English translation of the Book of Mormon. He experienced the process but he did not know through personal experience that it was correct or whether its modern translation represented a historical ontology or a nineteenth-century ontology. He simply could not know." (quote at p. 7). For a contrary view that Joseph was cognizant of what he was translating, see Chapters 6(B), 6(C) and 7(D) of this book and Richard Dilworth Rust, "Joseph Smith's Prodigious Memory and the Translation of the Book of Mormon," forthcoming, copy in possession of authors.

[55] Harold Bloom, *The American Religion: The Emergence of the Post-Christian Nation* (New York: Simon Schuster, 1992) and John Christopher Thomas, *A Pentecostal Reads The Book of Mormon: A Literary and Theological Introduction* (Cleveland, TN: CPT Press, 2016).

[56] See for example https://faenrandir.github.io/a_careful_examination/joseph-smith-capable-of-authoring-the-book-of-mormon/ (accessed November 12, 2022).

In Chapter 5(D), we will argue the opposite, that evidence of Joseph's intelligence and exposure to the world he lived in is actually strongly compatible with the Book of Mormon's authenticity. However, to do so requires reviving Joseph's original narrative that the Book of Mormon was his active translation of the plates with the help of God and the interpreters "that God had prepared ... for the purpose of translating the book."[57]

E. Evaluating the Three Approaches – the Language

We have only three indisputable sources for evaluating the Book of Mormon's origins: (i) the accounts of persons who were "on the scene," (ii) the English text of the Book itself, and (iii) the Original Manuscript written by Joseph's scribes.

Any reader of the Book of Mormon can see that the text draws on the King James translation of the Bible (hereafter the "KJV"). Most scholars have looked at the KJV as the primary source for Book of Mormon language. Some have concluded that the text is so complex that Joseph Smith could not have produced it, leading them to adopt the transcription narrative. For example, Royal Skousen concluded that based "on the linguistic evidence, the translation must have involved serious intervention from the English-language translator, who was not Joseph Smith."[58]

Others have examined the nonbiblical language in the text and have found a variety of potential sources that Joseph and/or his collaborators could have used to compose the text.[59] Yet others

---

[57] Joseph Smith – History 1:35.

[58] Royal Skousen, *Critical Text of the Book of Mormon, Volume 3, The History of the Text, Part Five, The King James Quotations in the Book of Mormon* (Provo, UT: FARMS and BYU Studies, 2019), p. 6.

[59] E.g., Benjamin L. McGuire, "Finding Parallels: Some Cautions and Criticisms," *Interpreter: A Journal of Latter-day Saint Faith and Scholarship* 5 (2013) pp. 1-59, available

conclude that such sources corroborate Joseph's claim that he translated the engravings on the plates.⁶⁰

Dissatisfied with the evidence and arguments for transcription and composition, Neville investigated the possibility that Joseph Smith actually translated the plates. For several years he reviewed the literature on the translation narratives and then conducted a comprehensive analysis of the Book of Mormon's text and available original sources about its production. Focusing on the non-biblical language in the text, he studied the sources of language realistically available in Joseph's environment. The result was a database with over 1,200 separate correlations between the non-biblical Book of Mormon and language sources readily available to Joseph.

Neville's research employed the concept of *intertextuality*, which involves comparing one text with other texts to see whether they are related, based on how much they resemble or differ from each other. The vocabulary in the Book of Mormon is fairly limited (5,360 words, of which 2,219 are used only once or twice). Biblical vocabulary in the text has an obvious source: the King James Version of the Bible. Significant portions of the Book of Mormon are duplicates of passages and chapters from the KJV, with some minor alterations. Much of the rest of the text consists of paraphrased passages and phrases blended from disparate biblical verses. While scholars have assumed these are based on the KJV, they could also originate in the works of Christian authors who paraphrased and blended Biblical passages in their own writings.

But there are about 750 nonbiblical words in the text (depending on how one categorizes word forms) and hundreds of nonbiblical phrases. Neville's research focused on these nonbiblical words and phrases and whether these instances of nonbiblical vocabulary were

---

https://journal.interpreterfoundation.org/finding-parallels-some-cautions-and-criticisms-part-one/. Also D. Michael Quinn, *Early Mormonism and The Magic World View* (Salt Lake City, UT: Signature Books, 1998, 2ⁿᵈ edition), Chapter 6.

⁶⁰ See Neville, *A Man That Can Translate*.

present in Joseph's world prior to the translation. His study found that nearly every verse in the Book of Mormon contains language and concepts found in one or more of five categories of sources, all available to Joseph before he translated the plates.

1. The King James Version of the Bible.
2. Books and other publications sold in Palmyra between 1818 and 1828, such as the works of Christian authors Jonathan Edwards and James Hervey, and publications available in Vermont and Massachusetts before the Smiths moved to Palmyra, such as the Deane sermons discussed in Chapter 5(D).
3. Newspapers published in the Palmyra area between 1818 and 1828.
4. So-called "pseudo-Biblical" books including *The Late War*, *The American Revolution*, *The First Book of Napoleon*, and *The First Book of the American Chronicles of the Times*.
5. Family speech as documented in their writings, primarily Lucy Mack Smith's history.

This database's over 1,200 entries (hereinafter referred to as the Nonbiblical Intertextuality Database, or "NID") track substantive nonbiblical words or phrases in the Book of Mormon to one or more of the sources 2 through 5. One of Neville's most interesting discoveries was the unexpected correlation between the Book of Mormon and the language and concepts of Jonathan Edwards, the great American theologian of the First Great Awakening. (This research is presented in Neville's *Infinite Goodness: Joseph Smith, Jonathan Edwards and the Book of Mormon*.[61]) The entire database is currently over 1,700 pages. The NID has been released in draft form online, but is being regularly expanded and edited.[62]

---

[61] Jonathan Edward Neville, *Infinite Goodness: Joseph Smith, Jonathan Edwards and the Book of Mormon* (Salt Lake City, UT: Digital Legends, 2021).

[62] https://www.mobom.org/nonbiblical-intertextuality-database

The NID enables us to evaluate possible sources of the Book of Mormon text. Were the nonbiblical words and phrases in the Book of Mormon present in Joseph's environment or not? If they were, where were they? Were they concentrated in particular sources, or were their sources scattered and apparently random? And perhaps most significantly, do any of these sources shed any light on the meaning of the Book of Mormon's text? In Chapter 5 we will explore these questions further in light of the NID research.

F. Evaluating the Three Approaches – the People

The NID shows plausible sources for the Book of Mormon's text, assuming the production of that text originated with only Joseph Smith and a few scribes. There are also many witness statements outside the canonical account which describe the origins of the Book of Mormon. However, all sources are not created equal. Sources written close in time to the events are generally considered more reliable than those written down long after the events. And firsthand sources are generally given more weight than secondhand sources. The authors are both attorneys, and the law has long and well-tested criteria for evaluating secondhand or hearsay testimony, which we apply to sources about the origins of the Book of Mormon.

Witness credibility (sincerity) and reliability (accuracy) are both critical. Honest, sincere witnesses can be persuasive because they believe their own observations, even if those observations are mingled with incorrect assumptions or inferences (not to mention the vagaries of memory).

Technically, "hearsay" is an out-of-court statement offered as evidence to prove the truth of the matter asserted in the statement. Hearsay is inherently unreliable and is not allowed in court because the original witness did not testify under oath, was not subject to cross-examination, and could not have her or his credibility assessed. A related rule requires witnesses to have personal knowledge of the matter, meaning witnesses had the ability and opportunity to perceive the event that they testify about. (Historical statements are by definition hearsay, but we do not apply courtroom rules of evidence to exclude such evidence from consideration. Even in court, the "ancient document" exception to the hearsay rule allows documents that are more than 20 years old. But we can apply the principles of evidence to assess historical statements.)

The classic case is a witness repeating what someone else said; e.g., "James told me that he saw the blue car run a red light." That is obviously hearsay, so we call James in to testify. James says, "the blue car ran a red light." Are we finished? Of course not. James could be completely sincere and believe what he said, but we can't tell whether his testimony was reliable without further questioning. Was he present at the scene (time and place) or was he repeating what someone else told him? Was he watching the car and the light or did he hear a collision and look up? Was he positioned where he could observe clearly? Did he dislike the driver of the blue car or have another reason to shape his testimony?

Obviously, historical figures are not available to testify in person. They cannot be cross-examined. Their credibility cannot be assessed based on their demeanor. But that does not mean we must either reject their statements or take their statements at face value. We can consider evidence of witness reliability and credibility, including bias, motive, opportunity to observe, amount of detail, accuracy of recall of other past events, contradictions, and other factors related to credibility. Sometimes what a witness does not say is as important as what she or he does say.

The importance of critically analyzing sources can be illustrated by the case of David Whitmer (1805-1888). In early June 1828, David traveled to Harmony, Pennsylvania to transport Joseph and Oliver to his parents' home in Fayette, New York, where, as instructed in Doctrine and Covenants 10:41, Joseph translated the plates of Nephi (1 Nephi through Words of Mormon). David was present through the

Book's publication and the early years of the Church until he left the Church in Missouri in 1838.

He was one of the Three Witnesses who saw an angel display the plates, a testimony he steadfastly maintained through the rest of his long life despite his disaffiliation from Joseph and the Church. And he left an extensive record of his recollections, especially in the 1870s and 1880s. Not only did he publish a book on his experiences but, living in Missouri, he was more accessible to newspapers than were other early Church members who had migrated to Utah.

Yet, in the end, he was mainly a hearsay witness to the dictation of the Book of Mormon. David Whitmer was never a scribe for Joseph. He visited Harmony, where about three quarters of the text was translated, only briefly to collect Joseph and Oliver after they had finished translating the abridged plates. David never saw the plates and the interpreters until after the dictation of the text in Fayette was completed, when the angelic manifestation that made him one of the Three Witnesses occurred. With one possible exception to be discussed in Chapter 2(F), he never witnessed the dictation process. Despite the certainty with which he gave them, almost all of his copious accounts about the coming forth of the Book of Mormon were based on what he heard or inferred, not on what he himself actually saw.

This difference in eyewitness status is central to one of the most important factual issues in the creation of the Book of Mormon – were the interpreters returned to Joseph after they were taken from him following the loss of the 116 manuscript pages containing the first part of Mormon's record? As per the canonical account, Joseph and Oliver said Joseph regained the interpreters, since they reported using the interpreters to produce the entire Book of Mormon as well as many revelations.⁶³ This was confirmed by a significant secondary witness, Lucy Mack Smith.⁶⁴

However, David Whitmer later consistently claimed that the interpreters were never returned to Joseph, and that the present Book of Mormon was entirely produced by Joseph looking at a stone in the bottom of his hat rather than at the plates.⁶⁵ Despite the efforts of some historians to blend the accounts, they are factually irreconcilable. So, whose account do we accept on this fundamental issue? Firsthand witnesses Joseph and Oliver, or secondhand hearsay witness David? This is the kind of analysis which must be applied to evaluate all sources, which we undertake in the next chapter.

A final point must be made. Unlike the Bible, with its complicated history of multiple sources stretched over centuries, the Book of Mormon seems to present a straight-forward either/or choice. Either its origins are in some way divine, or it is a purely human fabrication, even if piously motivated. Either it is an authentic history of people living in ancient America or it is a modern invention. This dichotomy is part of its central role as a witness of Christ.

Consequently, explanations about the Book of Mormon have historically fallen into a similar deductive dichotomy. Both defenders

---

⁶³ B. H. Roberts (ed), *Comprehensive History of the Church of Jesus Christ of Latter-day Saints* (Salt Lake City, UT: Deseret Book Company, 1930), volume 1, p. 23 recounts the return of the interpreters, and pp. 21-52 their use in receiving subsequent revelations. The full History of the Church is available online at https://byustudies.byu.edu/further-study/history-of-the-church/ The *History of the Church* account of the return of the interpreters comes from Joseph Smith's *History, circa June 1839–circa 1841* available at https://www.josephsmithpapers.org/paper-summary/history-circa-june-1839-circa-1841-draft-2/13.

⁶⁴ Lucy Mack Smith, *History 1845*, p. 138 available at https://www.josephsmithpapers.org/paper-summary/lucy-mack-smith-history-1845/145. The full text of this important source is available at https://www.josephsmithpapers.org/paper-summary/lucy-mack-smith-history-1845/1.

⁶⁵ For one of many examples see David Whitmer to *Kansas City Journal* 13 June 1881, in Dan Vogel, *Early Mormon Documents* (Salt Lake City, UT: Signature Books, 1996), volume 5, pp. 81–82.

and critics have sought definitive incontrovertible proofs, irrefutable "slam-dunks" that usually end as exercises in bias confirmation. A more productive approach would lead to agreement among all concerned regarding the historical facts while recognizing multiple hypotheses which are individually plausible even if inconsistent with each other.

We recognize that rational, informed people can reach different conclusions based on the same evidence. Our intent here is not to propose a definitive narrative that everyone must accept. Instead, we propose an addition to the existing spectrum of multiple working hypotheses. Obviously, we think ours is supported by the evidence and rational analysis. We even think it is the best explanation for the available evidence. But we recognize alternatives are plausible and we welcome additional insights and discussion.

2. Transcription and the SITH Narrative

> ... that Joseph had another stone called seers' stone, and peep stone, is quite certain. This stone was frequently exhibited to different ones and helped to assuage their awful curiosity; but the Urim and Thummim never, unless possibly to Oliver Cowdery.
>
> Zenas H. Gurley, Jr.[66]

A. The Stone-in-the-Hat (SITH)

In an effort to refute the argument that Joseph Smith himself created the Book of Mormon out of his own head, some believing scholars interpret Joseph's use of the term *translate* to mean a supernatural phenomenon whereby Joseph read words that appeared on a seer stone at the bottom of his hat. Again, for convenience, we will refer to this scenario as "SITH" (*stone-in-the-hat*).[67]

One such author frames the position this way: "To suggest that Joseph Smith, who lacked formal education and struggled to write a coherent letter in his early years, was the author of such unforgettable

---

[66] Zenas H. Gurley, Jr., "The Book of Mormon," *Autumn Leaves* (1892), Vol. 5, quote at pp. 452 – 453, available at https://hdl.handle.net/2027/nyp.33433075797161 and at https://babel.hathitrust.org/cgi/pt?id=nyp.33433075797161&view=1up&seq=485&skin=2021.

[67] Note that *transcription* — the idea that Joseph merely read words that appeared before him — could also apply to exact wording appearing on the interpreters (without reference to the plates) as well as the stone-in-a-hat. Advocates of transcription-based explanations typically adopt the seer stone as the mechanism, but the identical analysis applies if coming from the interpreters; i.e., it would be a transcription rather than composition or translation.

phrases at age twenty-three is simply untenable."⁶⁸ Others tend to characterize Joseph as "poorly educated and unbookish,"⁶⁹ assert Joseph could not have known big words⁷⁰ or nuances of Early Modern English,⁷¹ and that, at any rate, Harmony, Pennsylvania, Joseph's home when he dictated most of the text in 1828 and 1829, was a "resource vacuum."⁷²

This has led to the currently widespread narrative that, because Joseph Smith was unlearned, he could have produced the Book of Mormon *only* by reading exact English words that appeared on a seer stone he placed in a hat (either literally or in a visionary sense). The actual translation into English was performed supernaturally by unknown means so that Joseph could simply read the words that appeared.⁷³

This narrative was not invented out of whole cloth. There are several accounts (particularly David Whitmer's later accounts) which report that Joseph never consulted the plates during the production of the Book of Mormon we have today, a point we will address later in this chapter. The element of the SITH narrative which emphasizes

---

⁶⁸ Tad R. Callister, *A Case for the Book of Mormon* (Salt Lake City, UT: Deseret Book, 2019), p. 124.

⁶⁹ Richard L. Bushman, "The Mysteries of Mormonism," *Journal of the Early Republic* 15 (Autumn 1995): 506, quoted in Carmack, "Joseph Smith, Captain Kidd Lore, and Treasure-Seeking," p. 106.

⁷⁰ Roger Terry, "The Book of Mormon Translation Puzzle," *Journal of Book of Mormon Studies*: Vol. 23: No. 1 (2014), Article 10, p. 182, available at: https://scholarsarchive.byu.edu/jbms/vol23/iss1/10

⁷¹ Royal Skousen, *The History of the Text of the Book of Mormon—Part Four—The Nature of the Original Language* (Provo, UT: BYU Studies, 2018).

⁷² John W. Welch, "Was There a Library in Harmony, Pennsylvania?" *Insights: An Ancient Window* (January 1994) p. 2, quoted in Carmack, "Joseph Smith, Captain Kidd Lore, and Treasure-Seeking," p. 106.

⁷³ This consensus has been described in Richard L. Bushman, *Joseph Smith: Rough Stone Rolling* (New York: Alfred A. Knopf, 2005) and Royal Skousen, *The History of the Text of the Book of Mormon, The Nature of the Original Language* (Parts 3–5) (Provo, UT: FARMS/BYU Studies, 2018).

how "unlearned" Joseph was also serves the apologetic purpose of emphasizing the divinity of the text. (We will discuss to extent of Joseph's learning in Chapter 5(D)).

However, as Roger Terry pointed out, none of the existing explanations based on transcription account for all the evidence.[74] Further, by divorcing the Book of Mormon from the plates and the interpreters, the SITH narrative unmoors it from the earthy reality which Tolstoy admired, leading scholars to float into many ethereal variations, which we will discuss in the next chapter.

The key departure from the canonical account common to all transcription-based explanations is the proposition that Joseph did not use either the plates or the interpreters to produce the Book of Mormon we have today. The SITH accounts say that Joseph received the text by looking at a seer stone which he placed at the bottom of a hat to block out light which might interfere with his being able to read the words which appeared on the seer stone. Contrary to the canonical account, in these accounts the plates are put aside, covered and unused.[75] Most SITH accounts follow David Whitmer in claiming that the interpreters were nowhere to be found, having been retained by the heavenly messenger who took them after the lost manuscript fiasco.

The SITH narrative is based on a variety of sources. As noted in Chapter 1(C), the earliest newspaper reports of the Book of Mormon refer to Joseph putting the "spectacles" into a hat to produce his "gold

---

[74] Roger Terry, "The Book of Mormon Translation Puzzle," p. 178.

[75] In modern times the first appearance of the SITH narrative in the scholarly literature may have been Richard Van Wagoner and Steve Walker, "Joseph Smith - The Gift of Seeing" *Dialogue*, Vol. 15, No. 2 (Summer 1982), pp. 49-68 at https://www.dialoguejournal.com/wp-content/uploads/sbi/articles/Dialogue_V15N02_50.pdf. While the SITH narrative has been extensively promulgated, other widely available sources would include Gardner, *The Gift and Power*, Part 1 and chapter 21, MacKay and Dirkmaat, *From Darkness unto Light*, pp. 87 – 88, 123, and Dirkmaat and MacKay, *Let's Talk About the Translation*, pp. 62-107.

bible."[76] By 1834 when the first anti-Mormon book, E. B. Howe's *Mormonism Unvailed*, was published, both the SITH and the canonical narratives were well known.[77] It was also clear that they were contradictory alternatives, and Howe accurately presented them as such. Howe mocked the inconsistencies, pointing out that whether Joseph used the "peep stone" or the "big spectacles," the instrument was provided "to enable Smith to translate the plates *without looking at them!*"[78] (emphasis in original). Howe pointed out the implications for the Three Witnesses:

> Let us ask, what use have the plates been or the spectacles, so long as they have in no sense been used? Or what does the testimony of Martin Harris, Oliver Cowdery and David Whitmer amount to? They solemnly swear that they saw the plates, and that an angel showed them, and the engravings which were upon them. But if the plates were hid by the angel so that they have not been seen since, how do these witnesses know that when Smith translated out of a hat, with a peep-stone, that the contents of the plates were repeated and written down? Neither of the witnesses pretend that they could read the hieroglyphics with or without the stone; and, therefore, are not competent testimony—nor can we see any use, either in finding the plates or the spectacles, nor of the exhibition of them.[79]

---

[76] See Note 1 to Joseph Smith, Jr., "Letter to Oliver Cowdery," (October 22, 1829), available at https://www.josephsmithpapers.org/paper-summary/letter-to-oliver-cowdery-22-october-1829/1 as well as *Palmyra Freeman* available at https://contentdm.lib.byu.edu/digital/collection/BOMP/id/4381 and "Golden Bible," *The Gem: A Semi-Monthly Literary and Miscellaneous Journal* (Rochester, NY: 5 Sept. 1829), p. 70, available at https://contentdm.lib.byu.edu/digital/collection/BOMP/id/161. Note though that almost all early accounts speak of two stones and/or the spectacles rather than a single stone, which describes the interpreters rather than the lone seer stone. See Clements, "Before the Urim & Thummim: Pre-1833 Newspaper Accounts of the Book of Mormon Translation."

[77] Howe, *Mormonism Unvailed*. See specifically p. 18, available online at https://play.google.com/books/reader?id=KXJNAAAAYAAJ&printsec=frontcover&pg=GBS.PA18.

[78] Howe, *Mormonism Unvailed*, p. 18.

[79] Howe, *Mormonism Unvailed*, pp. 77-78.

When *Mormonism Unvailed* was published, Oliver Cowdery began a series of eight detailed essays, published as letters in the Church's Kirtland newspaper, giving the first known comprehensive history of the Church. Joseph assisted Oliver in writing the essays, which were republished several times during Joseph's lifetime. The excerpt in the note to Joseph Smith – History 1:71 in the Pearl of Great Price stating that Joseph used the Urim and Thummim, is a direct response to Howe's SITH narrative (see quote in Chapter 1(A)).

(SITH also contradicts Joseph's statement that the Title Page is a "literal translation taken from the very last leaf, on the left hand side of the collection or book of plates, which contained the record which has been translated; the language of the whole running the same as all Hebrew writing in general," because Joseph could not have known it was a "literal translation," where it was placed in the plates or how the writing ran unless he was actually translating the plates.[80])

Howe mocked the SITH narrative not only for its inconsistencies and its contradiction of the plates-and-interpreters narrative, but because it was common knowledge that Joseph always dictated from behind a blanket or screen. He had to; he had been explicitly commanded not to show the plates or interpreters to anyone until the translation was complete. If not for the concealment, there would be no basis for the Spalding theory. The title of the book, *Mormonism Unvailed*, focused on the question: who (or what) was behind the "vail" (veil) when Joseph was dictating?[81]

Howe's answer—the Spalding theory—was widely embraced by critics of the Book of Mormon. When Oliver Cowdery rejoined the Church in 1848, he made a point of denying that Sidney Rigdon or Solomon Spalding had written the book. The Spalding theory persisted as an impediment to missionary and retention work through the 19th century.

---

[80] Joseph Smith, Jr., *History, circa 1841,* p. 60 available at https://www.josephsmithpapers.org/paper-summary/history-circa-1841-fair-copy/60

[81] See Howe, *Mormonism Unvailed,* p. 278.

Transcription and the SITH Narrative

Decades after the SITH accounts in *Mormonism Unvailed,* a number of additional SITH accounts appeared. In nearly every case in the literature, these accounts have been accepted at face value without considering their context. While these are analyzed in detail in *A Man That Can Translate,*[82] in this book we focus on two of the most frequently cited SITH sources – two statements attributed to Book of Mormon scribes Emma Smith and Martin Harris, both first published after their deaths. Then we will examine the primary source of the SITH narrative, David Whitmer.

To analyze these accounts, we must introduce a concept – the "proof text." In its simplest form a proof text is just a biblical passage which one cites to support a scriptural or theological interpretation. This is something Christians have been doing since the beginning. However, this practice can have a pitfall, which is somewhat confusingly called "proof-texting." This is where the Bible passage is cited out of context, and in actual or possible contradiction to its real meaning when read as part of the larger selection of the Bible from which it is taken. Bible scholars use the expression "a text without a context is a pretext for a proof-text" to summarize this pitfall.[83]

Similarly, when looking at a passage from a historical source, especially one advanced as proving a religious position like the SITH narrative, we should not look at it in isolation. We need to ask what is its larger context, why it was said and, perhaps most importantly, what else did the source say on the same subject? As the Reverend Dr. Eugene A. Nida, the dean of modern Bible translation who for decades was the executive secretary of the American Bible Society, observed, the "answer to most problems of meaning come from extended contexts, whether within the text in question or in other texts by the

---

[82] Emma and Martin's accounts are discussed in detail in chapters 9 and 10 of author Neville's *A Man That Can Translate* and subchapters 2(B) and (C) below. *A Man That Can Translate* examines all known accounts of the translation process.

[83] https://www.theopedia.com/proof-texting

same writer ..."[84]. If a source said one thing once, but something different numerous times, or later in time after further consideration, or the entirety of their position conflicts with the one reference, to avoid the pitfall of proof-texting we have to question the reliability of the one-time reference. (We will hear more from Reverend Nida in Chapters 5 and 6 when we discuss how the Book of Mormon was translated.)

B. The "Last Testimony of Sister Emma"

Emma Hale Smith played many roles in the Restoration besides being the wife of Joseph Smith, Jr.[85] One of these was occasionally serving as scribe for the Book of Mormon, mostly on the early pages which Martin Harris lost, but also some of the Book we have today. After Joseph's assassination she stayed in Nauvoo with her children. She remarried a man named Lewis Bidamon, who turned out to be a drinker and philanderer. (Emma raised as her own a child produced by one of Bidamon's extramarital affairs.) She did not tell her children much about their family religion.

However, a number of Saints who did not follow Brigham Young and the other apostles west started working toward a reorganization of the Church, with the Book of Mormon and Doctrine and Covenants, but without plural marriage. After some years of effort, in 1860 they succeeded in inducing Joseph, Jr. and Emma's eldest son, Joseph Smith III (who had been only eleven years old in 1844 when his father was killed), to accept the presidency of this new Reorganized Church of

---

[84] Eugene A. Nida, *Contexts in Translating* (Philadelphia, PA: John Benjamins Publishing Company, 2001), p. 66.

[85] Well-regarded biographies of Emma include Linda King Newell and Valeen Tippetts Avery, *Mormon Enigma* (Champaign, IL: University of Illinois Press, 2nd edition 1994) and most recently Jennifer Reeder, *First: The Life and Faith of Emma Smith* (Salt Lake City, UT: Deseret Book, 2021).

Jesus Christ of Latter Day Saints (abbreviated RLDS until the name was changed to Community of Christ in 2001).[86]

We have very little of Emma's writing on any subject. Most of what is presented as Emma's words on the Book of Mormon come from an article published in 1879 by Joseph Smith III, six months after her death. Titled "Last Testimony of Sister Emma," it purported to be an interview by Joseph III with his mother in the weeks before her death.[87] It appears to follow the question-and-answer format of a newspaper interview. Here are some of the items relevant to the Book of Mormon:

Q. What of the truth of Mormonism?

A. I know Mormonism to be the truth; and believe the Church to have been established by divine direction. I have complete faith in it. In writing for your father I frequently wrote day after day, often sitting at the table close by him, he sitting with his face buried in his hat, with the stone in it, and dictating hour after hour with nothing between us.

Q. Had he not a book or manuscript from which he read, or dictated to you?

A. He had neither manuscript nor book to read from.

---

[86] The Community of Christ has produced many works on their history. A good short history by a great-great-grandson of Joseph and Emma is Paul M. Edwards, *Our Legacy of Faith: A Brief History of the Reorganized Church of Jesus Christ of Latter Day Saints* (Independence, MO: Herald House, 1991).

[87] Joseph Smith III, "Last Testimony of Sister Emma," *The Saints Herald*, , volume 26, No. 19, Oct. 1, 1879, available at https://archive.org/stream/TheSaintsHerald_Volume_26_1879/the%20saints%20herald%20volume%2026%201879#page/n287/mode/2up and http://www.latterdaytruth.org/pdf/100193.pdf

Q. Could he not have had, and you not know it?

A. If he had had anything of the kind he could not have concealed it from me.

Q. Are you sure that he had the plates at the time you were writing for him?

A. The plates often lay on the table without any attempt at concealment, wrapped in a small linen tablecloth, which I had given him to fold them in. I once felt of the plates, as they thus lay on the table, tracing their outline and shape. They seemed to be pliable like thick paper, and would rustle with a metallic sound when the edges were moved by the thumb, as one does sometimes thumb the edges of a book.

Q. Where did father and Oliver Cowdery write?

A. Oliver Cowdery and your father wrote in the room where I was at work.

Q. Could not father have dictated the Book of Mormon to you, Oliver Cowdery and the others who wrote for him, after having first written it, or having first read it out of some book?

A. Joseph Smith (and for the first time she used his name direct, having usually used the words, "your father" or "my husband") could neither write nor dictate a coherent and well-worded letter, let alone dictate a book like the Book of Mormon. And, though I was an active participant in the scenes that transpired, and was present during the translation of the plates, and had cognizance of things as they transpired, it is marvelous to me, "a marvel and a wonder," as much so as to anyone else. ...

Q. Mother, what is your belief about the authenticity, or origin, of the Book of Mormon?

A. My belief is that the Book of Mormon is of divine authenticity - I have not the slightest doubt of it. I am satisfied that no man could have dictated the writing of the manuscripts unless he was inspired; for, when acting as his scribe, your father would dictate to me hour after hour; and when returning after meals, or after interruptions, he could at once begin where he had left off, without either seeing the manuscript or having any portion of it read to him. This was a usual thing for him to do. It would have been improbable that a learned man could do this; and, for one so ignorant and unlearned as he was, it was simply impossible.

Taken uncritically at face value the document appears to be straight-forward, even inspiring, as long as one rejects Joseph and Oliver's testimonies and the canonical account of the translation in favor of the SITH narrative. However, when we step back and look at the "Last Testimony of Sister Emma" in its broader context the picture becomes much more complicated.

When he interviewed his mother shortly before her death, Joseph III was engaged in intense rhetorical battles on two fronts. One was with the LDS Church in Utah over whether Joseph Smith initiated plural marriage.[88] The other was with proponents of the Spalding theory of the Book of Mormon's origins. And the latter was pressing. Joseph III and his small RLDS community did not live in isolation in the western deserts surrounded by fellow believers, but in the Midwest in the midst of opponents of the Book of Mormon who accepted the Spalding explanation.

Read in this larger context, the "Last Testimony of Sister Emma" is custom designed to fill Joseph III's needs at that time. This same document has Emma denying that Joseph participated in plural marriage. Today few historians, including those in the Community of

---

[88] In his inaugural address on assuming the RLDS Church's presidency in 1860, Joseph III had declared that proving that his father had nothing to do with plural marriage was one his primary missions. See Edwards, *Our Legacy of Faith*), pp. 135-136.

Christ, accept Emma's claim in the "Last Testimony" that Joseph had nothing to do with plural marriage and that she knew nothing of it.[89]

The leading biographers of Emma, Linda King Newell and Valeen Tippetts Avery, see the "Last Testimony" interview as mother and son dancing around the issue, with Emma dodging directly addressing the subject because Joseph III did not use the code words for plural marriage that were employed in Nauvoo, and Joseph III deliberately avoiding asking or pressing questions which might have resulted in answers he did not want to hear.[90] Eliza R. Snow and others in Utah who participated in plural marriage with Joseph questioned whether Emma's "Last Testimony" was actually written by Joseph III—which, actually, he did, as the original documents from the interview show.[91]

Whether he accurately recorded what his mother may have said is ultimately unknowable. However, we can begin to analyze its reliability by looking at an earlier account by Emma of her work as a scribe. In an 1870 letter to a friend, Emma Pilgrim, in response to an unknown question (because we do not have Pilgrim's letter), Emma stated:

> Now, the first part my husband translated, was translated by the use of Urim and Thummim, and that was the part that Martin Harris lost. After that he used a small stone, not exactly black, but was rather a dark color. I cannot tell whether that account in the *Times and Seasons* is correct or not because someone stole all my books and I have none to refer to at present, if I can find one that has that account I will tell you what is true and what is not.[92]

---

[89] Merina Smith, *Revelation. Resistance and Mormon Polygamy: The Introduction of and Implementation of the Principle* 1830-1853, (Logan, UT: Utah State University Press, 2013), pp. 44, 47-51, 59-60, 64-85; Richard P. Howard, *The Church Through the Years*, (Independence, MO: Herald Publishing House, 1992), volume 1 pp. 293-296, volume 2 pp. 75-77; and Edwards, *Our Legacy of Faith*, pp. 107-110.

[90] Linda King Newell and Valeen Tippetts Avery, *Mormon Enigma*, pp. 300-302.

[91] See Neville, *A Man That Can Translate*, pp. 146 – 148 for some of these responses and "Joseph the Seer's Plural Marriages," *Deseret Evening News*, October 22, 1879, p. 13 available at https://newspapers.lib.utah.edu/details?id=2663429.

[92] Emma Smith Bidamon to Emma Pilgrim, March 27, 1870, in Vogel, *Early Mormon Documents*, volume 1, p. 532.

Transcription and the SITH Narrative

Emma's 1870 letter does not specify when, where, or what she wrote as a scribe. The absence of such details undermines the reliability of her statements because there is no way to verify or challenge the details of her claims. In her letter, Emma does not claim to be an eyewitness. She relates the account the same way anyone would who had heard someone else describe it. This passage can be read either as an eyewitness account by someone who forgot to mention she was an eyewitness, or as an explanation based on what she heard others say. Even if Emma acted as scribe for the unspecified "first part," she had not been authorized to see the Urim and Thummim or the plates, so her statement that "the first part... was translated by use of Urim and Thummim" is necessarily hearsay.

Emma implies but does not state that she saw the stone ("not exactly black, but was rather a dark color"), but she likely saw it even before Joseph obtained the plates, assuming it is the stone he found in a well and regularly carried around. Emma also fails to specify where, when or how Joseph used the stone or what he dictated with it. The statement "After that he used a small stone" is vague; Emma did not write "after that I observed him use a small stone," "after that, he used *only* a small stone" or "after that he used a small stone to dictate every word in the Book of Mormon we have today." People infer she meant to say Joseph used a small stone to "translate" the Book of Mormon but she does not specifically say even that.

In addition, her statement is consistent with what she may have observed during a demonstration using the seer stone as a stand-in for the interpreters which Joseph was not allowed to publicly display, even to Emma (we will discuss this further in subchapter F of this chapter).

Lucy Mack Smith quotes Joseph saying Emma wrote for him after he recovered the Urim and Thummim following the loss of the 116 pages.[93] That would directly contradict Emma's claim in the 1870 letter. Emma's account makes sense only if she never saw what was behind

---

[93] Lucy Mack Smith, *History 1845*, p. 145 available at https://www.josephsmithpapers.org/paper-summary/lucy-mack-smith-history-1845/145.

the screen when Joseph dictated; i.e., she had to be speculating or repeating hearsay in her letter. There is evidence she was a scribe for part of the 116 pages which were lost and part of the Original Manuscripts produced in both Harmony and Fayette, but she never claimed she saw the plates or the Urim and Thummim.

And Emma's letter directly contradicts Oliver's claims about the Urim and Thummim. Because he was not involved until after the 116 pages were lost, Oliver could not have been referring to the translation of those pages, and thus had to be referring to the pages Emma seems to say were translated with the stone.

Based on Emma's letter, we infer Pilgrim's question arose from an unspecified account in the *Times and Seasons*, possibly Oliver Cowdery's Letter I, the Wentworth letter, or Joseph Smith's History (now Joseph Smith—History in the Pearl of Great Price). Emma's reference to the *Times and Seasons* could mean either that she meant to say she could tell what was true or false about the account in the *Times and Seasons*, or that she needed that reference to refresh her recollection. The *Times and Seasons* was published 10 years after the events of the translation. Emma wrote this letter nearly 30 years after the *Times and Seasons* was published, but she did not know, or could not remember, what the newspaper's accounts said about the translation.

However, by 1870, numerous conflicting accounts of the translation had been published, but the Spalding theory had become the de facto explanation among all but the staunchest believers. And by 1870 even among believers the SITH account was being advanced, despite being initially spread by the anti-LDS book *Mormonism Unvailed*. That year William McLellin, one the original members of the Quorum of the Twelve Apostles, was writing to Joseph III actively advocating the SITH narrative as part of McLellin's claim to guide the direction of the restored church.[94] Lacking any earlier sources such as issues of the *Times and Seasons* from the 1840s, Emma reverted to the SITH

---

[94] William E. McLellin to "My Dear Friends" (February 1870), Community of Christ archives, Joseph Smith III transcript file 1 pp. 123-124.

claims of McLellin and others to provide an answer to refute the Spalding theory and support the divine origin of the Book of Mormon.

With this background, let us look at the specific factual claims of the "Last Testimony."

Emma wrote day after day with Joseph "sitting with his face buried in his hat, with the stone in it, and dictating hour after hour with nothing between us." As noted, this directly contradicts Joseph's accounts which can be seen in Chapter 1(A) and Appendix B. It also contradicts the 1870 letter to Emma Pilgrim, which states that the lost pages were translated using the Urim and Thummim, yet most of Emma's scribal work was done on those pages. The "Last Testimony" has Emma writing "day after day" (a phrase likely borrowed from Oliver Cowdery[95]), without indicating what, exactly, she wrote or when—or even where. We cannot help suspecting that more details would have lent credence to the Spalding theory because of the screen behind which Joseph translated. Most critically, as we will see below, even Joseph III later rejected the SITH narrative, which raises the question of whether Emma ever made these statements.

Joseph did not have "a book or manuscript from which he read, or dictated" including something concealed from Emma. Here we see how central the Spalding theory was to shaping the "Last Testimony," as the central claim of the Spalding theory was that Joseph was reading from a hidden manuscript. This was the claim that Joseph III focused on in a letter to James Cobb, with whom Joseph was carrying on an ongoing dispute over the Spalding theory, telling Cobb that "the larger part of this labor was done in her presence, and where she could see and Know what was being done; that during no part of it was did Joseph Smith have any Mss, or Book of any Kind from which to read, or

---

[95] "Day after day I continued... to write... as he translated with the Urim and Thummim." Joseph Smith-History 1:71, note.

dictate except the metalic plates which she knows he had."⁹⁶

(Note that in this account, written right after his visit to his mother and months before the "Last Testimony" was published, Joseph III has his mother saying Joseph worked from the "metallic plates," which is contrary to the SITH narrative that he was only looking at the seer stone in his hat with the plates covered and unused.)

Here we can apply some common sense. Most of the Book of Mormon translation (and Emma's scribing) was done in Harmony. There Emma and Joseph were living in what was basically a log cabin. Even if Joseph and Oliver were behind a screen, there was simply no place in those small quarters where Joseph could hide or dispose of dozens or maybe hundreds of pages of notes or manuscript. Even if Emma was very debilitated at the time of the interview, this seems the kind of detail a housewife would remember even decades later.

The plates "often lay on the table without any attempt at concealment, wrapped in a small linen tablecloth." Although SITH advocates infer that this means the plates were <u>always</u> concealed, the actual statement is also compatible with understanding the plates were under the cloth <u>except</u> when being used to translate.

Oliver and Joseph "wrote in the room where I was at work" and she was present for most of the translation. Being "present" is not the same as witnessing the actual translation, and greatly exaggerates her limited service as scribe. Indeed, she said she never saw the plates, which suggests Joseph and Oliver worked behind a screen or curtain that prevented Emma from seeing the plates. It is significant that she did not deny there was such a screen when Oliver was scribe. And Joseph III's follow-up was not to ask for more specifics of Emma's observations. Instead, he returns yet again to the Spalding theory.

Joseph could not have written Book of Mormon or read it out of a book because Joseph "could neither write nor dictate a coherent and well-worded letter, let alone

---

⁹⁶ Joseph Smith III to James T. Cobb, (February 14, 1879) Community of Christ archives, Joseph Smith III transcript file 5, quote at p. 478 and in Vogel, *Early Mormon Documents*, volume 1, p. 544.

dictate a book like the Book of Mormon." This an early example of a common apologetic trope which seeks to prove the Book of Mormon by portraying Joseph as a near-illiterate (see Chapter 1(D)). Yet we have a letter which Joseph wrote to Oliver Cowdery shortly after the Book of Mormon was finished, in Joseph's own handwriting, which is perfectly clear and understandable.[97] (We will discuss the question of Joseph's abilities in more detail in Chapter 5(D)).

When Emma acted as scribe Joseph "would dictate to me hour after hour; and when returning after meals, or after interruptions, he could at once begin where he had left off, without either seeing the manuscript or having any portion of it read to him. This was a usual thing for him to do. It would have been improbable that a learned man could do this; and, for one so ignorant and unlearned as he was, it was simply impossible." Even though Emma's work as a scribe was not as extensive as implied by the "Last Testimony," she was a scribe, and this seems like the kind of detail which one could remember even if one's faculties were failing.

So, what can we make of this document? It is entirely choreographed to rebut the Spalding theory. For example, Joseph III begins the interview by asking whether Sidney Rigdon performed the marriage of his parents which, if true, would support the Spalding theory. (Emma denied Rigdon's involvement.)

While there are some points which seem factually credible, Emma's brief responses, and Joseph III's failure to probe for specifics, accomplished their united purpose of refuting the Spalding theory, but we are left with unfortunate ambiguity. The "Last Testimony" is vague to the point of being evasive. When discussing the Book of Mormon translation, Emma and her son displayed the same evasive generalities

---

[97] Joseph Smith, Jr., "Letter to Oliver Cowdery," (October 22, 1829) at https://www.josephsmithpapers.org/paper-summary/letter-to-oliver-cowdery-22-october-1829/1

seen in their discussion of plural marriage.[98]

As noted, despite the ambiguities surrounding the "Last Testimony," SITH proponents accept the Book of Mormon related parts uncritically at face value, even as they have to acknowledge that the same document is completely unreliable on the subject of plural marriage. This incongruity suggests an outcome-oriented approach; i.e., SITH proponents are satisfied with the "Last Testimony" and so, like Joseph Smith III at the time, probe no further. Emma died within weeks of the interview, and therefore never had the opportunity to comment on it when it was published many months after her death.

However, her son, Joseph Smith III, lived into the 20th century. What did "young Joseph" think of the SITH narrative which relies so heavily on this article?

Our first clue came from an unexpected source. In the next subchapter we will meet a fascinating character, Edward Stevenson. Born in Gibraltar, he joined the Church after his family emigrated to the United States. He served many missions and spent the last few years of his life as one of the presidents of the Seventy of the LDS Church (a building at the Missionary Training Center in Provo is named after him.) One of his personal missions was to befriend surviving witnesses of the Book of Mormon. In the next subchapter we will review how he brought Martin Harris to Utah, where Martin

---

[98] On Emma's knowledge of Joseph's involvement with plural marriage in Nauvoo see Newell and Avery, *Mormon Enigma*, pp. 98, 142-145, 292, 303; Brian C. Hales, "Joseph Smith: Monogamist or Polygamist?" *Interpreter: A Journal of Latter-day Saint Faith and Scholarship* 25 (2017), at pp. 136-140, available at https://journal.interpreterfoundation.org/joseph-smith-monogamist-or-polygamist/ and Reeder, *First: The Life and Faith of Emma Smith*, pp. 2, 27-31, 70, 114-115, 134-135, 170-171. Immediately after the "Last Testimony" was published, numerous still living eyewitnesses in Utah specifically contradicted her incredible claim in the "Last Testimony" that she knew nothing of any involvement on Joseph's part in plural marriage. Andrew Jenson (editor and publisher), "Church Encyclopedia, Book 1," in *The Historical Record*, Salt Lake City, Utah (1889), pp. 219-234, available at https://archive.org/details/churchencyclopae58jens/page/218/mode/2up.

lived until his death in 1875. After Martin's death Stevenson set about establishing a relationship with David Whitmer, visiting him three times at his home in Missouri in the course of his mission travels.

Of his last visit with David in 1886, Stevenson made a curious notation in his journal:

> David Whitmer says that the Josephites was displeased with him because he maintained that the 116 pages which were translated & written by Martin Harris was translated by the Urim & Thummim or Interpreters as he preferred calling them, but after the loss of the 116 pages the remainder of the translation was done with the Seer stone ...[99]

The "Josephites" refers to the RLDS Church, whose leader was Joseph Smith III (in contrast to the "Brighamites," a term they used for those who accepted Brigham Young as Joseph Smith, Jr.'s successor). Were the RLDS displeased because David maintained that the first part of the Book of Mormon was translated using the interpreters? This would contradict the claim in the "Last Testimony" that Joseph used the stone in the hat rather than the plates and interpreters.

To find out if that was the reason Joseph Smith III was "displeased" with "Father Whitmer," we consulted the *Saints Herald*, a weekly newspaper which served (and still serves) as the primary organ of the RLDS Church. One might think of it as the equivalent of the *Liahona* in the current LDS Church, but that would understate its official status, for at that time Joseph Smith III served as its editor, and his chief associate editor, William W. Blair, was also the first counselor in the RLDS Church's First Presidency.

The answer was the exact opposite of what we expected. Indeed, the question of David Whitmer's seer stone claims had been addressed

---

[99] Edward Stevenson, *Book 4: Typescript journals (1886 January 14 - 1887 August 20)*, volume 28, page 52 at https://catalog.churchofjesuschrist.org/assets/bc546251-522d-430a-a259-964bd8bde02f/0/0

in the *Saints Herald*, and by Joseph Smith III himself. However, rather than referring to the "Last Testimony" as the definitive last word, as do modern SITH proponents, Joseph III makes no reference at all to the "Last Testimony." What does he look to as the authoritative word on how the Book of Mormon was translated? Joseph III quotes, at length, from Oliver Cowdery's Letter I (now a note to Joseph Smith – History in the LDS Pearl of Great Price) and his father's article for John Wentworth (best known as the source of the Articles of Faith), both of which emphatically state that the interpreters were the instrument used to translate the Book of Mormon.[100]

In a bit of rhetorical flourish, Joseph III does say that if the stone was used "it was in effect a Urim and Thummim." However, lest SITH proponents find comfort in that statement, Joseph III immediately continues that even then the stone was "evidently not the chief instrument." Referring to Joseph and Oliver, Joseph III notes that it "must be allowed that these men best knew by what means the Book of Mormon was translated" and that "chief instrument" was the interpreters. In contrast, David Whitmer was "neither translator or scribe, but only an occasional observer."[101]

Two years later the question of David Whitmer's SITH claims was again put to the *Saints Herald*. Joseph III was traveling so the response came from his second-in-command, William W. Blair. Referring to the same sources from Joseph and Oliver, Blair added citations from the Book of Mormon itself about the interpreters as the "'means' God had prepared for the interpretation of the plates from which the Book of Mormon was translated. The testimony of these texts and that of Joseph the Seer and Oliver Cowdery harmonize, therefore we endorse it instead of that which purports to be the testimony of David

---

[100] These are documents 15 and 20 in Appendix B.

[101] Joseph Smith III, "David Whitmer Reviewed," *The Saints Herald*, volume 33, No. 45, November 13, 1886, quotes at p. 707, available at https://www.google.com/books/edition/Saints_Herald/qmqsXWe1xFAC?gbpv=1&bsq=707.

Whitmer."[102] (We will discuss David Whitmer's SITH claims further below in subchapter D.)

So, is there no further mention of the "Last Testimony" until its elevation to near-scriptural status by modern SITH proponents? Yes, actually, it was referenced again in another RLDS publication in 1892, from which the opening quote to this chapter is taken. There another interesting character whom we will meet shortly, Zenas H. Gurley, Jr., notes the "Last Testimony," but only to conclude that since Emma, like David Whitmer, was never allowed to see the Urim and Thummim interpreters in use, their comments on the translation process are to be disregarded.[103]

What then are we to make of the SITH references in the "Last Testimony"? A full examination of that odd document is beyond the scope of this short book, but we would propose a new perspective: it is not a verbatim transcript of Emma's words, but rather Joseph III's summary, interpretation or characterization of his mother's "answers." It may be that they comport with whatever she actually said, if anything, on the topics then of concern to Joseph III, namely plural marriage and the Spalding theory. If this is the case, we still have the question of why Joseph III changed so decisively to an anti-SITH position.

A clue to this riddle could come from a seemingly out of place question in the "interview" (which should always be referred to with

---

[102] W. W. Blair, *The Saints Herald*, volume 35, No. 9, March 3, 1888, quote at p. 129, https://www.google.com/books/edition/Saints_Herald/vJD0EOEmJyYC?hl =en&gbpv=1&dq=%22saints+herald%22+%22march+3,+1888%22&pg=PA129 &printsec=frontcover

[103] Zenas H. Gurley Jr., "The Book of Mormon," p. 453 available at https:// hdl.handle.net/2027/nyp.33433075797161. It is worth noting that this article was published in 1892, six years after Gurley's 1886 resignation from the RLDS Church. That Joseph Smith III nonetheless permitted Gurley to publish this criticism can be seen as further evidence of Joseph III's dismissal of the "Last Testimony's" SITH statements. Gurley does try to minimize the contradiction stating the "only discrepancy between the statements of the witnesses is that relating to the detail of the translation." However, as we are seeing, the conflict between the seer stone and interpreter accounts is more than a "detail."

many caveats and scare quotes). Following the many questions focused on the Spalding theory, Joseph III asks, not apropos to anything else in the "interview," "what do you think of David Whitmer?" His ghostwritten "answer" is that David is an honest man, and what he says can be relied on.

In 1879, when the so-called "interview" took place, David was starting to put out his SITH views, but had not yet broadcast the extent to which he considered Joseph Smith to be a fallen prophet. Everyone, including the RLDS Church, was trying to curry favor with the last surviving Witness, who also was holding the printer's manuscript of the Book of Mormon and his late brother John's earliest records of the Church. (Note that this was true of the LDS Church as well, as shown by the visit of an official delegation led by Joseph F. Smith and Orson Pratt in 1878, and approval of Edward Stevenson's overtures beginning in 1877.)

We suggest that in the "Last Testimony" Joseph III and perhaps Emma as well were simply echoing David Whitmer in the "answers" Joseph III ghostwrote for his mother, "answers" which were also temporarily useful in his main objective of rebutting the Spalding theory. (He also could have been influenced by the SITH arguments William McLellin made to him a few years before.) For example, Emma's purported statement about the plates laying nearby covered by a linen and the absence of a screen is vague enough to support the anti-Spalding argument, but is also consistent with Emma having observed the covered plates when Joseph was not translating from them.

David Whitmer had been criticizing Joseph since before he left the Church in 1838, but in the mid-1880s, David launched an all-out attack on Joseph Smith, Jr. (We will discuss this further below in subchapter D.) Realizing that this supposed friend was actually a bitter enemy of his father and everything his father had worked to build (other than the Book of Mormon, which David continued to vouchsafe), Joseph III stopped accepting David's SITH claims at face value. Instead, he undertook serious research.

Unlike today, when records are accessible with a few keystrokes, for Joseph III this required digging up files of 40 and 50 year old copies of Church newspapers, such as the *Times and Seasons* issues Emma said she would have consulted if her copies had not gone missing. This research made it apparent that David Whitmer and William McLellin's SITH claims directly contradicted his father's testimony. Joseph III never directly repudiated the "Last Testimony," probably because it also contained his passionately held belief that his father was not involved with plural marriage. But never again, as long as he presided, would the RLDS Church support the SITH claims of a man who called Joseph III's father a liar and a fallen prophet.

We would argue that, when he uncovered this definitive contrary evidence, Joseph III was able to readily abandon the SITH claims in the "Last Testimony" either because he knew that his mother had not made them in the first place, or that she made them but with his coaching to fit his goal of refuting the Spalding theory. In either case, he had written them himself, using the best information he had available at the time, to fill out and add "color" to his mother's enfeebled memories.

Before we criticize Joseph III for possibly embellishing much of this lovely record of his mother's supposed last words, we must return to our theme of context, context, context. So common today, the very idea of an "interview" was still quite new in 1879. The first well-known published interview had been only 20 years earlier, when Horace Greeley printed in question-and-answer format his report of his meeting with Brigham Young. There were no established rules, guidelines or even customs for interviews, and in many quarters they were still seen as unseemly.[104]

And in 1879 the United States was on the verge of the great era of what its detractors were to call "yellow journalism." More neutrally

---

[104] Michael Schudson, "Questioning Authority: A History of the News Interview in American Journalism 1860-1930s," *Media Culture and Society* (1994), Vol 16, no. 4, pp. 565 – 587.

put, it was a time when journalists saw themselves first as writers rather than "reporters." Getting the facts right was respected, but flair and riveting writing took precedence over grubby facts. The epithet "yellow" was only used by newspapers who were less popular and influential than the practitioners of this livelier form of reportage.[105]

For Joseph III to fill out this "interview," particularly to make his own mother sound more eloquent, would not have been seen as untoward. And before we apply our supposed modern standards of journalistic "objectivity" retroactively to almost 150 years ago, we should remember that in our times many across the ideological spectrum regard this "objectivity" as simply a cover for hewing to the views accepted by the powers that be.[106]

And then, what of Emma and her supposed "Last Testimony"? By any measure, Emma's statements cannot resolve the issue of how Joseph translated the plates. Emma Smith is one of the enigmatic figures of the Restoration. An "elect lady" who was present at every stage almost from the very beginning, we want to know what she thought and experienced, a desire largely frustrated by the paucity of her writings.[107] Understandably we cling to the words of the "Last Testimony" because we have so little else from her. However, in the end, we must conclude that the document is not reliable.

Was Emma, as per Brigham Young, just "one of the damnedest liars I know of on this earth"?[108] Or, shortly before her death, was she choosing to remember an idealized beloved husband who never kept

---

[105] See David Mindich, *Just the Facts: How "Objectivity" Came to Define American Journalism* (New York: NYU Press, 1998) and Michael Schudson, *Discovering the News: A Social History of American Newspapers* (New York: Basic Books, 1978).

[106] Compare the conclusions of trans activist Lewis Raven Wallace, *The View From Somewhere: Undoing the Myth of Journalistic Objectivity* (Chicago, IL: The University of Chicago Press, 2019) and conservative commentator Mark R. Levin, *Unfreedom of the Press* (New York: Simon & Schuster, 2019).

[107] Reeder, *First: The Life and Faith of Emma Smith*, pp. 3-4.

[108] Brigham Young, October 7, 1866, "Brigham Young Addresses, 1865—69," 5:116—19, Brigham Young Papers, LDS Church Library.

confidential matters from her? Was she telling her beloved eldest son what she knew he wanted to hear, not what she actually may have remembered? Was her memory influenced by David Whitmer and others, especially since, as she indicated in her 1870 letter, she no longer had her old records to consult? Or, was she also focused to the exclusion of any other conflicting memories on rebutting the Spalding theory, the greatest threat at the time to her late husband's legacy?

Or, as we have theorized, were her "answers" in this posthumous account primarily the work of Joseph III, an accomplished writer who was perhaps giving his late mother an eloquence only loosely based on what she said?[109] Still another possibility is that Emma's memory and mental faculties were diminished as she approached her death. In a letter to his uncle William Smith shortly after Emma's death, Joseph III reported that he "found her fast failing."[110] This would have left

---

[109] RLDS historian Richard Howard asks if Emma had "'psychologically blocked out' the painful, distasteful memories of these things, so that in truth she could no longer call them to mind? Or, was Emma primarily protecting her son's crucial leadership situation, and feeling increasing freedom to do so in view of what she felt to be her own impending demise? ... Or, was Emma trying to protect the good name of the church with which she had cast her lot on April 6, 1860, at Amboy, Illinois?" In any case, Howard concludes that "a careful reading of these Emma Smith statements indicates caution in accepting them literally, at face value, without raising questions inherent in the dynamics of the 1879 situation in which Joseph Smith III interviewed his mother." Howard also points to Joseph III's delays both until the end of his mother's life in seeking her views and in posthumously publishing them as further reasons for caution in evaluating the "Last Testimony." Richard P. Howard, "The Changing RLDS Response to Mormon Polygamy: A Preliminary Analysis," *The John Whitmer Historical Association Journal*, vol. 3 (1983), pp. 14-29, at pp. 25, 29, https://www.jstor.org/stable/43200716. We note that Howard is specifically discussing the 'Last Testimony's" sections relating to plural marriage, but we believe that his cautions are equally applicable to the rest of the document.

[110] Joseph Smith III to William Smith, (May 6, 1879) Community of Christ archives, Joseph Smith III transcript file 5 page 548. See also Hales, "Joseph Smith: Monogamist or Polygamist?" p. 137 note 75. Another aspect of this story, beyond the scope of this book, is that the reason Joseph III delayed so long in seeking this

Joseph III no choice but to complete the "interview" with the best information he had, which at the time was the SITH claims advanced by David Whitmer, William McLellin and others. In any case, dear as the "Last Testimony" may be, it is too unreliable to support a revisionist narrative that rejects the canonical narrative of the translation of the Book of Mormon.[111]

C. Edward Stevenson's report of Martin Harris in Utah

Martin Harris was a peripatetic character, always wanting to be known and in the know.[112] Originally, he was one of Joseph's greatest supporters, serving as the first major scribe until he lost all of the pages he had scribed. Even though he was thereafter largely barred from scribing, he still mortgaged his farm to finance the first printing of the Book of Mormon, and he was a stalwart in the first years of the Church. However, he eventually broke with Joseph and was excommunicated in 1837.

After his break with the Church, at various times he affiliated with various Restoration break-offs as well as briefly with the Shakers. Martin remained in Kirtland, where he was a self-appointed custodian and tour guide for visitors to the Temple. With a couple of possible exceptions, all pre-1870 accounts of his descriptions of the translation

---

interview was the assertion of many older members of his church, who had been adults in Nauvoo, that his father had indeed been involved with plural marriage and that his mother knew about it.

[111] See William L. Davis, *Visions in a Seer Stone: Joseph Smith and the Making of the Book of Mormon* (Chapel Hill, NC: University of North Carolina Press, 2020), pp. 178-187. Although Davis accepts SITH, he reaches similar conclusion with regard to the unreliability of the "Last Testimony" as evidence of anything relating to the Book of Mormon. Rather he also finds Emma's remarks wholly skewed to serve Joseph III's need for evidence against the Spalding theory.

[112] The best recent biography of Martin is Susan Easton Black and Larry C. Porter, *Martin Harris: Uncompromising Witness of the Book of Mormon* (Provo, UT: BYU Studies, 2018).

mention only the use of the interpreters for the translation of the Book of Mormon.[113]

In 1870, at the age of 87, he finally went to Utah after Edward Stevenson organized a fund-raising effort among LDS Church members to cover his travel on the newly completed transcontinental railroad. Martin almost did not make the trip after suffering a blackout, possibly a stroke, one night shortly before his departure.[114] Stevenson accompanied Martin on the train ride to Utah, a journey that produced one of the more enigmatic statements attributed to Martin, as we will see below.

Martin arrived in Ogden on August 29, 1870, and in Salt Lake City a day later. On September 4, 1870, Martin spoke at a Sunday meeting, but the content of his speech was never published.[115] Eleven years later, in 1881 (six years after Martin's death in 1875), Stevenson published an article in the *Deseret News* that related Stevenson's recollections of his experiences with Martin. After mentioning Martin's arrival in Utah and quoting four newspaper articles about that event, Stevenson described a claim about the translation that Martin had made to him during the train ride to Utah back in 1870.

---

[113] Neville, *A Man That Can Translate*, pp. 167-183 reviews the various accounts of Martin's descriptions of the translation.

[114] Black and Porter, *Martin Harris*, p. 421.

[115] The September 5, 1870, issue of the *Deseret Evening News* contains a notice of the meeting where Martin spoke. See "Sabbath Meetings" *Deseret Evening News*, (September 5, 1870), p. 2 at https://news.google.com/newspapers?nid=AulkAQHnToC&dat=18700905&printsec=frontpage&hl=en. A longer article about Martin's arrival was published a few days later on September 7, 1870, but does not give any account of what he said. See "Martin Harris – One of the Witnesses of the Book of Mormon," *Deseret Evening News* (September 7. 1870) p. 3 at https://contentdm.lib.byu.edu/digital/collection/desnews2/id/43437/rec/36. A transcript of an 1870 interview of Martin by Stevenson also does not contain any record of either the use of the seer stone or the stone-swapping story. See Black and Porter, *Martin Harris*, pp. 431 – 433.

Martin Harris related an instance that occurred during the time that he wrote that portion of the translation of the Book of Mormon, which he was favored to write direct from the mouth of the Prophet Joseph Smith. He said that the Prophet possessed a seer stone, by which he was enabled to translate as well as from the Urim and Thummim, and for convenience he then used the seer stone.... Martin said, after continued translation they would become weary and would go down to the river and exercise by throwing stones out on the river, etc. While so doing on one occasion, Martin found a stone very much resembling the one used for translating, and on resuming their labor of translation, Martin put in place the stone that he had found. He said that the Prophet remained silent unusually and intently gazing in darkness, no traces of the usual sentences appearing. Much surprised, Joseph exclaimed, "Martin! What is the matter? All is as dark as Egypt." Martin's countenance betrayed him, and the Prophet asked Martin why he had done so. Martin said, to stop the mouths of fools, who had told him that the Prophet had learned those sentences and was merely repeating them, etc. Martin said further that the seer stone differed in appearance entirely from the Urim and Thummim that was obtained with the plates, which were two clear stones set in two rims, very much resembled spectacles, only they were larger Martin said there were not many pages translated while he wrote; after which Oliver Cowdery and others did the writing. [116]

---

[116] Edward Stevenson's account of Harris' Sunday Morning Lecture in Salt Lake City, September 4, 1870, appears in the *Deseret News* on December 28, 1881 (https://newspapers.lib.utah.edu/details?id=2634097) as a letter to the editor dated November 30, 1881. The article appears to indicate that the original account of Martin's remarks was published in the *Deseret Evening News* September 5, 1870, yet it is not in that 1870 issue of the newspaper. This 1881 article was reprinted in the *Millennial Star* 44 (February 6, 1882), 86-87 and elsewhere. This account of Martin's comment about Joseph's use of the seer stone thus appears in many different sources,

Transcription and the SITH Narrative

This story—Joseph using a "seer stone ... for convenience" and Martin swapping Joseph's seer stone leaving Joseph unable to translate—has been cited to support the SITH theory. The story contradicts not only what Joseph Smith and Oliver Cowdery taught, but also almost all of the dozens of accounts of Martin's description of the translation both before and after his arrival in Utah, which refer only to the Urim and Thummim interpreters.[117] Because the evidence points to Stevenson as the only direct source for the story, we have to consider if the article accurately related something Martin told Stevenson.

The first known publication of the story was this 1881 article, 52 years after the alleged events, eleven years after Martin allegedly related it to Stevenson on the train to Utah, and six years after Martin died in 1875. Stevenson apparently wrote the 1881 article based solely on his memory from the 1870 train ride. If he recorded it contemporaneously, the record is lost because there is a gap in his journal between January 1870 and 26 February 1871.[118]

---

but these are all reprints of or based on this one anomalous reference to the seer stone from a secondhand report first published years after Martin's death.

[117] See for example the Martin Harris collection in Vogel, *Early Mormon Documents*, volume 2, pp. 260 – 393, available beginning at https://archive.org/details/volume-2_202011/page/259/mode/2up. Aside from Stevenson and a few confused and hostile newspaper reports, all other accounts by Martin in those 130 pages refer only to the Urim and Thummim interpreters being used by Joseph. Note that in many of the accounts Martin is reported as only using the term "Urim and Thummim." As will be discussed later in this chapter, SITH advocates use the scholarly sleight of hand of claiming that the term "Urim and Thummim" came to be also used for seer stones. However, that Martin only used it to refer to the interpreters can be seen by Edward Stevenson's own report where he claims Martin said that Joseph "possessed a seer stone, by which he was enabled to translate as well as from the Urim and Thummim ....".

[118] Edward Stevenson *Book 1: Typescript journals (1852 April 6 – 1871 August 3)*, volume 11, p. 1 (p. 308/332 https://catalog.churchofjesuschrist.org/assets/559c8308-21e9-4edf-95c2-adabdcfc31c6/0/0.

During the train trip to Utah when Martin supposedly recounted the seer stone stories to Stevenson, Martin gave an interview to an Iowa newspaper which reported that:

> Mr. Harris describes the plates as being of thin leaves of gold, measuring seven by eight inches, and weighing altogether, from forty to sixty lbs. There was also found in the chest, the Urim and Thummim, by means of which the writing upon the plates was translated… By means of the Urim and Thummim "a pair of large spectacles," as Mr. Harris termed them, the translation was made, and Mr. Harris claims to have written, of the translations as they were given by Smith, "116 solid pages of cap [foolscap]."[119]

During the five years he lived in Utah until his death, Martin bore his testimony of the Book of Mormon on many occasions, and there are many written accounts by his listeners of hearing directly from one of the Three Witnesses.[120] Yet, none of these accounts record Martin telling the stone-swapping story or of Joseph using the seer stone.

This account from 1870, reported contemporaneously in a non-LDS newspaper, comports well with a firsthand report of an interview with Martin Harris by John A. Clark (also not LDS) 30 years earlier in 1840, where Martin told Clark that:

> The way that Smith made his transcripts and transcriptions for Harris was the following. Although in the same room, a thick curtain or blanket was suspended between them, and Smith concealed behind the blanket, pretended to look through his spectacles, or transparent stones, and would then write down or repeat what he

---

[119] A Witness to the Book of Mormon," *Des Moines Iowa State Register*, August 28, 1870; in Vogel, *Early Mormon Documents*, volume 2, p. 330 and available at http://www.sidneyrigdon.com/dbroadhu/IA/misciow2.htm#081670. We would note that, unlike the backdated 1881 "article," this account was published at the time of the original interview. Further, Stevenson himself noted this event in his journal.

[120] Many of the accounts of Martin's testimonies in Utah are gathered in Black and Porter, *Martin Harris*, pp. 465 – 511.

saw, which, when repeated aloud, was written down by Harris, who sat on the other side of the suspended blanket. Harris was told that it would arouse the most terrible divine displeasure, if he should attempt to draw near the sacred chest, or look at Smith while engaged in the work of deciphering the mysterious characters. This was Harris's own account of the matter to me.[121]

After Stevenson published the stone-swapping story in 1881, it became popular and has been often repeated, mostly recently appearing in the 2021 movie *Witnesses*. Inexplicably, historians have also accepted this tale uncritically at face value without addressing the fact that it conflicts with these and dozens of other reliable accounts of Martin affirming the use of the interpreters for the translation. On the other hand, despite the inherent problem of Stevenson's late and posthumous retelling of Martin's story, we have no reason to question that the incident occurred or that Martin did recount it to Stevenson.

A clue to understanding the incident may come from its timing. The first reference to the story in Stevenson's extensive journals does not occur until 1887 when he recounts his third and final visit to David Whitmer. There, after noting that Joseph III by this point had turned against David's SITH claims (quoted in the previous subchapter), Stevenson writes that David recounted a version of the stone-swapping incident, where David says that:

---

[121] John A. Clark, *Gleanings by the way*, (Philadelphia: W.J. & J.K. Simon, 1842), pp. 230-231, available at https://archive.org/details/gleaningsbyway00clarrich/page/230/mode/2up. SITH advocates Dirkmaat and MacKay attack Clark's account on the grounds that he was unfriendly to the Mormons (*Let's Talk About the Translation*, pp. 103-104). They assume that Clark was influenced by *Mormonism Unvailed*, making Clark unreliable, yet they also: (1) uncritically accept on their face any source that supports their SITH narrative and (2) never acknowledge that *Mormonism Unvailed* is the first published account of Joseph's use of a seer stone to produce the Book of Mormon.

after the loss of the 116 pages the remainder of the translation was done with the Seer stone, and that Martin wrote some & it was at this time when Martin put the wrong stone in the hat deceiveing [sic] the Prophet who looked into the hat when he exclaimed all is as dark as Egypt. Martin Said he done this to stop the Mouths of fools who said the Prophet knew by heart & would repeat. Martin Harris related more fully the same story when I brought him from Kirtland Ohio.[122]

While Martin is best known as the scribe for the 116 pages from April to June of 1828, he appears to have also been a scribe briefly in March 1829 after the return of the plates (and interpreters), but before the arrival of Oliver Cowdery in April 1829.[123] (As the main scribe for the Book of Mormon we have, Oliver always stated that Joseph

---

[122] Edward Stevenson, *Book 4: Typescript journals (1886 January 14 - 1887 August 20)*, volume 28, p. 52 (p. 200-202/330) at https://catalog.churchofjesuschrist.org/assets/bc546251-522d-430a-a259-964bd8bde02f/0/0. Stevenson does not explain where David heard of the stone-swapping account. David may have heard it directly from Martin at some point, or David may have read Stevenson's own 1881 account in the *Deseret News* and simply told Stevenson that the event occurred after the loss of the 116 pages because he, David, believed Joseph did not have the Urim and Thummim after the 116 pages were lost. David never related the story in the dozens of interviews he gave, so it seems more likely that he learned about it from Stevenson's 1881 article, particularly because David added no details beyond what was already published in the 1881 article.

[123] When Martin Harris lost the 116 pages in the summer of 1828, Joseph had to forfeit the plates and the Urim and Thummim. After he received them back again, he resumed the translation of the abridged plates in the Book of Mosiah with Emma writing for him. We are left to infer from Section 5:30 that Martin was an additional pre-Oliver scribe for "not many pages," as Stevenson related in his 1881 article. The extant Original Manuscript does not feature the handwriting of Emma or Martin so we cannot tell which part of the text they may have recorded. The pages they likely scribed in Harmony—much or all of Mosiah through the first few chapters of Alma—were lost or destroyed. The extant manuscript begins with the handwriting of Oliver Cowdery at Alma 10:31.

translated with the Nephite interpreters.[124]) In March 1829 a revelation (now Section 5 of the Doctrine and Covenants) was given at the request of Martin Harris. The possibility that the stone-swapping incident occurred close in time to the receipt of the revelation suggests the two may be linked.

The revelation begins by re-iterating the covenant Joseph made to not show the sacred translation materials (plates and interpreters) to anyone (verses 3 and 4), which means neither Martin or Emma, while still scribing some at this time, would have been allowed to see these objects. However, it also contains an oblique reference to Martin seeing "the things which he desires to *know*" (verse 24), which was changed for the 1835 Doctrine and Covenants to read "the things which he desires to *see*." While this can be referring to his eventual call as one of the Three Witnesses, it may also refer to Joseph going along with his stone-swapping gambit to satisfy Martin's curiosity and get him to stop pestering Joseph on the subject (verse 29).[125]

---

[124] Oliver's testimony on this point was consistent throughout his life. We have quoted his writings during the 1830s, and will discuss later in this subchapter what he said on returning to the Church at the end of his life. Soon after the beginning of the Church, a report published in 1831 states that in a trial "Oliver Cowdry, one of the three witnesses to the book, testified under oath, that said Smith found with the plates, from which he translated his book, two transparent stones, resembling glass, set in silver bows. That by looking through these, he was able to read in English, the reformed Egyptian characters, which were engraved on the plates" A. W. Benton, "Mormonites," *Evangelical Magazine and Gospel Advocate* (Utica, NY), vol. 2, no. 15 (Apr. 19, 1831), available at https://www.mrm.org/mormonites. See Appendix B for all of Oliver's statements on the translation.

[125] This timing would also allow us to place the stone-swapping incident into a broader context. Martin had been seeking external validation for a long time, including his trip to visit scholars (most famously Charles Anthon) and his persistence in pursuing permission to take the 116-page manuscript back to Palmyra to show his wife and a few others. Stevenson wrote that Martin's motive in carrying out the stone-swapping trick was to "to stop the mouths of fools, who had told him that the Prophet had learned those sentences and was merely repeating them, etc." If David Whitmer's proposed March 1829 timing is correct, these "fools" could have

With this perspective, let us take a fresh look at this episode. First, it is unlikely that Joseph would not have recognized that Martin had swapped a river stone for the stone Joseph had been supposedly staring at for years (starting before he got the plates). Even if, as we argue, Joseph was not using the seer stone for translation, he had been carrying it around for many years. Thus, it is unlikely that Martin really fooled Joseph with the substitute stone.

Second, it is likely that Martin was using the stone swap to bolster his faith. While Joseph never used the stone to translate (which Martin would not know, being on the other side of the blanket), he kept it nearby on the table for whatever reason. During a break in the translation, Martin sees the stone, assumes Joseph was using it to translate, picks it up and swaps it with the one he found at the river.

Another possibility, which we will discuss below, is that Joseph showed Martin the stone in an attempt to explain what he was doing behind the blanket while still obeying the charge to not show the interpreters.

Either way, when Joseph returned, he saw the similar, yet different, stone and indulged Martin's attempted test—thus allowing Martin to "know" what he wanted to know, while abiding by his covenant to not display the sacred objects. Alternatively, Joseph could have played along with Martin's prank, consistent with Joseph's playful disposition, hoping this would resolve Martin's incessant queries about the translation process.[126] (Joseph's use of the seer stone as a demonstration will be discussed further below in subchapter F.)[127]

---

been people in Palmyra to whom Martin showed the 116 pages, but who still did not believe his story. Most importantly, this could have included his wife, who remained dubious about Martin's involvement with Joseph. As always, the imprecision of the available historical records makes it impossible to come to any more exact conclusions.

[126] On Joseph's playful side, see Bushman, *Rough Stone Rolling*, pp. 6-7, 483-485.

[127] There are two earlier statements, possibly originating with Martin, that appeared in the August and September 1829 newspaper accounts mentioned earlier

Martin probably eventually realized that Joseph was humoring him during the stone-swapping incident. Although he regaled his traveling companion Edward Stevenson with the story during their long hours on the train to Utah, he did not appear to find it worth repeating to anyone else. It is possible that Martin never related the incident publicly precisely because he realized it was intended only to bolster his private faith. Far more significant to Martin was his direct angelic manifestation as one of the Three Witnesses. And, as evidenced by the dozens of accounts of his testimonies, Martin also came to understand that the translation was accomplished using the interpreters, not the seer stone.

The stone-swapping story came to us posthumously as second-hand hearsay that may or may not have included Martin's actual words and the entire context of the incident. So, is the story a pointless anecdote which should be forgotten despite Edward Stevenson's diligent efforts to preserve it? We would suggest that a spiritual insight is still available from this little event. If, as we believe, Martin failed to fool Joseph with the substitute stone, why did Joseph play along with Martin's rather silly gambit?

What we note is that Joseph did not rebuke or mock Martin. He understood that for Martin seer stones were real, and that at this point in his spiritual journey this episode was important to Martin. Therefore, Joseph went to where Martin was, and walked with him patiently and graciously while his seed of faith was still just budding. For his part, Joseph showed his faith that this superstitious older man

---

in this book. Both say that "by placing the spectacles in a hat, and looking into it, Smith could (he said so, at least) interpret these characters." Because Joseph was forbidden from showing the Urim and Thummim or Nephite interpreters to anyone, these accounts reflect a misunderstanding on the part of the reporter, or hearsay, or an assumption by Martin because he could not have seen the interpreters until after the translation was complete. In any case, Martin's own reference to the spectacles in these 1829 articles casts doubt on his stone swapping account if he gave it to Edward Stevenson in the 1870s.

would become the man who would sacrifice his farm to bring forth the Book of Mormon, and bear valiant testimony of it for the next 45 years.

And what of Edward Stevenson? Did he believe that the stone-swapping story and the lone sentence about Joseph being able to use a seer stone to translate overthrew Joseph's entire account of the coming forth of the Book of Mormon?

Edward Stevenson was the type of person who liked to see for himself. No sooner had he gotten Martin Harris to Utah in 1870, he was off again on the still brand-new transcontinental railroad on another mission to the eastern United States. He had joined the Church in 1834, emigrated to Missouri and therefore personally witnessed all the events from then onward. However, he had never seen the New York locations important to Church history. So on this trip, long before guided tours and travel study or the LDS Church's acquisition of properties there, in 1871 Edward Stevenson visited Palmyra, the Hill Cumorah and other important New York sites.

He claimed to have traveled over 100,000 miles on his missions. However, it was not mileage that was important to Edward Stevenson, but what was done on those travels. For example, many Saints called on Martin Harris in Ohio and David Whitmer in Missouri, but it was Edward Stevenson who worked to build a personal rapport with the Witnesses.

You may know the type, or be one yourself. Senior couples going on missions, the more exotic the destination the better, or travelers who always visit temples wherever they go. But it is not only love of travel, it is people who fill their accounts, not just sites. People they talked to about the Restored Gospel, the wonderful members they worked with and loved. If our religion had them, we would propose Edward Stevenson as a patron saint of these latter-day pilgrims.

Apparently always a raconteur as well, in his later life before his call to serve as one of the presidents of the Seventy, Stevenson would give presentations on these travels and experiences. In 1893, he published a short book of them, *Reminiscences of Joseph, the Prophet, and*

Transcription and the SITH Narrative

the coming forth of the Book of Mormon.[128] It briefly recounts the stone-swapping anecdote and reports that Martin "said that the Prophet possessed a seer stone as well as the Urim and Thummim by means of which he could translate the characters."[129] However, there are two significant differences with the 1881 account.

First, the *Reminiscences* uses the statement about seer stones directly as an introduction to the stone-swapping anecdote. Stevenson gives it no separate significance. Second, he drops the words "for convenience" in reference to why Joseph might have used the seer stone. Those words also apparently held no importance for Stevenson. However, SITH advocates have placed enormous importance on this concept. In sum, the argument is that the seer stone was easier to use than the interpreters, therefore, Joseph only used the seer stone.[130] Is this what Edward Stevenson intended to show in his book?

If we step back and look at the entirety of Stevenson's book, it is hard to see this SITH argument as anything other than proof-texting. In *Reminiscences* Stevenson spends only a few sentences on the stone-swapping anecdote. However, when it comes to the question of how the Book of Mormon was translated, Edward Stevenson firmly follows Joseph's account that it was through the Urim and Thummim interpreters. A fifth of the book's pages discuss the Urim and Thummim interpreters, including an illustration of Moroni delivering the plates and spectacle-like interpreters to Joseph.[131] Stevenson writes that Joseph "could not have accomplished the work entrusted to him

---

[128] Edward Stevenson, *Reminiscences of Joseph, the Prophet, and the coming forth of the Book of Mormon* (Salt Lake City, UT, published by the author, 1893) available at https://catalog.churchofjesuschrist.org/assets/665af85e-da18-4a2b-a5f5-2b4bbd033797/0/0.

[129] Stevenson, *Reminiscences*, p. 30.

[130] See, for example, Van Wagoner and Walker, "Joseph Smith - The Gift of Seeing," p. 53, MacKay and Dirkmaat, *From Darkness unto Light*, p. 92 and https://youtu.be/FKiJOAWNyAk?t=53 (March 19, 2018, accessed November 12, 2022).

[131] Stevenson, *Reminiscences*, pp. 7, 19 – 24, 27 – 28, 31 – 33. The illustration is on p. 21.

without the aid of the Urim and Thummim. It was therefore provided to him."¹³²

And here is the ultimate context. SITH advocates selectively cite a few generally late, often posthumous, secondhand accounts to support their position, but ignore the fact that the overwhelming consensus of then contemporary believers in the Book of Mormon was that Joseph used the interpreters to translate it. We have discussed the only two contrary accounts supposedly from actual scribes, and shown that they were either unreliable or proof-texting contrary to the total context of their sources.

Like the leadership of the RLDS Church, the senior leaders of the LDS Church all sustained Joseph and Oliver's plates-and-interpreters account, even making it part of the LDS Church's canon (Standard Works of scripture) in 1880. These men—we are talking about Brigham Young, John Taylor, Wilford Woodruff, Orson Pratt, etc.—were all contemporaries and close associates of Joseph and Oliver (and also knew David Whitmer personally).¹³³ Any use of these few out-of-context examples to challenge the canonical narrative should at least acknowledge these overwhelming teachings of actual prophets and

---

¹³² Stevenson, *Reminiscences*, p. 23, available at https://catalog.churchofjesuschrist.org/assets/665af85e-da18-4a2b-a5f5-2b4bbd033797/0/34.
Lest SITH advocates try here their usual obfuscation of the meaning of "Urim and Thummim," Stevenson continues to identify the Urim and Thummim with the interpreters described in the Book of Mosiah. "By the above we learn that the Urim and Thummim or interpreters was anciently used and answered the descriptions of these that Joseph is represented as receiving." *Reminiscences*, p. 24.

¹³³ See Neville, *A Man That Can Translate*, pp. 367 – 371. One might ask why the LDS Church did not correct this errant sentence at the time. We can think of several possible reasons. First, it was so obscure no one, including Edward Stevenson, probably could have imagined that LDS academics would someday use it to overthrow all that the first elders of the Church, Joseph and Oliver, taught about the Book of Mormon. Second, there was no correlation at the time to oversee such matters. Third, during the 1880s, the United States government was trying to destroy the LDS Church, which rather pre-occupied the attention of the LDS Church's leadership during this time.

apostles to the contrary. And, as we have seen, like them, Joseph Smith III, Martin Harris and Edward Stevenson were also all solid Urim and Thummim men.[134]

Which brings us to David Whitmer.

D. David Whitmer - leading source for the SITH narrative

The one figure in Restoration history who indisputably advanced the full SITH narrative was David Whitmer, one of the Three Witnesses. He claimed that Joseph did not receive back the interpreters after Martin Harris' loss of the first part of the translation, and that the entire Book of Mormon we have today came from the seer stone in the hat rather than the plates.

That David Whitmer's views on the translation should now prevail in LDS scholarly circles is surprising. David was never a scribe for Joseph. He was never in Harmony while the majority of the translation took place, and he admitted that he was not present for most of the translation even in Fayette. Everything he said about Joseph's mental process was hearsay or speculation.[135]

After carefully reviewing all of David's statements about the translation, Kenneth Godfrey concluded that "historians and teachers of Mormon history should be cautious in accepting Whitmer's version of the translation process." Godfrey found David's numerous accounts to be inconsistent and even contradictory, and advised that we "should remember that Whitmer, after all, was not an eyewitness

---

[134] Are you?

[135] See Joseph Fielding McConkie and Crag J. Ostler, "The Process of Translating the Book of Mormon," from *Revelations of the Restoration: A Commentary on the Doctrine and Covenants and Other Modern Revelation* (Salt Lake City, UT: Deseret Book, 2000), pp. 89-98, online at https://emp.byui.edu/satterfieldb/Rel121/Process%20of%20Translating%20the%20BofM.pdf at p. 4 of the pdf.

to the translation process."¹³⁶ And yet, inexplicably, David is accepted as a firsthand witness, while Joseph and Oliver's genuine firsthand accounts are ignored or minimized. ¹³⁷ Only the actual translator, Joseph, and possibly his primary scribe, Oliver, could speak from firsthand experience.¹³⁸

---

¹³⁶ Kenneth W. Godfrey, "David Whitmer and the Shaping of Latter-day Saint History," in Stephen D. Ricks, Donald W. Parry and Andrew H. Hedges (eds) *The Disciple as Witness: Essays on Latter-day Saint History and Doctrine in Honor of Richard Lloyd Anderson* (Provo, UT: The Foundation for Ancient Research and Mormon Studies, 2000) pp. 223 – 256, quotes at p. 236, available at https://scholarsarchive.byu.edu/cgi/viewcontent.cgi?filename=9&article=1083&context=mi&type=additional. See also the extensive analysis of David's unreliability as a witness to the translation process in Stoddard and Stoddard, *Seer Stone v. Urim & Thummim*, pp. 142 – 191.

¹³⁷ In MacKay and Dirkmaat, *From Darkness unto Light*, the authors admit that when "Cowdery told others how Joseph translated the plates, he apparently primarily referred to the spectacles, rather than an individual seer stone." (p. 127) However, instead of addressing the fact that a primary firsthand witness (who even these authors concede was the principal scribe for most of the Book of Mormon we have) directly refutes their entire hypothesis, the authors instead turn to David Whitmer's secondhand claim that he "believed that Joseph was using a single brown seer stone when he translated," and treat that as sufficient basis to thereafter simply ignore Oliver's witness and hide behind obfuscation of the meaning of the term Urim and Thummim (p. 129, emphasis added). In his chapter on "Translating and Printing the Book of Mormon" in John W. Welch and Larry E. Morris (eds), *Oliver Cowdery: Scribe, Elder, Witness* (Provo, UT: Neal A. Maxwell Institute for Religious Scholarship, 2006), available at https://criticaltext.byustudies.byu.edu/translating-and-printing-book-mormon, Royal Skousen cites almost entirely late David Whitmer statements and never refers to Joseph or Oliver's early accounts (see pp. 75-100).

¹³⁸ Richard Lloyd Anderson, universally recognized in the LDS scholarly community as the leading historian of the Three Witnesses, evaluated the evidence in exact opposition to the SITH proponents. Professor Anderson wrote in the *Ensign* that toward the end of the translation process "David Whitmer on occasion watched and afterwards spoke of the seer stone. Yet as an intimate assistant, Oliver Cowdery stressed the Urim and Thummim in his statements." Professor Anderson then quotes Oliver's 1834 statement now included as a note to Joseph Smith - History in the Pearl of Great Price that Oliver wrote Joseph's dictation "as he translated, with the *Urim* and *Thummim*, or as the Nephites would have said, 'interpreters,' the history,

And, as we have seen, Godfrey was hardly the first to make this observation. In his 1886 article, Joseph Smith III noted that Joseph and Oliver "best knew by what means the Book of Mormon was translated. ... it should be remembered that David Whitmer had nothing to do, directly, with the work of translating the Book of Mormon. He was neither translator nor scribe, but only an occasional observer."[139] RLDS First Presidency first counselor William W. Blair was even more blunt, writing that David Whitmer ...

> was not a competent witness as to the "means" used by the Seer in translating the Book of Mormon. He did not meet Joseph the Seer until at least two months after Oliver Cowdery had been writing the Book of Mormon as the Seer translated it. David Whitmer never wrote a line of the Book of Mormon; and there is no evidence at hand to prove that the Seer ever showed him the "means" by which he translated. The purported testimony of David Whitmer as to the "means" by which the Book of Mormon was translated, is that of a man who had no direct hand in that translation, being neither translator nor scribe, but simply a "witness" after its translation, while, on the other hand, the testimony of Joseph Smith and Oliver Cowdery is that of men who were the immediate agents in the translation ... . The testimony of Joseph and Oliver was given in the first years of the church, while these matters were fresh in the minds of these chief actors and the Saints; while that which purports to

---

or record called 'The Book of Mormon.'" Later in the article Professor Anderson cautioned against accepting David Whitmer's statements "at face value [as] ... David Whitmer had not personally translated [and] ... had no personal knowledge of the translation itself." Professor Anderson believed that David Whitmer's "highly rigid" views on scriptural inerrancy "may have influenced his view of the translation," a rigidity which was incompatible with the many changes Joseph made to later editions. (In subchapter F we will present two possible alternative origins for David's seer stone statements.) Richard Lloyd Anderson, "By the Gift and Power of God," *Ensign* (September 1977), pp. 78-85 available at https://www.churchofjesuschrist.org/study/ensign/1977/09/by-the-gift-and-power-of-god?lang=eng, quotes at pp. 80, 81, 82, 84.

[139] Joseph Smith III, "David Whitmer Reviewed," quote at p. 707.

come from David Whitmer was given when he had become feeble with infirmities and multiplied years.[140]

It must be of some weight that all those who knew David Whitmer personally and were cognizant of the issues, whether Joseph Smith III and W. W. Blair, or Orson Pratt, Brigham Young, John Taylor and Wilford Woodruff, rejected David's version of the translation. And they did understand what David Whitmer (and modern SITH advocates) were contending.

We have already seen that Joseph III and W. W. Blair were responding directly to David's claims. Similarly, Edward Stevenson recorded in his journal that David told him "that the Prophet translated first by the urim & thumin & after by a Seer Stone." He included this with his notes that David said that the publication of the Doctrine & Covenants "would result in Evil & that the Prophet had Gone astray & he did not believe in Revelations Received by the Prophet since that time." These claims lead even the genial Edward Stevenson to bear a "faithful testimony" to David "of the work being onward & invited him to give heed & search for the mind of the Lord & gather up to Zion …".[141]

Yet David's SITH statements seem so sure, so firm, that they have convinced modern scholars to reject Joseph and Oliver's testimony and give preference to David's version. Why did David Whitmer late in life so forcefully contradict Joseph and Oliver and, for that matter, even his own earlier statements?[142]

---

[140] W. W. Blair, *The Saints Herald*, (March 3, 1888), quote at p. 129.

[141] Stevenson, *Book 2: Typescript journals (1871 August 13 - 1882 October 22)*, volume 15, pp. 5 – 6, available at https://catalog.churchofjesuschrist.org/assets/b2a3c8cc-3f2f-4563-91ed-7f43a1259907/0/0.

[142] On David Whitmer's changing and inconsistent statements regarding the translation, see Lee H. Pearson, "David Whitmer: Man of Contradictions – An Analysis of Statements by David Whitmer on Translation of the Book of Mormon" (February 10, 2019), at https://josephsmithfoundation.org/papers/an-analysis-of-

To understand we must remember that David eventually denounced Joseph as a fallen prophet, and rejected the principles of continuing revelation, priesthood restoration, and the entirety of the Doctrine and Covenants.[143] We raise this point not to make an ad hominem attack on David as an apostate. He testified to the divine authenticity of the Book of Mormon through opposition and dangers throughout his life. However, he did come to reject everything Joseph did in his prophetic ministry after the publication of the Book of Mormon.

In Chapter 1(F) we discussed the difficulties with witness testimony, and how hard it can be to distinguish what a witness really saw from suppositions and assumptions they project on to their memories. This can be seen in David Whitmer's case by comparing two incidents from the earliest history of the Church as described by David.

---

statements-by-david-whitmer-on-translation-of-the-book-of-mormon/, Neville, *A Man That Can Translate*, chapter 8, and Godfrey, "David Whitmer and the Shaping of Latter-day Saint History." David's contradictions continued well into the 1870s as can be seen by comparing two different interviews, both published in the *Saints Herald* in 1879. Thomas Wood Smith claims that David told him the translation was done with the Urim and Thummim (Thomas Wood Smith, "Origin of the Mormon Bible," *Fall River (MA) Herald*, 28 March 1879; reprinted in the *The Saints' Herald* 26 (15 April 1879) available at https://archive.org/stream/TheSaintsHerald_Volume_26_1879/the%20saints%20herald%20volume%2026%201879#page/n125/mode/2up) whereas J. L. Traughber Jr. claims David said the translation was done "by means of one dark colored, opaque stone, called a "Seer Stone," which was placed in the crown of a hat, into which Joseph put his face" (J. L. Traughber Jr., "Testimony of David Whitmer," *Saints' Herald* 26 (November 15, 1879), p. 341 and in Vogel, *Early Mormon Documents*, volume 5, p. 58).

[143] David Whitmer, *An Address to All Believers in Christ* (Richmond, MO, 1887) available at https://archive.org/details/addresstoallbeli00whit/mode/2up. There is a tendency to cite the first pages of David's book, where he strongly re-affirms his witness of the Book of Mormon, but ignore the rest of the book where he elaborates at length on these views and Joseph's alleged perfidy. This is where he repeats his SITH claims. To give David credit for consistency, he renounced Joseph Smith III as well as Brigham Young and John Taylor as successors to Joseph.

After the majority of the Book of Mormon (taken from the abridged plates) had been translated (as per Joseph and Oliver by using the interpreters), Oliver wrote to his friend David Whitmer to ask him to come to Harmony, Pennsylvania and transport Joseph and Oliver to the Whitmer family home in Fayette, New York to finish the translation. This David did, after a miraculous experience in which three strangers plowed overnight the fields for which David was responsible.

On the trip from Harmony back to Fayette, the men encountered a white-haired stranger walking along the road with a backpack. David offered to have the stranger ride with them, but he declined, telling them he was going to a different destination. Where? David never forgot the man's answer, for the stranger said he was going to Cumorah, the first time David had ever heard that name. Then they could no longer see the man, even though it was a sunny day and they were in the midst of open fields. David and Oliver turned to Joseph who, deeply moved, told them that the stranger was "one of the Nephites," and that he was carrying the plates.[144]

---

[144] David recounted this story to Edward Stevenson on each of his visits as well as to Joseph F. Smith and Orson Pratt when they visited him in 1878. David apparently recounted the event as well in the 1830s, because Zina Young remembered hearing it as a young woman and asked Edward Stevenson to ask David about it on his first visit to David in 1877. Edward Stevenson, *Book 2: Typescript journals (1871 August 13 - 1882 October 22)*, volume 15, pp. 6 – 7, available at https://catalog.churchofjesuschrist.org/assets/b2a3c8cc-3f2f-4563-91ed-7f43a1259907/0/0. Shortly thereafter a man meeting the identical description visited David's mother, and showed her the plates. In all of his accounts David said that Joseph identified the man as "one of the Nephites," and Mary Whitmer always said that the man called himself "Brother Nephi." Although the names of the Three Nephites were not given in the Book of Mormon, it would seem a reasonable surmise that this is Nephi, son of Nephi and grandson of Helaman (3 Nephi 1:2), the Nephi of the Book of Third Nephi (as opposed to Nephi, son of Lehi) who led the church in the Nephite lands before Christ's appearance and was the senior of the twelve disciples. Nonetheless many years later one of Mary's grandsons and historian Andrew Jenson decided that

Here we have an incident to which David was a firsthand personal eyewitness. (We would note that the same would apply to the angelic manifestation that made him one of the Three Witnesses.) Contrast this with David's assertion (discussed in Chapter 1(F)), that the interpreters were not returned to Joseph after the loss of the first part of the manuscript because of Joseph's "transgressions." This assertion portrays Joseph as unworthy of using the plates or interpreters even during the translation, which in turn re-enforced David's eventual contention that Joseph was on the verge of failure as a prophet even as the Book of Mormon was going to press.[145]

Yet, David was not even present in Harmony when the first pages were lost. Nor did he ever even attempt to offer an explanation of how he knew the angel had refused to ever return the interpreters to Joseph due to his transgressions, when there is no question that David was personally over a hundred miles away when these events occurred. Nor does he explain how Joseph could be unworthy of the interpreters yet worthy of the plates themselves.

Why would David Whitmer make such baseless claims when both his personality and his culture led him to be scrupulously precise about events to which he was a true eyewitness? We do not need to say that

---

the old lady did not know what she was talking about, and that the man was Moroni. Andrew Jenson, "Mary Musselman Whitmer" in *Latter-day Saint biographical encyclopedia: a compilation of biographical sketches of prominent men and women in the Church of Jesus Christ of Latter-day Saints* (Salt Lake City, UT: The Andrew Jenson History Co., 1901), p. 283 available at https://archive.org/details/latterdaysaintbi01bjens/page/282/mode/2up. This error has been perpetuated through today, appearing in volume 1 of the *Saints* series. This is rather ironic, since one of the goals of the *Saints* books is supposedly to bring forward stories of women's contributions to the Restoration, and yet it completely disrespects the testimony of the thirteenth, and only female, Witness to the Book of Mormon.

[145] The evolution of David's discontent with Joseph and how it affected his changing versions of early events is described in H. Michael Marquardt, "David Whitmer: His Evolving Beliefs and Recollections," in Newell G. Bringhurst and John C. Hamer (eds) *Scattering of the Saints: Schism within Mormonism* (Independence, MO: John Whitmer Books, 2007) pp. 46 – 77.

David was deliberating lying. (Indeed, in subchapter F below we will suggest that David may have even seen Joseph use the seer stone as a demonstration or in connection with other revelations.) David made these claims only many decades after the events, decades during which he brooded over his disenchantment with Joseph's post-Book of Mormon prophetic ministry.

More than 40 years of dwelling on resentments can lead one to reform one's memories to justify those resentments, especially when the memories are based on assumptions and hearsay rather than actual observation. These perhaps subconscious adjustments would include exaggerating a one-time demonstration by Joseph using the seer stone in the hat to infer that that was the normal process. Another would be inflating the Lord's rebuke of Joseph following Martin's loss of the first pages to permanent withdrawal of the interpreters as punishment, despite David not being a witness to any of the events, and despite those who were witnesses saying the interpreters were returned for use with the rest of the translation.

These versions of events to which David was not a witness do not fit the facts as given by those who were witnesses, but they do fit David's later contention that Joseph was on the path to failure as a prophet and rejection by the Lord even during the translation.

In a review of a collection of David Whitmer interviews, Professor Richard Lloyd Anderson, the preeminent modern historian of the Three Witnesses, noted the conflict between the "early Cowdery and late Whitmer" translation accounts, with the early Cowdery accounts speaking of the interpreters while the late Whitmer accounts claim a single seer stone as the medium of translation. His view was that while a long passage of time "does not necessarily block out accurate recall, ... long-sustained rationalization is another thing." Professor Anderson summarized his "skepticism of David's interpretation of what he at times saw Joseph doing: 'Having left the Church, Whitmer developed a theory to explain Joseph's 'fall,' then explained translation in a way that fit his theory."'[146]

As we have said before, we have no explanation as to why modern scholars are so enthralled by David's account. As with the "Last Testimony," these LDS scholars accept David's SITH accounts on their face but presumably reject the rest of David's claims against Joseph's prophethood. Could it just be due to the frequency and certainty with which David recounted it at the end of his life, overwhelming far more reliable earlier firsthand accounts through sheer repetition and quantity?

Whatever the reason, in evaluating David's assertions about the translation process, we need to take account not only of their secondhand hearsay nature and their rejection by knowledgeable contemporaries, but of the probability that they were significantly distorted to conform to this larger agenda which rejected all that Joseph claimed and did after producing the Book of Mormon.

E. Was the seer stone also called a Urim and Thummim?

Joseph Smith - History 1:35 implies that it was Moroni who first identified the interpreters as the "Urim and Thummim." Similarly, our earliest and most detailed account of Moroni's visit, written by Oliver Cowdery with Joseph's assistance and published as Letter IV in the first history of the Church, also describes Moroni using the term.[147] However, because the term does not appear in the historical record until 1832, historians have inferred instead that Joseph (or another

---

[146] Richard Lloyd Anderson, "David Whitmer Interviews: A Restoration Witness" (book review), *Journal of Mormon History* (Spring 1994), vol. 20, no. 1, pp. 186 – 193, quotes at pp. 190, 191, available at http://digitalcommons.usu.edu/cgi/viewcontent.cgi?article=1022&context=mormonhistory. Professor Anderson attributed the phrasing of his summation to Richard L. Jensen.

[147] Oliver Cowdery, Letter IV, available at https://www.josephsmithpapers.org/paper-summary/history-1834-1836/69

contemporary such as W.W. Phelps) borrowed the term from the Bible and applied it to the spectacles.[148]

Regardless of the original application of the term, the interpreters obviously bore little resemblance to the biblical objects, which were jewels in the Jewish high priest's regalia.[149] However, the term came to have a broader meaning. For example, Joseph used the term figuratively in an 1843 revelation to describe the world where God dwells, the earth's post-millennial state and a gift to celestial beings.[150]

Some proponents of replacing the canonical narrative with the SITH narrative have argued that Joseph and Oliver used the term "Urim and Thummim" to apply to both the seer stone and the Nephite interpreters. These proponents argue that Joseph's 1843 broader use of the term should apply retroactively so that references to the Urim and Thummim even in 1834 also include the seer stone.[151]

---

[148] In July 1832, W.W. Phelps wrote that scattered Israel "were even to do without the Teraphim, [Urim & Thumim, perhaps] or sacred spectacles or declarers" *Evening and Morning Star* I.2:14 ¶4. In August 1832, a Boston newspaper reported that Samuel Smith and Orson Hyde said Joseph translated with the Urim and Thummim.. Abner Kneeland, "Questions proposed to the Mormonite Preachers and their answers obtained before the whole assembly at Julien Hall, Sunday Evening, August 5, 1832," *Boston Investigator* (August 10, 1832), Vol. 2, No. 20, available at http://www.sidneyrigdon.com/dbroadhu/NE/miscne01.htm#081032.

[149] Kenneth Sowers, Jr., "The Mystery and History of the Urim and Thummim," in Maurice L. Draper and A. Bruce Lindgren (eds), *Restoration Studies II* (Independence, MO: The Temple School, 1983), pp. 75 – 79.

[150] Doctrine and Covenants 130:8-11.

[151] See for example Van Wagoner and Walker, "Joseph Smith - The Gift of Seeing," pp. 61 – 63; Gardner, *The Gift and Power*, pp. 127 – 129; Nicholson, "The Spectacles, the Stone, the Hat, and the Book," pp. 148 – 153; MacKay and Dirkmaat, *From Darkness unto Light*, p. 129 and MacKay and Frederick, *Joseph Smith's Seer Stones*, pp. 128 – 130. The latter cite an incident when Hyrum Smith asked Joseph to dictate the revelation on plural marriage, but after he has done so Hyrum asks Joseph to do it again using a seer stone, which Hyrum calls a Urim and Thummim. The authors see this as evidence that seer stones are holy objects, (*Joseph Smith's Seer Stones* at p. 130). We see it as an example of the persistence of superstitious beliefs among his

However, *Mormonism Unvailed* in 1834 laid out a clear distinction between the "peep" stone and the Urim and Thummim. Joseph's 1838 history (now Joseph Smith – History in the Pearl of Great Price) and his 1842 Wentworth letter unambiguously identify the Nephite interpreters that accompanied the plates as the Urim and Thummim.[152] Oliver reiterated the point in his testimony upon rejoining the Church.

Even major sources cited by SITH proponents, such as Emma's 1870 letter to Emma Pilgrim and Edward Stevenson's recollections of his conversations with Martin Harris, both discussed above, use the term "Urim and Thummim" to refer only to the Nephite interpreters, whereas the seer stone is referred to as being a separate object. And in Edward Stevenson's journal, he quotes David Whitmer as making the distinction, noting that Whitmer preferred to refer to the Urim and Thummim as the Interpreters, and then referred to the "Seer stone" as a different object.[153]

Craig Ostler, a professor of religious education at Brigham Young University, has undertaken a comprehensive review of descriptions of the instruments used to translate the Book of Mormon. His research shows that until the 1843 revelation, no one used the term "Urim and Thummim" to mean anything other than the interpreters and that, in fact, in the 1830s and 1840s, almost the only written references to the use of a lone seer stone are from *Mormonism Unvailed*.[154] Almost all of the seer stone claims do not appear until decades later, and no one

---

followers which Joseph had to accommodate. See Chapter 5(C) for a discussion of a modern understanding of these objects and how to regard such continuing superstitious beliefs among early Saints.

[152] Joseph Smith, Jr., "Church History," *Times and Seasons* (1 March 1842) vol. 3, no. 9, p. 707 (Wentworth letter) at https://www.josephsmithpapers.org/paper-summary/church-history-1-march-1842/2

[153] Edward Stevenson, *Book 4: Typescript journals (1886 January 14 - 1887 August 20)*, volume 28, page 52 at https://catalog.churchofjesuschrist.org/assets/bc546251-522d-430a-a259-964bd8bde02f/0/0

[154] Craig Ostler, "Book of Mormon Translation Instrument Descriptions: Interpreters, Urim & Thummim and Seer Stones."

attempted to conflate the seer stone with the Urim and Thummim until modern scholars needed to confuse the two in order to account for this large time discrepancy between the early accounts of the interpreters and the much later appearance of the seer stone claims.

Most important to the subject of this book, when referring to the translation of the Book of Mormon, Joseph and Oliver used the term "Urim and Thummim" only to refer to the interpreters. In Appendix B we have collected all of Joseph and Oliver's recorded statements relating to the translation, and we invite the reader to review them to see the care that the two primary witnesses took to make this distinction clear.

F. The Demonstration and Pop-Out Hypotheses

The Demonstration Hypothesis. When faced with diametrically opposite witness statements, observers are tempted to pick one side and label contradictory witnesses on the other side as dishonest. For years, LDS authorities reiterated what Joseph and Oliver taught, implicitly rejecting SITH accounts as lies. Famously, Brigham Young called Emma a liar in the context of plural marriage. Critics predictably labeled Joseph and Oliver as the liars.

Some modern scholars seek to still the water with the oil of word thinking by claiming that both Joseph and Oliver used the term "Urim and Thummim" for both the interpreters and the seer stone, but as discussed above, that approach contradicts the historical record. For believers, it is problematic to label as liars either (i) Joseph and Oliver, or (ii) the other two of the Three Witnesses.[155]

---

[155] We should note that there were two other SITH accounts from people who were certainly around the Whitmer home during the translation there, 14 year old Elizabeth Whitmer (who later married Oliver Cowdery) and Joseph Knight. These accounts are also questionable (especially an 1870 affidavit allegedly from Elizabeth, of which a substantial part is missing and whose only source is hardline SITH

The common dilemma of conflicting witness statements is even more acute when dealing with historical documents because witnesses are unavailable for cross-examination or contemporaneous investigation of corroborating evidence. We cannot send a disinterested investigator back in time to interview all the witnesses, review all the facts, and render a balanced evaluation. However, astonishingly, there may have been such an investigator with regard to the production of the Book of Mormon.

During the 1870s and 1880s, Zenas H. Gurley, Jr., undertook to study all the material available on the source of the Book of Mormon, including interviewing both John and David Whitmer, the only surviving witnesses. Although his material has long been available to scholars, Gurley's observations and conclusions have generally been overlooked. On the LDS side, even though his work was reprinted in LDS publications, his conclusions may have been disregarded because he was an apostle of the RLDS Church who, among other ministries, had gone to Utah to denounce the "Brighamite" leadership. Yet, on the RLDS side he is generally only remembered for resigning from the church in 1886 after a major dispute with Joseph Smith III.[156]

As part of his research, Gurley interviewed John Whitmer who, in contrast to his brother David, had actually been a scribe for Joseph (and was also one of the Eight Witnesses). In direct contradiction to David's SITH account, Gurley reported that John Whitmer affirmed that when "the work of translation was going on he [John] sat at one table with his writing material and Joseph at another with the breastplate and Urim and Thummim. The latter were attached to the breast-

---

advocate William McLellin), but are in the historical record. They are addressed in detail in Neville's *A Man That Can Translate* at pp. 81, 239 - 244. Both Elizabeth Whitmer and Joseph Knight were likely present for the demonstration described here, and their accounts can also be explained by the demonstration hypothesis.

[156] Edwards, *Our Legacy of Faith*, pp. 154 -159 and Roger D. Launius, *Joseph Smith III: Pragmatic Prophet* (Urbana and Chicago, IL: University of Illinois Press, 1988), pp. 273 – 286. The LDS reprint of Gurley's work is at http://www.boap.org/LDS/Early-Saints/BOM-Witn.html.

plate and were two crystals or glasses, into which he looked and saw the words of the book."[157]

After considering all his research, in an article published in 1892, Gurley noted that David Whitmer (who Gurley interviewed in 1885) maintained his SITH views, and that Emma was reported as making such a statement in the "Last Testimony." However, Gurley concluded that "David and Emma, in the nature of things, did not know just how the Urim and Thummim were used, as they had never seen them" which led Gurley to discount their statements, explaining that "no one was allowed to see either the plates or the Urim and Thummim, except permitted by command of God."[158]

This strict prohibition did not apply to the seer stone, however: "that Joseph had another stone called seers' stone, and peep stone, is quite certain. This stone was frequently exhibited to different ones and helped to assuage their <u>awful curiosity</u>; but the Urim and Thummim never, unless possibly to Oliver Cowdery."[159]

This suggests an alternative solution: everyone was telling the truth about what they actually *observed*, but some also reported hearsay and inferences as fact. A careful reading of the record suggests that Joseph performed demonstrations with the seer stone to satisfy (or deflect) curiosity about his work. This left Joseph and his scribes free to perform the actual translation in private with the interpreters and the plates in compliance with Moroni's instructions that neither the plates nor the interpreters were to be shown to any unauthorized persons.[160]

---

[157] S. F. Walker, "Synopsis of a Discourse by Zenas H. Gurley," *The Saints Herald* (December 15, 1879, vol 26, issue 24), pp. 369 – 371, quote at p. 370, available at https://archive.org/details/TheSaintsHerald_Volume_26_1879/page/n369/mode/2up.

[158] Gurley, "The Book of Mormon," at p. 453.

[159] Gurley, "The Book of Mormon," at pp. 452 – 453 (emphasis added).

[160] Neville, *A Man That Can Translate* includes a more detailed examination of the "stone-in-the-hat" incidents and the demonstration hypothesis. See especially pp. 79 – 122. The commandment to keep the plates and interpreters private is in Joseph Smith – History 1:42, cited in Chapter 1(A) above.

To appreciate the significance of that "awful curiosity," we need to put ourselves back into the circumstances Joseph faced at the beginning of his prophetic ministry. The Church had not yet been organized. Everyone was new to the Restoration. Joseph's early followers sought revelations at his hand mainly because of their excitement about the new book of scripture and the wonders surrounding it, including Joseph's ability to translate the ancient plates.

And Joseph and his early followers lived in a culture where belief in folk magic persisted side-by-side with Christianity and Enlightenment rationalism. People who accepted folk beliefs were open to accepting that stones were capable of yielding guidance and information.[161] They would not understand the difference between a seer stone and the two stones in the interpreters. But the Lord, and Joseph Smith, did.[162]

In Chapter 5(C) we will argue that the interpreters (unlike the seer stone) are entirely plausible in the context of 21st century technology. But in the early 1800s, Joseph's contemporaries knew nothing of advanced technology. Given the strict command he was under, showing the seer stone to his supporters to "assuage their awful curiosity" was likely Joseph's only alternative, particularly because he was dependent on Martin Harris and the Whitmer family for the material sustenance necessary to permit him to carry out his work of translation.

A suggestion of how Joseph addressed this "awful curiosity" is seen in an interview which appeared in 1885 in the *Chicago Tribune*.

---

[161] Bushman, *Rough Stone Rolling*, pp. 48-52, 57.

[162] Orson Pratt observed that "this Urim and Thummim was formed in the first place. It was not something that existed on the earth in a natural state, it was something made by the Lord. He is a good mechanic, he understands how to make things." Orson Pratt, "King Limhi's Enquiry, From The Book Of Mormon—Ammon Replies—Seership And The Urim And Thummim—The Brother Of Jared, etc." (December 9, 1877) in *Journal of Discourses* (Liverpool, UK: William Budge, 1878) volume 19, quote at p. 214, available at https://contentdm.lib.byu.edu/digital/collection/JournalOfDiscourses3/id/929

There David Whitmer describes an event which occurred in his parents' home in Fayette, New York, where Joseph and Oliver were living while translating the plates of Nephi. Normally, Joseph and Oliver (and the other scribes) worked in privacy in an upstairs room. However, the Whitmers and other supporters were curious about the translation. A young woman working for the Whitmers threatened to quit if she was not told what the two young strangers were doing upstairs all day.[163]

In the *Tribune* article, David says the translation was in the main downstairs room of the Whitmer home and "was performed in the presence of ... the entire Whitmer household and several of Smith's relatives besides." Joseph commenced reciting sitting "on one side of a table and the amanuensis, in turn as they became tired, on the other." Note that in this account Joseph dictates so rapidly that three scribes (including Emma) took turns keeping up with his dictation.

As with all SITH accounts, there is no extant record of what, exactly, Joseph dictated at the session(s). No one reported that Joseph dictated the words of Nephi, or Jacob, or Isaiah, let alone recorded what he said (independently of the scribes).[164] Although the article implies that this public display was the normal translation procedure, in fact this event differed substantially from the normal translation process, which David separately described as "laborious" and which continued from "morning till night" (a 14-hour day in New York in

---

[163] The young woman, Sarah Conrad, joined the Church and lived to old age in Utah, where she recounted her story to Oliver Huntington. Of note is that she said Joseph and Oliver worked in the upstairs, out of sight of her and others in the house. From Diary of Oliver B. Huntington 1847-1900, Part II p. 415 in BYU Library, quoted in Richard Lloyd Anderson, "The House Where the Church Was Organized," *Improvement Era* 73 (April 1970) at p. 21 available at https://catalog.churchofjesuschrist.org/assets/af8e45bb-cf4a-43f4-8fb8-18a2f094d283/0/0.

[164] Historians have merely assumed that whatever he dictated ended up in the Original Manuscript, but the dictation could just as easily have been discarded. There is no "chain of custody" that directly ties the dictation during this event to the text.

June).¹⁶⁵ Instead of one scribe writing for a day or longer at a time, which we can see from the handwriting on the extant Original Manuscript for 1 Nephi, David describes three scribes taking turns as they tired.¹⁶⁶

Another indication that this demonstration was out of the norm was that the young woman who was so curious about the translation (Sarah Conrad, a relative of the Whitmers who later joined the Church) would have known what was going on if the translation was being carried out in public downstairs. Instead, her curiosity was piqued precisely because Joseph and Oliver were doing the translating upstairs out of sight of others in the household (which would include David).

The *Chicago Tribune* article is problematic because it conflates, combines and confuses many different sources. For example, it says that Joseph put the "spectacles" on his face in front of the crowd (which would be contrary to the strict command he was under), yet later gives David Whitmer's oft-repeated claim that the plates and "spectacles" were taken from Joseph and replaced with a "seer's stone [which] he was instructed to place in his hat, and on covering his face with the hat the character and translation would appear on the stone." Nonetheless, the article relates details that we can corroborate with other evidence. David's recollection of such a memorable dictation

---

¹⁶⁵ Bushman, *Rough Stone Rolling*, p. 76; James H. Hart, "About the Book of Mormon," *Deseret Evening News* (Salt Lake City), March 25, 1884 available at https://newspapers.lib.utah.edu/ark:/87278/s6d22s6w/2648947. Although he was not a scribe and therefore only a secondhand hearsay witness to the actual translation process, David was in his family home while the later translation was happening, and thus would be a firsthand witness as to the length of Joseph and Oliver's workdays, and how exhausted they appeared as a result of their labors.

¹⁶⁶ In *A Man That Can Translate*, Neville argues that, assuming whatever Joseph dictated ended up in the Original Manuscript, the demonstration probably consisted of Joseph reciting some of the Isaiah chapters from 2 Nephi which he memorized for the occasion from the KJV. Some of those chapters do in fact show the dropped and switched words that one would expect from a lengthy memorized recitation. Neville, *A Man That Can Translate*, pp. 89-115.

event may be part of what Zenas Gurley describes as Joseph's efforts to deal with his new supporters' "awful curiosity."[167]

As noted above, Martin Harris also is used as a SITH source (although the posthumous single source attributed to Martin is questionable), yet David Whitmer does not name him as being present at the demonstration in the Whitmer home. However, an 1831 newspaper article, which appears to derive from information from Martin, also describes Joseph dictating from a hat using a memorized Bible passage. The unfriendly newspaper account garbles facts and is obviously secondhand at best, but it also describes Joseph using the stone in the hat to allay his supporter's curiosity.[168]

Given the lack of detail in such accounts, we cannot say how much Joseph explained to his listeners, whether to an individual such as Emma or Martin, or to the crowd in the Whitmer home. The witness statements do not specifically quote Joseph as saying either that this was the actual translation or that it was a demonstration of the general nature of the process, but Joseph and Oliver claimed the actual process involved sacred objects (the plates and the interpreters) which could not be publicly displayed, a claim corroborated by John Whitmer. Whatever explanation Joseph gave, as attorneys we can say from experience that people generally do not pay much attention to disclaimers, especially when they are driven by "awful curiosity."

The Pop-Out Hypothesis. Another possible explanation for the SITH accounts is based on the fact that the interpreters were not used only

---

[167] "The Book of Mormon," *The Chicago Daily Tribune*, Vol. XLV Thursday, December 17, 1885, p. 3. The article is available at https://en.wikisource.org/wiki/Chicago_Daily_Tribune,_December_17,_1885 but is very difficult to follow. An annotated easier to read transcript is available at https://www.mobom.org/annotation-of-chicago-tribune-article.

[168] "Mormonites," *The Sun*, August 18, 1831, available at http://www.sidneyrigdon.com/dbroadhu/PA/Phil1830.htm#081831.

for translation.[169] Joseph made other inquiries through the interpreters, including those leading to a number of early revelations.[170] All modern accounts of the interpreters describe them as being set in a metal rim. However, the original description of the interpreters in the Book of Mormon (Ether 3:23-24) speaks only of the stones. (Mention of the rims does not appear until Nephite times in Mosiah 28:13.)

This raises the possibility that the stones could be removed from the rims and used independently of the plates for purposes other than translation. In such cases, Joseph may have placed the stone from the Urim and Thummim interpreter instrument in a hat, both the exclude exterior light and to hide it from the view of unauthorized persons, as per Moroni's instructions.

Four such revelations received through the Urim and Thummim were directed to David Whitmer's father and brothers (Sections 14, 15 and 16) and, most significantly, Section 17 authorizing the call of the Three Witnesses was directed to David along with Oliver and Martin.[171] The record does not explicitly say that any of these were present when Joseph received these revelations through the Urim and Thummim, but with the Urim and Thummim stone concealed from

---

[169] This concept originated from discussions with Jerry Grover and notes in the papers of the late Professor Richard Lloyd Anderson, but we are solely responsible for this particular formulation of the proposal.

[170] The 1832 Book of Commandments did not mention the Urim and Thummim. The 1835 Doctrine and Covenants added the Urim and Thummim to what became Section 10 and added what became Section 17, which also mentions the Urim and Thummim. We believe that the added references to the Urim and Thummim should be seen simply as clarifications, perhaps intended to respond to the SITH accusations which appeared the previous year in *Mormonism Unvailed*. References to use of the Urim and Thummim were to be added to the headings to Sections 3, 6, 7, 11, 14, 15, 16 and 17 of the LDS Doctrine and Covenants. See the footnotes following for sources for these references.

[171] Joseph Smith, Jr., *History, 1838–1856*, volume A-1 [23 December 1805–30 August 1834], p. 22, The Joseph Smith Papers, available at https://www.josephsmithpapers.org/paper-summary/history-1838-1856-volume-a-1-23-december-1805-30-august-1834/28.

view in the hat, the recipients may well have been present to see the process of receiving the revelation.¹⁷² Watching this process of receiving revelations through one of the Urim and Thummim "stones" placed in a hat could easily have led David and others who did not have direct knowledge of the actual translation process to assume that that was how the translation was done as well.

Either "translation" demonstrations as proposed by Gurley or seeing revelations unrelated to the translation (and hence not requiring the plates) through the Urim and Thummim stones secreted in a hat are likely the source of most, if not all, of the SITH accounts.

G. Early Modern English

Probably the most sophisticated effort to deflect evidence of Joseph Smith's active involvement in the creation of the Book of Mormon as either author or translator is the approach taken by Royal Skousen and Stanford Carmack. They claim that details in the vocabulary, grammar and syntax of the original manuscript of the Book of Mormon (dictated by Joseph Smith) constitute indicia of Early Modern English that predated even the KJV, so they were already obsolete by 1829. It would be impossible, they claim, for Joseph Smith or anyone else in his day to understand and properly implement these relics from Early Modern English.

Their research is impressive. They use sophisticated statistical analysis of large databases.¹⁷³ They generated a two-volume, 1383-page

---

[172] Joseph Smith, Jr., *History, 1838–1856*, volume A-1 [23 December 1805–30 August 1834], p. 23, The Joseph Smith Papers, available at https://www.josephsmithpapers.org/paper-summary/history-1838-1856-volume-a-1-23-december-1805-30-august-1834/29.

[173] For one critique of the statistical element, see Jonathan Green, "Of early modern English and the Book of Mormon," (April 1, 2019) at https://www.timesandseasons.org/index.php/2019/04/of-early-modern-english-and-the-book-of-mormon/

work that documents the basis for their theory.[174] Space will not permit us to detail why we disagree with their conclusions (although we accept their data), but the main problems with this approach are:

1. The only evidence we have of how Joseph Smith actually spoke is the verbatim record of his actual speech in the text of the Book of Mormon and early revelations that he dictated. No other verbatim transcripts of his speech are extant; even the few records of his later sermons are summaries of varying accuracy, such as the four accounts of the King Follet sermon. Skousen and Carmack turn this evidence on its head by claiming this only verbatim record of what Joseph dictated is *not* evidence of how Joseph spoke. Instead, they cite Joseph's 1832 *written* history to show how he *spoke* in 1829.[175]

The problems are obvious. Much of the 1832 history is in Joseph's own handwriting, showing it was not dictated; in fact, it may have been copied from a prior draft (and was therefore likely edited). Speaking and writing are two different skills; people do not write the way they talk. By 1832, Joseph was living in Kirtland among more educated people who taught him better grammar. The language of the revelations Joseph received shifted around 1832, reflecting Joseph's improved understanding of English grammar. In fact, the language of the pre-1832 revelations was edited before publication to correct some of Joseph's earlier grammar, and Joseph's 1837 revisions to the Book of Mormon reflect the same type of grammar changes that appear in the post-1832 revelations. These realities leave little reason to assume that what Joseph *wrote* in 1832 is an accurate representation of how he *spoke* in 1829.

2. While it is true that the Original Manuscript contains elements of Early Modern English that do not appear in published materials from the early 1800s, everyday experience teaches us that people do not speak the way they write. Consulting databases of published

---

[174] Royal Skousen, *The History of the Text of the Book of Mormon* (2018).

[175] Joseph Smith, Jr., *History, circa Summer 1832*, available at https://www.josephsmithpapers.org/paper-summary/history-circa-summer-1832/1.

material to detect regional dialects and speech patterns would be difficult even in today's society, but there is no reason to conclude that 19th century published material would capture everyday speech in rural New York.

Grandin's typesetter, John H. Gilbert, said the manuscript was not ready for publication. He wanted to correct the grammar and insert punctuation. Hyrum allowed him to punctuate the text but Martin Harris instructed him to leave the grammar as it was. Gilbert recalled,

> On the second day—[Martin] Harris and [Hyrum] Smith being in the office—I called their attention to a grammatical error, and asked whether I should correct it? Harris consulted with Smith a short time, and turned to me and said: "The Old Testament is ungrammatical, set it as it is written."[176]

Had Gilbert been permitted to correct the grammar, as any other editor or printer would have been, many if not most of the indicia of "Early Modern English" would not have survived. This renders inapposite any comparison between the uncorrected Book of Mormon and other properly edited published material of the time.

Joseph's speech patterns were the product of his environment. Colonial lag and other factors can account for elements of Early Modern English persisting among "common folk," even when these elements do not appear in published materials around Joseph's lifetime. Like all people in every society, Joseph's normal speech patterns retained archaic elements he incorporated from his family and peers. (Today's baby boomers sometimes catch themselves saying "groovy," a term their children consider obsolete at best.) Also, Joseph actually could have been exposed to Early Modern English because the T C

---

[176] Royal Skousen, "John Gilbert's 1892 Account of the 1830 Printing of the Book of Mormon," in *The Disciple as Witness: Essays on Latter-day Saint History and Doctrine in Honor of Richard Lloyd Anderson*. (Provo, UT: FARMS, 2000) available at https://criticaltext.byustudies.byu.edu/john-gilberts-1892-account-1830-printing-book-mormon-0.

Strong bookstore in Palmyra sold books from the 1600s, such as *Pilgrim's Progress* and Increase Mather's *History of the War with the Indians*.

3. The theory does not offer any explanation of why Early Modern English would be used, as opposed to any other form of English, such as that contemporaneous to Joseph Smith (which Skousen and Carmack assume was devoid of Early Modern English artifacts). We can think of no reason, nor have Skousen and Carmack proposed any reason, why God would choose an outdated and archaic form of a target language to put forth a book which claims to be meant for the modern world.[177] Adding a layer of supernatural mystery to the matter raises more questions than it answers.

4. The Early Modern English version of the transcription explanation does not explain the NID findings that the text of the Book of Mormon consists of vocabulary, phrases, concepts, and allusions which could all be found in sources available in Joseph's environment. This defeats the main premise of this approach, which is that the Early Modern English words and phrases could not have been known by Joseph.

For example, Skousen proposes that the word "ceremony" in Mosiah 19:24 is out of place because in context the proper terms in the 1820s should be words such as "discussion" or "conversation."[178] "And it came to pass that after they had ended the ceremony that they returned to the land of Nephi." Oliver spelled the word as "cerimony" in the Printer's manuscript, which Skousen proposes was Oliver's erroneous copying of the hypothetical "cermon" in the Original Manuscript (which is not extant for Mosiah). His rationale is that "sermon" in Early Modern English meant "talk, discussion." However, Lucy Mack Smith's *History 1845*, uses "ceremony" in the same sense as Mosiah 19:24, indicating a family usage that would be known to Joseph

---

[177] Mormon 8:34-35

[178] Skousen, *The History of the Text of the Book of Mormon, The Nature of the Original Language Part 3*, p. 165.

Smith. "When the Elders cam [sic] in and after the ceremony of introduction &c was over…"[179]

Skousen claims that the phrase "accept of" in Mosiah 28:10 is an Early Modern English usage: "there was not any of his sons which would *accept of* the kingdom." He makes the point that "In modern English we expect the phraseology "to accept the kingdom."[180] Similarly, we expect people to say that they accept Christ. However, in the 1740s Jonathan Edwards used: "To *accept of* Christ as our bread of life is to *accept of* him as our Savior and portion." "They that avouch the Lord to be their God, do profess to *accept of* Jehovah as their God."

Skousen points out that "arrive to" (e.g., "we did *arrive to* the promised land," 1 Ne. 18:23) is both the preferred usage in the original Book of Mormon and "is perfectly acceptable only in Early Modern English usage, from approximately 1560 to 1750."[181] Books written in the early to mid-1700s were readily available to Joseph Smith in the early 1800s Palmyra, including the 8-volume set of Edwards' works published in 1808. Edwards used the phrase, such as "when I arrive to Portsmouth" and "when we shall *arrive to* our journey's end." Skousen also notes that "disappointment" had an earlier meaning: "to frustrate the expectation or desire (of a person),"[182] as in Alma 51:31, 49:3-4, 11 and 16-17, 56:23-25, and 3 Nephi 4:8-10. Again, Edwards wrote "We may remark that Jonah's affliction, which was so great as to make him weary of his life, proceeds from a disappointment of his ambition and cross of his pride." As noted, the NID research suggests that Joseph was familiar with Edwards' works, including these "obsolete" phrases.

---

[179] Lucy Mack Smith, *History 1844 – 1845*, p. 12, book 12, at https://www.josephsmithpapers.org/paper-summary/lucy-mack-smith-history-1844-1845/152

[180] Skousen, *The History of the Text of the Book of Mormon, The Nature of the Original Language Part 3*, p. 215.

[181] Skousen, *The History of the Text of the Book of Mormon, The Nature of the Original Language Part 3*, p. 216.

[182] Skousen, *The History of the Text of the Book of Mormon, The Nature of the Original Language Part 3*, p. 231.

3. Assessing SITH

I know that good inspiration is based upon good information.

Russell M. Nelson[183]

Creating categories is helpful in presenting material. However, sometimes categories do not quite fit everything. While "transcription" describes most of the explanations for the Book of Mormon which reject the use of the plates and interpreters but still claim some kind of divine involvement, not all of these explanations argue that Joseph was merely reciting words generated by someone else. But all the explanations we are looking at in Chapters 2 and 3 share in common the abandonment of use of the plates or interpreters in any meaningful way.[184] In this chapter we will briefly describe explanations that go to the opposite extreme of those in the last chapter, explanations which are too loose rather than too rigid. Then we will look at an unsuccessful attempt at a solution, and evaluate where abandoning the plates and interpreters leads us.

A. The Shamanist Explanations

Some explanations which treat the plates as nugatory go to the opposite extreme of those described in the last chapter by arguing that even the seer stone was irrelevant. Rather Joseph Smith received the

---

[183] Russell M. Nelson, "Revelation for the Church, Revelation for Our Lives," *Ensign* (May 2018), p. 93-96, quote at p. 94, also available at https://www.churchofjesuschrist.org/study/general-conference/2018/04/revelation-for-the-church-revelation-for-our-lives?lang=eng

[184] See Dirkmaat and MacKay, *Let's Talk About the Translation*, pp. 93-102, for a survey of the myriad SITH-based models.

text of the Book of Mormon by direct inspiration. We refer to this as the "shamanist" theory because it asserts that the Book of Mormon text was essentially revealed directly into the mind of Joseph as with a shaman in a trance-like state. Another example might be the way the words of the Quran were said to have been revealed directly into the mind of Muhammad, who then dictated them to his scribes, much as Joseph dictated the Book of Mormon to his. Like with a shaman or the Quran, the source of the inspiration is left to the subjective preference of each individual. Believers accept a divine source, while non-believers ascribe it to other sources.

A recent example is Samuel Brown's view that "hybrid translation approaches, dominated by spiritual gifts and perhaps relying on panoramic visions, were central mechanisms of the translation process."[185] Other variations keep the seer stone, but treat it as only a talisman to activate direct inspiration into Joseph's mind.[186]

Perhaps the most influential variation seeking to separate the translation process from objective reality has been offered by Blake Ostler. He rejects the view that God revealed a (nearly) word-for-word text to Joseph. Indeed, Ostler argues that significant portions of the Book of Mormon came entirely from Joseph (with divine inspiration) and bear no relationship to the text on the plates; i.e., Joseph "expanded" the text. For him, neither the Urim and Thummim nor the seer stone actually did anything. They were just "instruments to spark human creativity in response to the divine lure." Instead, we have a mystical abstract process in which Joseph "did not perceive the ancient text and then consciously interpret it … rather, the text is the revelation he experienced within his own conceptual paradigms."

---

[185] Samuel Morris Brown, *Joseph Smith's Translation* (New York: Oxford University Press 2020), p. 146.

[186] Gardner, *The Gift and Power*, pp. 288 – 291; Nicholson, "The Spectacles, the Stone, the Hat, and the Book," pp. 183 – 184, 187 - 188.

It also appears that the usual relationship existing between a translator and an identifiable, objective text did not exist for Joseph Smith, for the ancient text merged with his own thought processes. Though Joseph Smith did not lose self-consciousness, the distinction between the text being revealed and the person receiving the revelation apparently dissolved. What we have therefore is neither an ancient document nor a translation rendering an ancient document from one language into another.[187]

Shamanist explanations not only reject Joseph as translator; they also ask readers to accept that the incredible detail of the Book of Mormon was all received in some kind of inchoate, even unconscious, experience. As will be discussed in Chapters 4(B)(4) and 7(B), the Book of Mormon has far more detail than any other revelation in the LDS canon, ancient or modern. Chapter 7 will discuss the issues created by thus divorcing the Book of Mormon from the plates and the interpreters.

B. Why not both the interpreters and the seer stone?

As we mentioned above, one recent effort to resolve the question is to conflate the two narratives, to both have your seer stone and eat it too.[188] However, this conflated narrative—sometimes Joseph used

---

[187] Blake T. Ostler, "The Book of Mormon as a Modern Expansion of an Ancient Source," *Dialogue: A Journal of Mormon Thought* 20, no. 1 (Spring 1987), pp. 66-123, quote at pp. 111-112, available at https://www.dialoguejournal.com/wp-content/uploads/sbi/articles/Dialogue_V20N01_68.pdf, updated April 26, 2005, at https://www.timesandseasons.org/harchive/2005/04/updating-the-expansion-theory/.

[188] Unfortunately, this untenable middle position is seen in the Gospel Topics Essay on Book of Mormon Translation, https://www.churchofjesuschrist.org/

the interpreters and sometimes he used the seer stone—requires a contrived reading of the sources that disregards the SITH sources' main argument. The primary SITH witness, David Whitmer, claimed the reason Joseph used the seer stone was because he no longer possessed the interpreters after the lost manuscript episode. This directly contradicts the canonical narrative as corroborated by Oliver Cowdery and Lucy Mack Smith's accounts.

While superficially appealing, the "have-it-both-ways" position is untenable. All of the Book of Mormon we have today was produced after the lost manuscript episode. Although we questioned David's reliability in the previous chapter, his accounts definitely did come from him. David's statements are not posthumous, hearsay, or otherwise suffer from dubious sourcing like the other SITH accounts. And David Whitmer explicitly excluded the interpreters from the translation process after the 116 pages were lost. Even if we allow that David did not know the interpreters were returned to Joseph because David was not among those authorized to see them, David's nonetheless averred that *all* of the Book of Mormon we have today was translated using the seer stone in the hat, and none of it using the plates and the interpreters. If true, the canonical narrative, and all the other statements by Joseph and Oliver, are false.[189]

---

study/manual/gospel-topics-essays/book-of-mormon-translation?lang=eng&_r=1. The Church's web page teaches Primary children that "Joseph used a special rock called a seer stone to translate the plates" and that "Joseph didn't have much schooling, so he wasn't good at writing or spelling." https://www.churchofjesuschrist.org/study/friend/2017/02/golden-plates-to-book-of-mormon?lang=eng. See Chapter 5(D) on the subject of Joseph's education. For an extended analysis of the Gospel Topics essay on translation see Neville, "Analysis: The Gospel Topics Essay on Book of Mormon Translation" at http://www.ldshistoricalnarratives.com/2022/09/analysis-gospel-t opics-essay-on-book-of.html, Appendices 3 and 4 in Neville, *A Man That Can Translate*, pp. 315 – 356, and Duffy, "The 'Book of Mormon Translation' Essay in Historical Context."

[189] LDS SITH advocates seek to avoid acknowledging this inevitable conclusion of their position. The option of saying David was right about the seer stone in the

And even if one accepts that Joseph did receive back the interpreters, but instead used the seer stone to translate in public, we still have a scenario where the Book of Mormon does not come from the plates. This defies the divine economy by wasting the efforts of the Nephite authors, relegating their work to the status of a mere talisman. It leaves the Three and Eight Witnesses to testify of an artifact that has no direct connection with the text. And it leaves unanswered the question, "If Joseph didn't translate the engravings on the plates into English, then who did?"

Arguments which attempt to square the circle on the Book of Mormon's translation almost always rely heavily on the one lone sentence attributed to Martin Harris in Edward Stevenson's 1881 article which says that Joseph used both, but the seer stone more often *for convenience*. In Chapter 2(C) we discussed the problems with this lone posthumous reference. We will not repeat that discussion here, but emphasize again that, even if Martin actually used the expression "for convenience" (which we doubt), it would only apply to the pages he scribed, which were mostly or entirely lost. He had little, if any, involvement in the writing of the Book of Mormon we actually have today.[190] (And, again, those who did produce the Book of Mormon we have today, Joseph and Oliver, consistently and repeatedly said it was done using the interpreters.)

---

hat but wrong about the interpreters not being returned to Joseph is not really credible. David affirmed both fact claims with equal (although we think dubious) certainty. David claimed that it was Joseph's loss of the interpreters that led him to use the seer stone. The first claim flows into the next. There is no logical way to separate them. See, for example Edward Stevenson's report of David Whitmer's account in *Book 4: Typescript journals*, volume 28, page 52.

[190] It is possible that Martin scribed a few pages in our current Book of Mormon in the short time between the return of the plates and interpreters and the arrival of Oliver Cowdery in Harmony at the beginning of April 1829. We cannot tell because the Original Manuscript of most of the Book of Mosiah was destroyed.

C. Whither SITH?

SITH enables believers to respond to criticisms of the Book of Mormon (anachronism, copying of KJV including italicized words, etc.) by appealing to inexplicable supernatural phenomena that must be taken on faith and cannot be disproven. For many believers, such explanations suffice. Others prefer pragmatic, plausible, evidence-based explanations, accompanied by spiritual confirmation as described in Doctrine and Covenants 9:8.

One common characteristic of the SITH accounts is imprecision. As we mentioned, no one reported what Joseph actually dictated when they claimed they saw him using the stone in the hat. No one gave a specific date or dates, or even time of day, when the SITH sessions occurred. We are left to speculate whether the lack of detail in the SITH accounts was intentional or merely an oversight.

Another common characteristic, when viewed as a whole, is the inconsistency among the SITH accounts, which are contradictory among themselves. Emma says Joseph used the interpreters until Martin lost the 116 pages; Martin (according to Edward Stevenson) says Joseph used the interpreters and the seer stone interchangeably. Emma and David say Joseph used only the stone after the pages were lost, but Martin's supposed statement implies both could have been used throughout the entire process, which is the basis for the untenable 'middle' ground attempts to reconcile everything. David described the SITH event downstairs in the Whitmer home, but admitted he was not present for most of the translation, which he said took place in the upper room of the house and in Harmony. The "Last Testimony" has Emma claiming that she wrote "day after day," yet Martin (and Joseph) say Martin wrote the lost pages.

Finally, and perhaps most important for this analysis, is the Spalding theory. The SITH accounts, particularly Joseph Smith III's "Last Testimony of Sister Emma" and David Whitmer's *An Address to*

All Believers in Christ, are aimed at the Spalding theory.[191] They emphasize there was no screen or curtain and that Joseph had nothing to read from. That is a gratuitous observation if not for the Spalding theory. But they knew the Spalding theory relied on the common understanding that there *was* such a visual barrier. Had there been no such barrier, there would have been no reason for Joseph to emphasize that he had been threatened with destruction if he allowed anyone to see the plates or interpreters before the translation was completed. The warning served no purpose if Joseph never used the sacred objects. For that matter, the entire narrative of the ancient metal plates and the specially prepared interpreters is superfluous if Joseph used neither to produce the Book of Mormon as we have it.

Another appeal of the SITH narrative to the midwestern Saints at the time of the "Last Testimony" (1879) may also have been to tweak their greatest *bête noire*, the LDS Church in Utah. The LDS Church had remained true to Joseph's account, making it part of its official canon in 1880 just as other followers of the Restoration, to refute the Spalding theory, were inflating the SITH narrative over that given by Joseph and Oliver.[192]

However, we recognize that believers such as David Whitmer and Joseph Smith III (in the "Last Testimony") were primarily motivated by their zealous desire to defend the Book of Mormon against the Spalding theory, even if that zeal led them to exaggerate accounts of the use of the seer stone and to downplay the interpreters. (Again, we note that Joseph III later repudiated the SITH narrative after he researched the question himself rather than rely on David Whitmer and William McLellin.)

---

[191] See discussion of the "Last Testimony" in Chapter 2(B) and David Whitmer, *An Address to All Believers in Christ*, pp. 10-12.

[192] See quotes in Neville, *A Man That Can Translate*, pp. 367–372 and Appendix B to this book. Joseph and Oliver's accounts are also now in Joseph Smith – History in the LDS Pearl of Great Price. Joseph dictated the entire Book of Mormon we have, and Oliver says he wrote the entire manuscript "save a few pages only," yet SITH proponents simply ignore the testimony of these two primary witnesses.

There is a certain irony here, and a cautionary tale for would-be apologists. In defending the Book of Mormon against the all-pervasive Spalding theory, these apologists of the 1870s and 1880s exaggerated the one-time seer stone demonstration into the primary, or sole, method of translation. This refuted the Spalding theory, but at the cost of ignoring (or for David Whitmer outright rejecting) Joseph and Oliver's testimonies. It is these inaccurate late apologetics 50 years after the Book of Mormon's publication, narrowly focused on the Spalding theory, which now serve as the basis for inaccurate modern apologetics which similarly reject Joseph and Oliver's testimonies, to the detriment of the testimonies of many modern Saints.

One may ask how these 19th century Saints could have responded to Spalding theory attacks on the Book of Mormon without resorting to SITH. Unlike today, they did not have an extensive apologia to fall back on, no Sidney Sperry or Hugh Nibley, no John Tvedtnes or John Welch. But they needed nothing more than the reaffirmation made by the main scribe, Oliver Cowdery, upon returning to the Church in 1848:

> I wrote with my own pen the entire book of Mormon (save a few pages) as it fell from the lips of the prophet as he translated by the gift and power of God by means of the Urim and Thummim, or as it is called by that book holy Interpreters. I beheld with my eyes and handled with my hands the gold plates from which it was translated. I also beheld the Interpreters. That book is true. Sidney Rigdon did not write it. Mr. Spaudling did not write it. I wrote it myself as it fell from the lips of the prophet.[193]

---

[193] Recorded by Reuben Miller from remarks by Oliver Cowdery at Council Bluffs, Iowa, in Reuben Miller Journal 1848 original available at https://catalog.churchofjesuschrist.org/assets/22222322-f4fe-41e3-aa86-bfc54b94df92/0/16 and transcribed in John W. Welch (ed), *Opening the Heavens: Accounts of Divine Manifestations* 1820-1844 (Provo and Salt Lake City, UT: BYU Press/Deseret Book, 2005), at p. 143. It is worth noting that Oliver had the seer stone at this time, which

Assessing SITH

Critics emphasize that the SITH accounts had previously been ignored in LDS Church histories, which is a valid point.[194] But embracing the SITH narrative goes far beyond simply filling out the historical record. Modern SITH proponents are privileging the SITH narrative over the canonical narrative, simply accepting the SITH accounts at face value without subjecting them to critique or evaluation.[195] And many do advocate the SITH narrative in its most

---

he had received from Joseph years before. Oliver could have easily produced the seer stone and declared how he saw Joseph use it. However, instead, he insisted on crediting the now unavailable interpreters. The story of Oliver's return to the Church is recounted in Scott H. Faulring, "The Return of Oliver Cowdery," in Ricks, Parry and Hedges (eds) *The Disciple as Witness:*, pp. 117 - 173. Reuben Miller, who recorded Oliver's testimony quoted above was no a casual witness, but rather Oliver's close friend who supplied the financial means to enable Oliver and his family to travel to rejoin the Saints (at pp. 141-143). See also Richard Lloyd Anderson, "Reuben Miller, Recorder of Oliver Cowdery's Reaffirmations," *BYU Studies Quarterly* (1968) Vol. 8, no. 3, pp. 277 – 293, available at https://scholarsarchive.byu.edu/byusq/vol8/iss3/5, where Professor Anderson positively evaluates Miller's reliability as a recorder of Oliver's remarks.

[194] In retrospect, early Church historians—especially Joseph's contemporaries—could have avoided the modern criticism by explicitly acknowledging and addressing the SITH accounts based on their personal knowledge and insights which led them to accept what Joseph and Oliver taught instead of the SITH accounts.

[195] E.g., see the following articles in Michael Hubbard MacKay, Mark Ashurst-McGee and Brian M. Hauglid (eds) *Producing Ancient Scripture: Joseph Smith's Translation Projects in the Development of Mormon Christianity* (Salt Lake City, UT: The University of Utah Press, 2020): Michael Hubbard MacKay, "Performing the Translation," p. 81; Samuel Morris Brown, "Seeing the Voice of God," p. 138; Richard Lyman Bushman, "Nephi's Project: The Gold Plates as Book History," p. 187; and Grant Hardy, "Ancient History and Modern Commandments," p. 209. Hardy's recent article "The Book of Mormon Translation Process," *BYU Studies* (2021) Vol 60, no. 3 (2021), pp. 203 – 211, available at https://byustudies.byu.edu/article/the-book-of-mormon-translation-process/, purports to be survey of all views, but simply assumes the SITH narrative and does not even address the historically most common explanation that Joseph translated from the plates using the interpreters. Another very recent example is Becerra, Easton-Flake, Frederick and Spencer, *Book of Mormon Studies: An*

extensive form, arguing or implying that the Book of Mormon was produced without examining the plates at all, let alone studying them with the help of the interpreters supplied by God for that purpose.

As noted in Chapter 1, critics have exploited this energetic shift by LDS scholars to prioritize the SITH accounts over the canonical narrative to urge members to leave the Church because Church authorities have been "lying about Church history." We do not propose ignoring the SITH accounts; their existence is historical fact, whether or not they relate accurate observations, hearsay, inference, or assumptions.

Instead of simply rejecting or accepting the SITH accounts on their face, we propose the demonstration and "pop-out" hypotheses as evidence-based, nuanced interpretations that are both (i) supported by the historical evidence (including the documentary evidence from the Original and Printer's Manuscripts), and (ii) consistent with the canonical narrative.

D. Applying Neutral Scholarly Criteria

We acknowledge that so far this book has been somewhat "inside baseball," an argument by a pair of believers responding to another set of believers. One of our core arguments for the canonical translation narrative is that it comes from Joseph and Oliver, and that to reject it in favor of the SITH narrative is to treat the two as lying. As we have just seen, there is no middle ground. If you believe Joseph and Oliver, you cannot believe the SITH narrative which David Whitmer propounded in the latter part of his life.

Introduction and Guide, where the SITH narrative is described as the scholarly consensus (see pp. 35 and 86) but which further, while supposedly surveying all literature discussing the Book of Mormon, contains not a single reference to the term "Urim and Thummim" or otherwise to the interpreters despite their prominence in all the accounts of the Book of Mormon's origins.

However, there are other actors in this play. Critics of the Book of Mormon, for example, have no problem accepting that Joseph and Oliver were lying. They support the SITH narrative because it confirms their preexisting biases. The SITH proponents have tried to deflect their reliance on David Whitmer's attack on Joseph and Oliver's credibility by pointing to a few statements purportedly from other credible parties, particularly Emma Smith and Martin Harris. In the previous chapter, we argued that these accounts were of dubious reliability, and presented alternate ways of understanding these. In this chapter we have described their contradictions and inconsistencies.

Unfortunately, neither history nor the historical record are tidy and consistent. Perhaps Joseph Smith III and Edward Stevenson recorded Emma's and Martin's statements exactly word-for-word. And there had to be some early talk of the seer stone for Eber Howe and other hostile reporters to have picked up on the idea, even if most of the recorded seer stone accounts do not appear until many decades later. So, are there any criteria that can help us other than just appealing to different preexisting biases?

An unclear and even contradictory historical record is all too typical in historical research. Researchers have developed general criteria to evaluate conflicting historical accounts. These are not hard tests that indisputably determine historical truth, but rather guidelines to compare the relative credibility of historical accounts.

First, accounts recorded nearer in time to the events are considered more reliable than those recorded much later. Memories fade, and intervening events can lead us to re-imagine what happened long ago. A written account close in time to an event is most likely to record something accurately without being affected by either forgetfulness or re-interpretation.

Second, accounts by third parties after the principal witness has died are particularly suspect because the witness has no opportunity to clarify or rebut what the third party claims they said.

Third, accounts recorded by or directly from primary firsthand witnesses are more credible than hearsay passed through one or more intermediaries.

Fourth, the more specific and detailed the account, the more reliable.

Fifth, even if a source is a firsthand witness, we also ask if their accounts are consistent over time.

The accounts from Joseph and Oliver better satisfy these criteria than any of the SITH accounts. Obviously, there is a supernatural element involved with each faithful alternative, but Joseph as an inspired translator is a more natural explanation than Joseph merely reading words supplied by entirely supernatural means. We leave to each reader to judge for themselves the comparative credibility of our witnesses.

E. Summary – Issues Transcription Cannot Resolve

1. *Why the saga?* Faithful SITH accounts still accept the basic story of how Joseph came to possess the plates: four years of preparation with visits from Moroni, the dangerous struggles to secure and protect the plates, the arduous labor involved in making the translation, losing the 116 pages, struggling through poverty to even get paper, opposition from Emma's family, etc. Everyone accepts the canonical account's statement that Joseph was forbidden to show the artifacts to anyone.

> Again, he told me, that when I got those plates of which he had spoken—for the time that they should be obtained was not yet fulfilled—I should not show them to any person; neither the breastplate with the Urim and Thummim; only to those to whom I should be commanded to show them; if I did I should be destroyed. (Joseph Smith—History 1:42)

On top of the modern plate narratives, the Book of Mormon itself recounts in detail the trials, labor, and challenges of the Nephite scribes in keeping and producing the records that Mormon abridged to create the Book of Mormon.[196] SITH forces us to question why God would require all this effort and struggle if the English text of the book was simply provided directly to Joseph Smith's eyes (or mind). If the stone Joseph found in a well was all he needed, why was Joseph burdened with lugging around and protecting sixty pounds of gold plates which constantly put his and his family's safety in danger? And why would God compound the risk by threatening his destruction if he showed the artifacts to anyone?

Apart from invoking God's "mysterious ways," the transcription model renders the plates and interpreters not only superfluous but an unnecessary additional burden. Transcription advocates have proposed that the plates served as a catalyst for Joseph to receive the revelation he dictated.[197] However, adding one more supernatural explanation for the otherwise inexplicable merely compounds the problem created by the supernatural transcription theory in the first place.[198]

---

[196] Richard Lyman Bushman, "Nephi's Project: The Gold Plates as Book History," in *Producing Ancient Scripture*, MacKay, Ashurst-McGee, Hauglid, (eds.), pp 187-204

[197] See, for example, Stan Spencer, "Seers and Stones: The Translation of the Book of Mormon as Divine Visions of an Old-Time Seer," *Interpreter: A Journal of Latter-day Saint Faith and Scholarship* 24 (2017), pp. 27-98, available at https://journal.interpreterfoundation.org/seers-and-stones-the-translation-of-the-book-of-mormon-as-divine-visions-of-an-old-time-seer/; MacKay and Dirkmaat, *From Darkness unto Light*, p. 87, MacKay and Frederick, *Joseph Smith's Seer Stones*, pp. 45 – 64, and Dirkmaat and MacKay, *Let's Talk About the Translation*, pp. 105-107.

[198] A similar approach has been proposed for the Book of Abraham papyri, but in that situation there was no claim that Joseph had or used the Urim and Thummim. See Gospel Topics Essay on the Book of Abraham, https://www.churchofjesuschrist.org/study/manual/gospel-topics-essays/translation-and-historicity-of-the-book-of-abraham?lang=eng

In Chapter 7 we will discuss our views as to why all this struggle on the part of American prophets both ancient and modern was needed. For now, we pose the question to readers – what was the point of all that struggle and drama? Relegating the plates and the interpreters to mere talismans transforms the saga of the coming forth of the Book of Mormon from a real-world, tangible necessity into inexplicable mysticism.

2.   *Is the Book of Mormon a Bible or a Quran?* Long established scholarship has shown that the Bible is an amalgam of numerous sources, many not identified in the biblical text itself. Although disturbing to believers in biblical inerrancy, this "documentary hypothesis" (when applied to the five books of the Pentateuch) or form criticism does not, according to scholars who accept the Bible's divine authority, detract from the Bible's authority, but rather enhances its power by showing how God interacts with human actors to communicate His words and will.[199]

The Book of Mormon openly lays out the process by which scripture is made in a way which is largely hidden in the Bible. Internally, the Book of Mormon is transparent on who wrote what, when and why and how the text was created and transmitted and by whom. It wonderfully shows how God works through men to teach us. However, this magnificent affinity between the Bible and Book of Mormon is lost if Joseph's role is reduced to being merely half of a transcription team.

Instead of resembling the Bible, the Book of Mormon becomes like the Quran, fundamentally inerrant, untouched by human participation. With all respect to the Moslem holy book, this is not how

---

[199] Even the harshest conservative Christian critics of higher criticism agree that the Bible is composed of many different texts by many different authors whose work "had to come in the language of the prophets and apostles and employ the cultural background of figures, illustrations, analogies, and other elements generally associated with linguistic communication." Josh McDowell, *The New Evidence That Demands A Verdict* (Nashville, TN: Thomas Nelson, 1999), pp. 4-7, 341.

most Christians (or Jews) view scripture or the participatory interactions between God and humanity. With Joseph's numerous revisions, and the Book of Mormon's own declarations that it is also the product of fallible humans, the Book of Mormon is very Christian in how it presents itself, an aspect that is lost if we insist instead that it was divinely dictated rather than the result of Joseph in some way studying it out in his own mind.[200]

3. *What was there for Joseph to study out in his mind?* Further to this last point, the revelation which tells us the most about the translation process, now found in Section 9 of the Doctrine and Covenants, indicates that the translation process began with the translator studying something out in his mind. If one is just reading specific predetermined wording off of a small rock, or through direct dictation into one's head, there is nothing to study out in one's mind. (We will propose a possibility consistent with this requirement in Chapter 6.) Also, if Joseph was not using the plates at all, the Lord's commandment to translate the plates of Nephi (Doctrine and Covenants Section 10) is both pointless and misleading because Joseph would have no idea which plates were being channeled through the stone.[201]

4. *How could alterations in later editions be permissible?* If the text of the Book of Mormon was divinely or supernaturally dictated word-for-word or close to that, altering the text would be unthinkable. (Among others, this was one of David Whitmer's arguments.) Yet, Joseph

---

[200] On comparing the Book of Mormon with the Quran, also see Givens, *By the Hand of Mormon*, p. 182 and Grant Hardy, *Understanding the Book of Mormon: A Reader's Guide* (New York: Oxford University Press, 2010), pp. 9 – 10.

[201] See Doctrine and Covenants 10:38-46. Author Neville has proposed that Joseph did not obtain the plates of Nephi from Moroni's stone box combined with the plates containing Mormon's record, but that they were separate and that Joseph only received the plates of Nephi after he arrived in Fayette. Among other things, this explains why the Title Page of the abridged plates does not mention any original records. See Jonathan Neville, *Whatever Happened to the Golden Plates?* (Salt Lake City, UT: Digital Legend, 2016), chapter 9.

made (or allowed) hundreds of changes to subsequent editions of the Book of Mormon during his lifetime—and he never justified the changes. Royal Skousen calculates that Joseph personally made more than 200 changes to these later editions.[202] As Stephen Ricks has noted,

> Joseph's many changes in the Book of Mormon argue strongly against the idea that he rendered it into English by automatic translation. If he had, then he would certainly have considered the text inviolate and refrained from making any changes. ... The actual translation was Joseph's alone and the opportunity to improve it in grammar and word choice still remained open. All who have had experience in translating are aware of the often considerable cleavage between being able to construe a sentence and actually rendering it in a felicitous translation. All who have translated are also keenly aware that it is a rare translation which cannot be improved. Thus, while it would be incorrect to minimize the divine element in the process of translation of the Book of Mormon, it would also be misleading and potentially hazardous to deny the human factor.[203]

5. *Where did the 19th century language come from?* If the text of the Book of Mormon was divinely or supernaturally dictated word-for-word or close to that, the presence of terms and concepts found in Joseph's immediate environment suggests the actual translator drew directly from Joseph's lexicon in the first place—complete with the errors in the text noted by Skousen and others. Divine dictation produced a book that reads precisely how it would read had Joseph translated it, as he claimed he did. Perhaps most tellingly, Neville's nonbiblical intertextuality research shows numerous instances where the Book of Mormon text repeats misquotes and paraphrases of the

---

[202] Royal Skousen, "Changes in the Book of Mormon," *Interpreter: A Journal of Latter-day Saint Faith and Scholarship* 11 (2014) pp. 161-176 at p. 175, available at https://journal.interpreterfoundation.org/changes-in-the-book-of-mormon/

[203] Stephen D. Ricks, *Joseph Smith's Translation of the Book of Mormon* (Provo, UT: FARMS, 1986), available at http://farms.byu.edu/display.php?table=transcripts&id=10.

KJV by religious figures such as Jonathan Edwards who were influential in Joseph's time.[204]

6. *Why is the Book of Mormon so dependent on the KJV?* In addition to these misquotes and paraphrases, the Book of Mormon not only lifts extended quotes from the KJV, but extensively adapts and adopts KJV language even when it is not directly tracking the KJV. Even if one sets aside recent scholarship that has shown the KJV to be a less than optimal version of the original sources (in LDS terminology "not correctly translated"), the Book of Mormon's usual use of the exact phrasing of the KJV strongly argues that the translator was deliberately following the KJV.[205] (In Chapter 5(B) we will propose an explanation as to why Joseph as translator would adhere so closely to the KJV.)

7. *Where did all the other 19th century material come from?* That the text of the Book of Mormon is so loaded with 19th century language and concepts is one of the primary grounds for arguing that Joseph Smith composed the Book. To claim otherwise, that the exact text of the Book has no such influences because the early 19th century American who produced it was merely a transcriber rather than an active translator, denies the composition explanation but does not refute it. The Early Modern English variation attempts to separate the text from the 19th century but is unpersuasive for the reasons discussed above.

Transcription explanations may satisfy those who accept purely supernatural explanations, but transcription ignores the substantial evidence that Joseph Smith was actively involved in creating the text of the Book of Mormon (including particularly Joseph's own claim that he translated the plates).

In the next three chapters we will argue that translation is the most credible explanation for the Book of Mormon. In the next chapter we will show how the arguments used for Joseph as author actually better

---

[204] This research is discussed in detail in Neville's *Infinite Goodness*.
[205] See Philip L. Barlow, *Mormons and the Bible: The Place of the Latter-day Saints in American Religion* (New York: Oxford University Press, 1991, Updated Edition 2013), pp. 26 – 39.

fit Joseph as translator, and in Chapters 5 and 6 we will propose an understanding of the translation process which we believe better explains the Book of Mormon we have than any of the transcription theories.

In fairness we would consider "evidence suggesting that Joseph was reading from a pre-existing translation," such as presented in a 2021 article in *BYU Studies*.[206] Unfortunately, in that article the author simply assumes the SITH narrative without considering a scenario where Joseph actually translated the engravings on the plates. The author describes "translation" as the kind of mystical, free-form, free-wheeling "shamanist" exercise described above, which would render precision difficult, and cites instances where the Book of Mormon is precise and detailed. However, his examples are readily explained if Joseph was translating from the plates in the ordinary sense of the term.[207]

---

[206] Hardy, "The Book of Mormon Translation Process," at pp. 209 – 210.

[207] One example comes from scribes' statements that when Joseph began a new translation session, he would be able to pick up where he left off without having to have the immediate previous work read back to him. This would seem difficult if one accepts Hardy's concept of translation as a vague spiritualistic experience. However, it is not surprising if Joseph was working directly from the plates. Mormon and the other writers already organized the flow of the text, which Joseph would just track from the plates. See the discussion at https://www.mobom.org/byu-studies-on-the-translation-process for a detailed analysis of Hardy's article and Chapter 4(B)(4) for more on the Book of Mormon's complexity.

4. Composition

It is not unlikely that this work of God's Spirit, so extraordinary and wonderful, is the dawning, or, at least, a prelude of that glorious work of God, so often foretold in scripture, which, in the progress and issue of it, shall renew the world of mankind. If we consider how long since the things foretold, as what should precede this great event, have been accomplished; and how long this event has been expected by the church of God, and thought to be nigh by the most eminent men of God in the church; and withal consider what the state of things now is, and has for a considerable time been, in the church of God and world of mankind, we can't reasonably think otherwise, than that the beginning of this great work of God must be near. And there are many things that make it probable that this work will begin in America.

Jonathan Edwards[208]

Almost from the moment of its first publication, critics have argued that Joseph Smith or others composed the Book of Mormon.[209] Although they have generated a vast literature over the last two

---

[208] Jonathan Edwards, "Some Thoughts Concerning the Revival of Religion in New England," (1742) in David Turley (ed) *American Religion: Literary Sources and Documents* (London and New York: Routledge, 1998, 2019), at pp. 145-146 at https://books.google.com/books?id=DwwLEAAAQBAJ&pg=PA145&lpg=PA135&dq=American+Religion+literary+souces+turley&source=bl&ots=J_tcorGlCV&sig=ACfU3U37gXgym_jXVU29BKXlf075RL7z_g&hl=en&sa=X&ved=2ahUKEwjs4qj56az6AhWblIkEHXllB_kQ6AF6BAgXEAM#v=onepage&q=American%20Religion%20literary%20souces%20turley&f=false.

[209] A good recent survey of composition theories is Brian C. Hales, "Naturalistic Explanations of the Origin of the Book of Mormon: A Longitudinal Study," *BYU Studies* (2019), Vol 58, no. 3, pp. 105-148, at https://byustudies.byu.edu/article/naturalistic-explanations-of-the-origin-of-the-book-of-mormon-a-longitudinal-study/

centuries, a succinct summary of the "obstacles to accepting the golden plates as the source of the Book of Mormon," is provided by Grant Palmer, a former LDS religion teacher turned critic:

> First, although these records were said to have been preserved for generations by Nephite prophets, Joseph Smith never used them in dictating the Book of Mormon. If we accept the idea that he dug up a real, physical record, then we must account for the fact that he never used it in the translation process. Second, much of the Book of Mormon reflects the intellectual and cultural environment of Joseph's own time and place. We find strands of American antiquities and folklore, the King James Bible, and evangelical Protestantism woven into the fabric of the doctrines and setting.[210]

In sum, the SITH narrative is the foundation upon which is laid the currently prevailing composition argument that the Book of Mormon came from Joseph's imagination as stimulated by his environment, not that of ancient Americans.

Even neutral observers like historian Daniel Walker Howe, who calls the Book of Mormon "a powerful epic written on a grand scale" which "should rank among the great achievements of American literature" notes that the "idiom is that of the King James Version, which most Americans assumed to be appropriates for a divine revelation. ... It contains elements that suggest the environment of New York in the 1820s (for example, episodes paralleling the Masonic/Antimasonic controversy) ...".[211]

---

[210] Grant H. Palmer, *An Insider's View of Mormon Origins* (Salt Lake City, UT: Signature Books, 2002), quote at p. 259.

[211] Daniel Walker Howe, *What Hath God Wrought: The Transformation of America 1815-1848* (Oxford History of the United States, New York: Oxford University Press, 2007), quote at p. 314. The presence of KJV style English and allegedly anti-masonic rhetoric in the Book of Mormon will be discussed in Chapters 5(B) and 4(C)(1), respectively.

However, Joseph Smith's active involvement in creating the text of the Book of Mormon does not mean that he originated it. Joseph Smith's imprint on the Book would also appear if he were an actively participating translator.

In this chapter, we will weigh these alternatives, and examine whether the obvious evidence of Joseph's imprint on the Book means that he was an author or an active translator. To perform this evaluation, we need to recognize this fundamental point:

Evidence of composition is also evidence of translation.

A corollary to this proposition is:

Evidence of 19th century language and subject matter does not require a 19th century source.

The critics have been so intent on showing that Joseph (and/or others) composed the Book of Mormon that they have not considered that if Joseph actually translated the ancient record into English in the normal sense of the term, we would find exactly the artifacts from other sources that are present in the text; i.e., as translator, Joseph could only draw from his own lexicon, or mental language bank, and his life experience. The critics have not realized that their evidence of similarities to other sources supports a translation explanation as well as a composition explanation.

Ironically, many faithful scholars reject the evidence of similarities developed by the critics because they do not realize such evidence supports Joseph's claim in the canonical account that he translated the plates. It seems that neither critics nor apologists take Joseph's claim of actual translation seriously. Yet, in the remainder of this book, we will argue that translation is the most comprehensive explanation for the evidence.

A. Similarities As Evidence of Composition and Translation

In 1887 a non-member of the Church wrote to the Editor of the *Millennial Star*:

> I know very well that whatever ideas an original writer or translator expressed, he could not go beyond his vocabulary. As Joseph Smith was confessedly a man of limited education, and the English Bible of 1611 was his one familiar book, of course he wrote or dictated to another to write in the very style and vocabulary which he possessed. An angel or spirit in using man's brain of course finds it a limited instrument, and cannot make it act differently for him any more than an artist can sketch a fine cut line with a blunt pencil, or a coarse one with a fine point, or a musician draw from an instrument harmonies beyond its powers. Suffice it to say, thinking men should not rule a book out of a claim to genuineness on account of its style, when the style and stated facts of Joseph Smith's education are so consistent. [212]

The author here assumed that the KJV was the only book familiar to Joseph when he translated the plates but, as the NID research shows, the translated text can be linked directly to several additional sources, all readily accessible to Joseph before he began the translation. The same point was made in a book published by the LDS Church's press written by former BYU president Franklin S. Harris (a great-grandnephew of Martin Harris), in 1953:

> Joseph Smith in his translating under the inspiration of God obtained the meaning of the Book of Mormon text. [footnote omitted] Joseph Smith neither had a Ph.D. in English nor had he been trained as a linguist. He gave the ideas in the English language in such phraseology and diction as he could master, and not being

---

[212] C (anonymous), "Are They of Israel," *Millennial Star*, No. 3, Vol. LXIX (49), Jan. 17, 1887, p. 37.

learned in the knowledge of the English, his expressions were oftentimes ungrammatical and the local expressions of his community sometimes occurred.²¹³

Whether Joseph composed or translated the text, the evidence of outside influences would be the same.²¹⁴ Joseph claimed he translated the ancient plates.²¹⁵ The question is whether the available evidence points toward composition or translation as the more plausible explanation.

Here we will examine one example, a study which compared digital files of over 100,000 books that predated the 1830s.²¹⁶ The authors, Chris and Duane Johnson, conclude that, due to the number of similarities between the two books, "Joseph most likely grew up reading a school book called *The Late War* by Gilbert J. Hunt and it

---

²¹³ Franklin S. Harris, Jr., *The Book of Mormon: Messages and Evidences* (Salt Lake City, UT: The Church of Jesus Christ of Latter-day Saints, Deseret News Press, 1953), p. 109.

²¹⁴ Thomas E. Donofrio itemized many of these possible influences in his article, "Early American Influences on the Book of Mormon – Part II Book of Mormon Historical Influences," at available at http://www.mormonthink.com/influences.htm#part2 (accessed November 12, 2022). A more comprehensive list is Rick Grunder, *Mormon Parallels* (2014) available at http://www.rickgrunder.com/parallels.htm.

²¹⁵ E.g., "Two days after the arrival of Mr. Cowdery (being the 7th of April) I commenced to translate the Book of Mormon, and he began to write for me." (JS-H 1:67). "Day after day I continued, uninterrupted, to write from his mouth, as he translated with the Urim and Thummim, or, as the Nephites would have said, 'Interpreters,' the history or record called 'The Book of Mormon.'" See note to Joseph Smith-History 1:71, from Letter I, *Messenger and Advocate*, vol. 1 (October 1834), pp. 14-16.

²¹⁶ Chris and Duane Johnson, "A Comparison of the Book of Mormon and The Late War Between the United States and Great Britain," March 9, 2014, published at http://wordtree.org/thelatewar/. There is little explanation of methodology and no list of the 100,000 books studied or even the database used, and the link to the authors' notes is broken.

heavily influenced his writing of the Book of Mormon."[217]

The Johnson study provoked significant (and ongoing) reaction from both believers and nonbelievers, which we find fascinating because both sides seem to misread the evidence. This provides us with a good case study for evaluating whether this intertextuality suggests composition or translation.

The first point to consider is that all language is derivative. That is what makes it a common language. The Johnsons themselves used vocabulary chunks and syntax that they borrowed from prior works they had read. Such unconscious recombination of language is not only unavoidable but necessary. But that does not make it plagiarism, and it does not detract from the originality of their work. It is simply how we process language, whether we are composing or translating.

The parallels in the Johnson study consist mostly of chunks of language sprinkled throughout the text of both books. The authors extract these chunks and string them together to make the parallels appear more striking than they do in either text separately. Nevertheless, the parallels exist for everyone to see.

The initial reaction of LDS commentators was denial. For example, in his discussion of *The Late War*, Tad R. Callister, an emeritus LDS General Authority and former General Sunday School President, wrote, "I doubt that Joseph read any of the books alleged by the critics to be sources for the Book of Mormon before the translation process commenced. There is no historical evidence confirming that he did."[218]

When we consider the historical context, though, *The Late War* fits solidly into Joseph's environment in both Vermont and New York. The book covered the War of 1812, which lasted from 1812 to 1815. In August 1813, the British attempted an invasion of Burlington,

---

[217] Several editions of *The Late War* were published. The final and most comprehensive was Gilbert J. Hunt, *The Late War, between the United States and Great Britain, from June, 1812, to February, 1815* (New York: Daniel D. Smith, 1819, originally published 1816) available at https://archive.org/details/latewarbetweenun00inhunt.

[218] Callister, *A Case for the Book of Mormon*, p. 79.

Vermont, the site of a major U.S. military base, but were repelled. Burlington is about 95 miles north of Lebanon, Vermont, where the Smiths were living at the time. Vermont troops (the "Green Mountain Boys" Joseph later appealed to) served in both militia and U.S. Army regiments during the war.

Separately, the British invaded Pultneyville (located only 16 miles north of Palmyra) in 1814, killing two citizens, wounding three, and taking two prisoners. This was just two years before the Smiths arrived in Palmyra, where they lived among veterans of the war. Joseph's older brother Alvin, who died on November 19, 1823, was buried in the General John Swift Memorial Cemetery, named after a local hero of the War of 1812. Swift's tombstone explains that he was "killed by the Enemy of his Country [the British] July 12, 1814" in Canada.

To assume Joseph Smith was unaware of *The Late War* is akin to assuming that a nine-year-old boy living in the eastern United States in 2003 would be oblivious of accounts of the 9/11 attacks on New York City and Washington, DC.

The Late War was "Written in the Ancient Historical Style" (1816 and 1817 editions) or in the "Scriptural Style" (1819 edition), meaning it read like the KJV (*It came to pass, the fourth day of the seventh month, the face of the whole earth,* etc.). The book contains an endorsement by Samuel L. Mitchill, the professor in New York City whom Martin Harris visited to solicit a similar endorsement. Plus, the 1830 edition of the Book of Mormon resembles *The Late War* in design (Title page, full copyright notice, Preface).

The totality of the evidence, including the linguistic parallels and the social context of *The Late War*, suggest that Joseph likely read *The Late War* and that the book formed part of Joseph's mental language bank. Consequently, the Johnson study provides evidence that Joseph used his own English vocabulary to dictate the text of the Book of Mormon, whether as composer or translator.

LDS scholars point out that there are more differences than similarities between *The Late War* and the Book of Mormon. While this argues against outright plagiarism, it does not refute the critics' point that *The Late War* influenced at least some of the vocabulary Joseph used in producing the Book of Mormon. Differences between the two books do not erase similarities, and the similarities are specific enough to raise a reasonable inference that there was at least some influence involved.

Key point: if Joseph Smith actually translated the ancient plates into English, we should expect exactly the kind of evidence the Johnson study produced; i.e., chunks of language scattered through the text of the Book of Mormon drawn from Joseph's mental language bank that he acquired by reading books such as (and probably including) *The Late War*. Critics, of course, point to the same facts as evidence that Joseph composed the Book of Mormon.

B. Translation More Persuasive Than Composition

Joseph's claim that he translated the plates is the only viable starting point, the default proposition that places the burden of proof to overcome on critics. The only difference between Joseph's claim and the claim of any other translator is the absence of the original source material. That requires us to review extrinsic evidence for corroboration.

1. The Consistency of Joseph's Description

Unlike with his accounts of the First Vision, Joseph gave no differing versions of the Book of Mormon's origins with disparate details.[219] Joseph consistently stated that he translated from the plates with the aid of the interpreters. He never claimed or implied he composed the text he dictated, and no one else claimed credit for composing it. Joseph never claimed or implied he saw the text, either

---

[219] On the disparate accounts of the First Vision and subsequent struggles, see Steve C. Harper, *First Vision: Memory and Mormon Origins* (New York: Oxford University Press, 2019).

on a stone or in vision, and merely read it off. No witnesses claimed or implied that he had a manuscript (other than the plates) to read from; several of them specifically denied that he had such a manuscript. Critics may dismiss this point as self-serving, but consistency is one mark of a reliable witness.

2. Scattered Distribution of Intertextual Elements

Continuing with *The Late War* as an example, the "influenced" vocabulary appears throughout both books in discrete chunks that are separated by intermittent text. They are not long passages (plagiarism) or even complete sentences. The Johnson presentation merges the chunks together, but when put in context, the influence is less direct. Here is an excerpt from the Johnson presentation that Callister evaluated.[220] The Johnson's used colors to show the corresponding vocabulary. Here we **bold** it.

TABLE 1 - THE LATE WAR COMPARISON 1

The Late War	Book of Mormon
35:5-6	Alma 53:18-20
two thousand hardy **men**, who ... fought freely for **their country** ... Now the men **of war** ... were ... **men** of **dauntless courage**.	**two thousand** of those young **men** ... to defend **their country**. ... they took their weapons **of war**, ... were all young **men**, and they were exceeding **valiant for courage**, ...

Presented this way, the similarities appear significant. *Two thousand* is a specific number, *dauntless* is a rough synonym for *valiant*, etc. However, Callister puts this example in context, which dilutes the similarities.[221] We see that rather than a precise count, *two thousand* likely

---

[220] Third entry at http://wordtree.org/thelatewar/
[221] Callister, *A Case for the Book of Mormon*, p. 74.

reflects a military unit (like a brigade) instead of an exact number; i.e., in neither case would the author write 1,999 or 2,001.

TABLE 2 - THE LATE WAR COMPARISON 2

The Late War	The Book of Mormon
The Late War 35:5–6 5 Immediately Jackson took **two thousand** hardy **men**, who were called volunteers, because they had, unsolicited, offered their services to **their country**, and led them against the savages. 6 Now the men **of war** that followed after him were mostly from the state of Tennessee, and **men of dauntless courage**.	Alma 53:18-20 18 Now behold, there were **two thousand** of those young **men**, who entered into this covenant and took their weapons of war to defend **their country**. 19 And now behold, as they never had hitherto been a disadvantage to the Nephites, they became now at this period of time also a great support; for they took their weapons **of war**, and they would that Helaman should be their leader. 20 And they were all young **men**, and they were exceedingly **valiant for courage**, and also for strength and activity; but behold, this was not all—they were men who were true at all times in whatsoever thing they were entrusted.

When viewed in this context, this evidence does not support the Johnson's unquantified and subjective claim that *The Late War* "heavily" influenced the Book of Mormon, but instances of similar chunks of language are specific enough to suggest they came from Joseph's mental language bank, which likely included his familiarity with *The Late War*.²²²

A composition based primarily on *The Late War* would have more similarities in theme and vocabulary than a translation of a foreign-language text in which the translator simply used his/her own vocabulary to restate the original material into English. In the above example, intertextuality may offer additional insights.

TABLE 3 - INTERTEXTUALITY

Phrase	BofM	KJV	Late War	Edwards
Period of time	6	0	0	30
Great support	1	0	0	4
This was not all	3	0	0	3
At all times	5	8 (OT)	0	256
Whatsoever thing	12	3 (OT) 1 (NT)	0	5
Dauntless	0	0	1	0
Unsolicited	0	0	1	0
Entrusted	5	0	1	37
Activity	1	1 (OT)	0	280
Disadvantage	1	0	0	176
Followed after	1	3 (OT) 4 (NT)	9	22
Courage	14	19 (OT) 1 (NT)	9	285
Their country	16	2 (OT) 1 (NT)	3	60

"Entrusted" is the only nonbiblical term in the Book of Mormon common to *The Late War* passage, but it is far more common in Jonathan Edwards' works. No non-biblical Book of Mormon terms are absent from Edwards.

---

²²² See Neville, *Infinite Goodness*, Appendices 2 and 3. This analysis used BYU's Wordcruncher program, which includes *The Late War* in the database so anyone can compare words and phrases. https://www.wordcruncher.com/

Neville's NID database bears out this conclusion for the entire Book of Mormon. While space will not permit detailing the over 1,200 entries in the NID, the variety and distribution of sources can be illustrated just by analyzing the first two verses of the Book of Mormon, 1 Nephi 1:1-2. This is the first sentence in the 1830 Book of Mormon and presumably the first verse Joseph translated in Fayette from the small plates of Nephi.

Strings of two or more words are more significant than single words. For example, the term "goodly" is found in the Bible, Jonathan Edwards (and several other Christian authors), Shakespeare, and two books written in the "biblical style" (*The American Revolution* and *The First Book of Napoleon*), but the combination "goodly parents" is rare outside of the Book of Mormon. That said, "goodly parents" appears in pre-1828 sources such as a poem published in 1801 by Peter Pindar ("of goodly parents she was born") and an 1809 New Family Bible's footnote to Genesis 34:1-5 ("Let not goodly parents that are lamenting the miscarriage of their children suppose their case singular").

In the footnotes, nonbiblical terms are shown as 0 OT, 0 NT, and bolded. Because some of these terms may appear in the Doctrine and Covenants (DC) or Pearl of Great Price (PGP), terms unique to the Book of Mormon (BM) are so indicated and bolded. JE stands for Jonathan Edwards.

1. I, Nephi, **having been born**[223] of goodly parents,[224] therefore was[225] **taught somewhat**[226]

---

[223] "having been born" **unique to BM**, but it appears 5 times in Edwards (shown as 5 JE).

[224] "goodly parents" **unique to BM**. "goodly" 31 OT, 4 NT, 2 BM, 4 DC, 0 PGP, 52 JE, 3 AmRev, 3 Nap, 87 Shakes.

[225] "therefore I was" 1 OT, 0 NT, 4 BM, 0 DC, 0 PGP, 3 JE.

[226] "taught somewhat" **unique to BM**. "somewhat" 14 OT, 10 NT, 44 BM, 0 DC, 1 PGP-JS-H, 260 JE. High prevalence in LDS = JE. Edwards: "It appears to me obvious, also, that, in connection with all this, they should be **taught somewhat** relating to the chronology of events, which would make the story so much the more distinct…"

Composition

in all the learning²²⁷ of my father;²²⁸ and having seen²²⁹ **many afflictions**²³⁰ **in the course**²³¹ of my days,²³² nevertheless, having been²³³ highly favored²³⁴ of the Lord in **all my days;**²³⁵ yea, having had²³⁶ a **great knowledge**²³⁷ of the goodness²³⁸ and the mysteries of God,²³⁹ therefore I make a record²⁴⁰ of my **proceedings**²⁴¹ in my days;

2 Yea I make a record²⁴² in the language of²⁴³ my father, **which**

---

²²⁷ "the learning" 1 OT, 0 NT, 4 BM, 0 DC, 0 PGP, 27 JE.
²²⁸ "of my father" 13 OT, 15 NT, 41 BM, 22 DC, 0 PGP, 103 JE. High prevalence in LDS = JE.
²²⁹ "having seen" 0 OT, 2 NT, 5 BM, 0 DC, 0 PGP, 19 JE.
²³⁰ "many afflictions" **0 OT, 0 NT**, 8 BM, 1 DC, 0 PGP, 1 JST, 7 JE. Edwards: "it may be God's hand is upon them in **many afflictions**."
²³¹ "in the course" **0 OT, 0 NT**, 3 BM, 0 DC, 0 PGP, 231 JE. Edwards: "the same is now proposed **in the course** of a sinner's convictions in these days…"
²³² "my days" 18 OT, 0 NT, 14 BM, 0 DC, 0 PGP, 34 JE. "of my days" 3 OT, 0 NT, 3 BM, 0 DC, 0 PGP, 8 JE.
²³³ "having been" 0 OT, 1 NT, 53 BM, 1 DC, 6 PGP (1 AB, 5 JS-H), 286 JE. High prevalence in LDS = JE.
²³⁴ "highly favored" 0 OT, 1 NT, 7 BM, 0 DC, 0 PGP, 19 JE; "highly favored of" **0 OT, 0 NT**, 3 BM, 0 DC, 0 PGP, 2 JE. Edwards: "highly favored by the Lord."
²³⁵ "all my days" **0 OT, 0 NT**, 3 BM, 0 DC, 0 PGP, 2 JE. Edwards: "went to bed resolving to live devoted to God all my days."
²³⁶ "having had" 0 OT, 1 NT, 7 BM, 0 DC, 0 PGP, 56 JE.
²³⁷ "great knowledge" **0 OT, 0 NT**, 6 BM, 0 DC, 1 PGP, 27 JE. Edwards: "they have a very great knowledge of the natural glory of God."
²³⁸ "goodness" 41 OT, 9 NT, 31 BM, 2 DC, 1 PGP, 2897 JE.
²³⁹ "mysteries of God" 0 OT, 1 NT, 8 BM, 3 DC, 0 PGP, 0 JE (mysteries of God's providence, mysteries of God's universe, mysteries of God's eternal duration)
²⁴⁰ "a record" 1 OT, 1 NT, 19 BM, 4 DC, 0 PGP, 42 JE. Edwards: "how much more may we expect that God gives the world a record of the dispensations of his divine government that doubtless is infinitely more worthy of an history…"
²⁴¹ "proceedings" **0 OT, 0 NT**, 10 BM, 2 DC, 1 PGP (JS-H), 207 JE. "my proceedings" **unique to BM** (3x). Edwards: "A Just & faithful account of my Proceedings & Conduct…"
²⁴² "make a record" 0 OT, 0 NT, 7 BM, 1 DC, 0 PGP, 0 JE.
²⁴³ "language of" 4 OT, 0 NT, 17 BM, 0 DC, 2 PGP, 402 JE.

consists[244] of **the learning of the Jews**[245] and the **language of the**[246] Egyptians.

The NID analysis shows a similar dispersion and variety of possible sources for most nonbiblical passages in the Book of Mormon. This argues for a diversity of sources for the Book of Mormon's language, all readily available to Joseph. This also rules out composition explanations which rely on an inference of plagiarism or copying from sources such as *The Late War*.

3. Unavailability of Supposed Source Texts

The translation narrative is re-enforced by the absence of evidence that Joseph (or anyone close to him) had a copy of *The Late War* or other alleged physical sources available during the dictation process in Harmony (1828 and 1829) or in Fayette (1829). To compose the text by copying from multiple sources as the critics argue, Joseph would have needed the sources available during the dictation. Yet no one, not even the critics, can cite evidence that Joseph brought books to Harmony or Fayette or that such sources were available to him there. Meanwhile, all witnesses agree that Joseph had the plates, even if some say the plates were under a cloth when Joseph dictated.

4. The Difficulty of Tracking Narrative Detail and Literary Forms and Structure

These first three factors would allow the possibility that Joseph entirely composed the text from memory or imagination. But once

---

[244] "which consists" **unique to BM**; 146 JE. "which consists of" 12 JE.
[245] "the learning of the Jews" **unique to BM**; Edwards: "the apostle Paul, who was famed for his much learning, as you may see, Acts 26:24; and was not only skilled in the learning of the Jews"
[246] "language of the" **unique to BM** (8x); 110 JE. Edwards "the language of the people," "the language of the Indians."

critics concede that Joseph did not rely on particular extraneous sources (other than the plates) during the dictation, distinguishing between composition and translation becomes easier. All the evidence points to a continuous dictation of a coherent document. Scribes reported that Joseph resumed work after breaks without asking for the previous work to be read back to him. That is exactly what we would expect if Joseph translated an original, edited text as he claimed because he could pick up where he left off—say, at the bottom of a plate.

Translators do not need their prior work to be read back because they know what they have already translated. They use the organization, structure, concepts, and narrative from the original text. They just convert one language to another. By contrast, dictating such a complex document from one's memory or imagination without making changes or edits is unimaginable—and unprecedented.[247]

The Book of Mormon contains over 200 named individuals, including their family connections, following 26 record keepers, 41 Jaredite kings (including rival lines), and dozens of other family relationships. It follows several different chronologies in precise annual detail over a thousand years and lays out a convoluted geography with over 100 named locations which is internally consistent (even if it has not been mapped definitively onto a known real-world setting). The track of the narrative is never lost even as it constantly switches to numerous different literary formats and back and forth in time. Yet, other than the plates, no witness ever saw evidence of any notes or papers laying out this incredibly complex thousand-year long story (and longer if one includes the Jaredites).[248]

---

[247] One recent composition advocate spends most of an entire book arguing on the basis of no evidence that Joseph must have had some form of notes to work from since reciting a book as long and as complicated as the Book of Mormon entirely from memory is inconceivable. Davis, *Visions in a Seer Stone: Joseph Smith and the Making of the Book of Mormon*, (2020).

[248] Hardy, *Understanding the Book of Mormon*, pp. 6 – 7.

The text's complexity is not just a matter of numerous names, places and story lines to keep track of. The Book uses complicated literary forms and structures. According to literature scholar Richard Dilworth Rust, the Book of Mormon has "the timelessness, sweep of significance and scope of meaning of cosmic drama. ... the breadth and inclusiveness ... characteristic of an epic: scope, nationalistic emphasis, with narrative motifs including warfare and rulership; a historical impulse, with allusions to key events in the life of a nation; a supernatural context in which the action occurs; and an epic structure of episodic plot with recurrent patterns or situations."[249]

Non-LDS historian Daniel Walker Howe has written that whether

> true or not, the Book of Mormon is a powerful epic written on a grand scale with a host of characters, a narrative of human struggle and conflict, of divine intervention, heroic good and atrocious evil, of prophecy, morality and law. Its narrative structure is complex. ... It tells a tragic story, of a people who, though possessed of the true faith, fail in the end. Yet it does not convey a message of despair; God's will cannot ultimately be frustrated.[250]

The epic is one of the oldest forms of human literature. It reaches back to national masterpieces such as *Gilgamesh*, the *Iliad* and *Odyssey*, and the Norse sagas. They are found in many ancient nations, and the form continues to grip moderns through works by a professor of philology and medieval literature at Oxford University named J. R. R. Tolkien, and many others. (But no epics were originally composed within a few months by oral dictation!)

In addition to its epic sweep and structure, the Book of Mormon is full of sophisticated literary devices. Professor Rust explains that the "impact of *what* the Book of Mormon says is often created through *how* it is said ... literary elements such as form, imagery, poetry and

---

[249] Richard Dilworth Rust, ""The Book of Mormon as Epic," *AML Annual 1998*, Lavina Fieldling Anderson (ed), pp. 24-30, quote at p. 24.

[250] Howe, *What Hath God Wrought*, quote at p. 314.

narrative, help teach and motivate us in ways that touch our hearts and souls as well as our minds."[251] Professor Rust and other scholars have written articles and entire books analyzing the many literary forms the Book of Mormon authors employed to convey God's message.[252] These are not things anyone can spin out off the top of their head with no notes or outlines, even if they have been thinking about it for years.

5. Hebraisms and Other Ancient Linguistic Artifacts

The fifth factor is the presence of subtle Hebrew linguistic patterns, structures and themes which are not obvious from the KJV. Beginning in the mid-20th century with scholars such as Sidney Sperry and Hugh Nibley, a massive quantity of work has explored Hebraisms and other features of the Book of Mormon which would be unexpected in a 19th century composition.[253] A well-known example is Jack Welch's work

---

[251] Richard Dilworth Rust, *Feasting on the Word: The Literary Testimony of the Book of Mormon*, (Salt Lake City and Provo, UT: Deseret Book and FARMS, 1997), quote at pp. 2 – 3, emphasis in original.

[252] See for example Rust, *Feasting on the Word*; James T. Duke, *The Literary Masterpiece Called the Book of Mormon* (Springville, UT: Cedar Fort, Inc., 2003); Hardy, *Understanding the Book of Mormon*; and Val Larsen, "In His Footsteps: Ammon$_1$ and Ammon$_2$," *Interpreter: A Journal of Latter-day Saint Faith and Scholarship* 3 (2013), pp. 85-113 at https://journal.interpreterfoundation.org/in-his-footsteps-ammon-and-ammon/.

[253] The literature is vast, but a representative sample over time might include Sidney B. Sperry, "The Book of Mormon as Translation English." *Improvement Era* 38 (March 1935): 141, 187-88 (reprinted in *Journal of Book of Mormon Studies* 4/1 1995): 209–17 available at https://scholarsarchive.byu.edu/cgi/viewcontent.cgi?article=1106&context=jbms); Sidney B. Sperry, "Hebrew Idioms in the Book of Mormon" *Improvement Era* 57 (October 1954): 703, 728-29, available at https://scholarsarchive.byu.edu/jbms/vol4/iss1/24; Hugh W. Nibley, *Since Cumorah: The Book of Mormon in the Modern World* (Salt Lake City, UT: Deseret Book, 1967); Noel B. Reynolds (ed), *Book of Mormon Authorship: New Light on Ancient Origins* (Provo, UT: Brigham Young University, 1982); John A. Tvedtnes, "The Hebrew Background of the Book of Mormon" in John L. Sorenson and Melvin J. Thorne (eds), *Rediscovering*

on chiasmus, a Hebrew poetic form, in the Book of Mormon.[254] Another would be the presence of ancient ritual and festival patterns such as the Feast of Tabernacles and enthronement ceremonies.[255] (In Chapter 6 we will propose a process by which these literary and linguistic features flowed into Joseph's English translation.)

6. Transliteration

The sixth factor that favors translation is the presence of transliteration in the text. "Transliteration is the process of transferring a word from the alphabet of one language to another."[256] Translators use transliteration when there is no known equivalent in the target language. By one count, there are 188 unique proper names in the

---

the Book of Mormon (Provo, UT: FARMS, 1991), pp. 77-91; Donald W. Parry, *Poetic Parallelisms in the Book of Mormon* (Provo, UT: Maxwell Institute Publications. 2007), available at https://scholarsarchive.byu.edu/mi/61/ and most recently Donald W. Parry, *Preserved in Translation: Hebrew and Other Ancient Literary Forms in the Book of Mormon*, (Salt Lake City and Provo, UT: Deseret Book and BYU Religious Studies Center, 2020). The latter includes a recent bibliography of such works at pp. 149-163. Many of these resources are also available at websites like www.fairlatterdaysaints.org and www.bookofmormoncentral.org.

[254] John W. Welch, "How Much Was Known about Chiasmus in 1829 When the Book of Mormon Was Translated?," *Review of Books on the Book of Mormon 1989–2011*: Vol. 15 : No. 1 (2003), available at https://scholarsarchive.byu.edu/msr/vol15/iss1/7.

[255] Stephen D. Ricks, "King, Coronation and Covenant in Mosiah 1-6" in John L. Sorenson and Melvin J. Thorne (eds), *Rediscovering the Book of Mormon* (Provo, UT: FARMS, 1991), pp. 209-219 and John A. Tvedtnes, "King Benjamin and the Feast of Tabernacles" in John M. Lundquist and Stephen D. Ricks (eds), *By Study and Also by Faith: Essays in Honor of Hugh W. Nibley* (Salt Lake City and Provo, UT: Deseret Book and FARMS, 1990), vol 2, pp 197–236.

[256] "transliteration", vocabulary.com https://www.vocabulary.com/dictionary/transliteration (accessed November 12, 2022)

text,[257] including kinds of animals that appear as transliterations such as *curelom* and *cumom*. These are non-English words. While it is possible to create non-English words when composing a manuscript in English, Joseph's scribes reported that he spelled out some of these names, exactly as one would do if transliterating the original language.

7. Journey through the Arabian Peninsula

Although not strictly linguistic in nature, another feature of the Book of Mormon that Joseph Smith as author could not have known involves Lehi's journey in Arabia. While there is no agreement on any geographical location for the Book of Mormon events in the Americas (other than the Hill Cumorah in New York), a consensus has emerged among faithful scholars that 1 Nephi accurately describes the journey of Lehi's party across the Arabian Peninsula circa 600 BCE.[258] Because it is unlikely that Joseph could have had any familiarity with that geography, the more plausible explanation is that he was translating the writings of someone (Nephi) who had actually made that journey.

---

[257] Paul Y. Hoskisson, "Book of Mormon Names," *Encyclopedia of Mormonism* (New York: Macmillan Publishing Company, 1992) Vol. 1, pp. 186-187, available at https://eom.byu.edu/index.php/Book_of_Mormon_Names

[258] Warren P. Aston and Michaela Knoth Aston, *In the Footsteps of Lehi: New Evidence for Lehi's Journey across Arabia to Bountiful* (Salt Lake City, UT: Deseret Book Company, 1994); Lynn M Hilton and Hope A. Hilton, *Discovering Lehi: New Evidence of Lehi and Nephi in Arabia* (Springville, UT: Cedar Fort, Inc, 1996); Noel B. Reynolds, "Lehi's Arabian Journey Updated" in Noel B. Reynolds (ed) *Book of Mormon Authorship Revisited: The Evidence for Ancient Origins* (Provo, UT: Foundation for Ancient Research and Mormon Studies, 1997), pp. 379-389; George Potter and Richard Wellington, *Lehi in the Wilderness: 81 new documented evidences that the Book of Mormon is a true history* (Springville, UT: Cedar Fort, Inc., 2003); S. Kent Brown and Peter Johnson (ed.), *Journey of Faith* (Provo, UT: The Neal A. Maxwell Institute for Religious Scholarship, 2006).

C. Are 19th Century Concepts Evidence?

The apparent 19th century influences on the Book of Mormon pointed out by critics go beyond Joseph's 19th century language. In one of the earliest extended critiques of the Book, Disciples of Christ founder Alexander Campbell wrote that:

> This prophet Smith, through his stone spectacles, wrote on the plates of Nephi, in his book of Mormon, every error and almost every truth discussed in N. York for the last ten years. He decides all the great controversies – infant baptism, ordination, the trinity, regeneration, repentance, justification, the fall of man, the atonement, transubstantiation, fasting, penance, church government, religious experience, the call to ministry, the general resurrection, eternal punishment, who may baptize, and even the question of freemasonry, republican government, and the rights of man. All these topics are repeatedly alluded to.[259]

However, the presence of subjects and concepts of Joseph's environment do not prove authorship. They would only definitively prove authorship if they appeared exclusively in Joseph's environment. If they (or their functional equivalent) appear in other times and places, their presence in the Book of Mormon could be attributable to the Nephite authors, expressed in a 19th century translation using 19th century terminology.

Campbell as much as admitted this by using terms that do not even appear in the text, such as "trinity," "regeneration," "transubstantiation," "penance," and "freemasonry." When he claims the text "repeatedly alluded" to these unmentioned topics, he in effect re-translates the text to suit his audience. That Joseph did not use such

---

[259] Alexander Campbell, "Delusions: An Analysis of the Book of Mormon: With an Examination of Its Internal and External Evidences, and a Refutation of Its Pretences to Divine Authority," *The Millennial Harbinger*, February 7, 1831. Reprint available at https://archive.org/details/delusionsanalysi01camp, quote at p. 13.

common terms suggests he was not composing a 19th century religious argument, but instead was constrained by the material in his ancient source. Whatever the ancient religious controversies were, a 19th century Christian translator would naturally express those controversies using 19th century Christian terminology—particularly when the ancient text was explicitly Christian itself.

In Chapter 1(F) we argued for a broader standard of proof in evaluating the Book of Mormon, one that realistically admitted that, given the uncertainties of historical evidence, in some cases the best we can hope for are multiple plausible explanations. With many of the issues, certain proof is not possible. Instead, we must look to the plausibility of different explanations, and then weigh the totality. Here are some examples of applying this approach to concepts present in Joseph Smith's environment which appear in the Book of Mormon.

1. Secret Combinations

One long-standing trope in criticism of the Book of Mormon is that Mormon's obsession with "secret combinations" derives from the anti-Masonic political fervor, or at least the rhetoric, prevalent in 1820s New York.[260] Even in 1831 Campbell included "the question of freemasonry" in his list. However, concern over conspiracies and insurgencies is a ubiquitous feature of human society; it is hardly limited to New York in the 1820s. Consider this description by the Roman historian Sallust (Gaius Sallustius Crispus) of the last days of the Roman Republic in the century before Christ:

---

[260] Brodie, *No Man Knows My History*, p. 65; Brent Lee Metcalfe, "Apologetic and Critical Assumptions about Book of Mormon Historicity," *Dialogue* 26/3 (1993), p. 171 available at https://www.dialoguejournal.com/wp-content/uploads/sbi/articles/Dialogue_V26N03_163.pdf; and Dan Vogel, "Mormonism's 'Anti-Masonick Bible,'" *The John Whitmer Historical Association Journal* 9 (1989), p. 29, https://www.jstor.org/stable/43200831.

> Frequent mobs, seditions, and at last civil wars, became common, while a few leading men on whom the masses were dependent, affected supreme power under the seemly pretense of seeking the good of senate and people; citizens were judged good or bad, without reference to their loyalty to the republic (for all were equally corrupt); but the wealthy and dangerously powerful were esteemed good citizens, because they maintained the existing state of things.[261]

This account of "leading men" with "supreme power" compares with Mormon's description of the Nephite nation in the same time period preceding the appearance of Christ. The description continued to be invoked by St. Augustine of Hippo in the *City of God* four centuries later.[262] Such concerns remain relevant to the condition of many modern states.

Indeed, research has shown that even in Joseph's time the term "secret combination" was not limited to anti-Masonic rhetoric, being used among other instances by Alexander Hamilton to describe political parties (again a use which might find resonance today).[263]

Another example comes from 1799, when David Edmond delivered a 4th of July oration "before a large concourse of people" in

---

[261] Gaius Sallustius Crispus, *Historiae Fragmenta*, 1:12, available at https://www.goodreads.com/quotes/8254253-frequent-mobs-seditions-and-at-last-civil-wars-became-common or in Sallust, *Catiline's Conspiracy, The Jugurthine War, Histories*, trans. William W. Batstone (New York: Oxford University Press, 2010), at p. 134. It is interesting to note that Sallust attributed this decline to the end of wartime pressures following Rome's victory over Carthage. Similarly, Mormon is constantly warning of the dangers of peace and prosperity, and situates the decline in the morality of the Nephite state after the defeat of the Lamanites by Captains Moroni and Moronihah.

[262] St. Augustine, *Concerning the City of God Against the Pagans*, Book 3, chapter 17, available at https://www.gutenberg.org/files/45304/45304-h/45304-h.htm#Page_114.

[263] Paul Mouritsen, "Secret Combinations and Flaxen Cords: Anti-Masonic Rhetoric and the Book of Mormon," *Journal of Book of Mormon Studies*: Vol. 12, No. 1 (2003), pp. 65-118 available at https://scholarsarchive.byu.edu/jbms/vol12/iss1/9.

which he said of French intellectuals that "the first object of these secret combinations was only the abolishment of Christianity."[264]

Critics may argue that Joseph Smith reflected the anti-Masonic politics of his surroundings in putting anti-Masonic rhetoric into the mouths of his fictional narrators, Mormon and Moroni. But it is also plausible that Joseph used anti-Masonic language familiar to him to translate the writings of the historical soldier/statesmen Mormon and Moroni, who were contending with political struggles which have risen, and still arise, in most human societies.

Plausibility is subjective; people can interpret the text to confirm whatever bias they want. But readers can ask themselves, does the text of the Book of Mormon read like the romantic imaginings of a young man in his early 20s? Or does it read like the realist hard-bitten reflections of a man who has seen "a continual scene of wickedness and abominations ... since I have been sufficient to behold the ways of man"?[265] A man who resigns his high military command to protest the war crimes of his own people, and then faces the excruciating moral dilemma of whether to accede to their pleas to return to command in order to save them, even though they will not change their ways? A man whose portrait of his personal hero, Captain Moroni (who would have been a contemporary of Gaius Sallustius Crispus), gives a full description of his hero's short temper, errors and defeats?[266] A historian who uses precious space on his laboriously engraved plates to give his account's antagonists their say in their own words?[267] Would Joseph Smith have heard the Norse myths of the *Götterdämmerung* or *Ragnarok*, a civilization-ending conflict, a half

---

[264] David Edmond, *An Oration delivered at Ridgfield on the Fourth of July* (Danbury: Dougles & Nichols, MDCCXCIX)

[265] Mormon 2:18 and Jonathan Edwards "a scene of wickedness and abomination" *History of the Work of Redemption.*

[266] On Captain Moroni's temper see Alma 44:17-18, 46:11, 51:14, 54:7, 59:13, 60:18.

[267] See Alma 30:13-18, 23-29, Alma 54:16-24, 3 Nephi 3:2-10.

century before Richard Wagner turned them into opera, or does the Book of Mormon read like it was written by men who lived it?

2. A "Christian" Old Testament

Richard Bushman once described the Book of Mormon to a seminar at the Union Theological Seminary as reading as if St. Paul had made an abridgement of the Hebrew Bible.[268] There is no question that the Book of Mormon text for the time preceding the appearance of Christ is far more explicitly Christian than anything in the Hebrew Bible. One plausible explanation for this is that the Book was written by a Christian named Joseph Smith. But a close reading of the text presents another plausible explanation.[269]

There are two components to this analysis. The first component is that, according to the Book of Mormon itself, the Christian who produced it was not Jospeh Smith but Mormon, son of Mormon.[270] Mormon and his son Moroni were chronological (but not geographically proximate) contemporaries of many of the early Fathers of the Christian Church in the Old World, such as St. Jerome, St. John Chrysostom, and St. Augustine of Hippo. Mormon and Moroni openly declared their agenda: to convince the "Jew and the Gentile that JESUS iis the CHRIST."[271] Consequently, we would expect Mormon's

---

[268] Personal recollection of James Lucas.

[269] We should note that another explanation advanced by Blake Ostler is that during the translation process Joseph Smith wrote the Christian additions into the original ancient source. We will discuss this expansion theory in Chapter 5. For purposes of this immediate discussion, we focus on the most obviously Christian elements, Lehi and Nephi's explicit prophecies of the coming Messiah.

[270] In this book we will occasionally refer to the Book of Mormon's principal author as "Mormon, son of Mormon" because (1) his father was also named Mormon (Mormon 1:5) and using a patronymic was common practice among ancient peoples and (2) to remind us that he was a real person.

[271] Title Page, Book of Mormon.

abridgement of his national history to emphasize every Christian element.

The second component concerns the first section of the Book of Mormon which was not composed by Mormon or Moroni. This record from the sixth century BCE has some of the Book of Mormon's most explicit Christian prophecies and teachings. (Note that we need not assume the term "Christ" is a transliteration, despite 2 Nephi 25:19. It can be a translation of whatever term the ancient Nephites used.) The account itself says these Christian prophecies and teachings came directly as revelations to Lehi and Nephi.

The Bible does not relate similar revelations among the Israelites of the Old World. Perhaps they were among the "plain and precious" matters that have been lost from the Bible.[272]

In any case, critics have understandably pointed to this Christian material in a pre-Christian era as evidence of 19th century composition. A close reading of the text, however, supports the plausibility of this material as a translation of Nephi's writings

In the Words of Mormon, Mormon recounts his discovery of the small plates of Nephi – "After I had made an abridgment from the plates of Nephi… I searched among the records had been delivered into my hands, and I found these plates."[273] Mormon seems surprised to find these records, presumably because he did not know about the Christian material despite having abridged the more secular plates of Nephi. He writes, "the things which are upon these plates pleasing me, because of the prophecies of the coming of Christ."

There is no indication in the text that Nephi's Christian prophecies were available to his descendants until Mormon found them. The later history of the Nephites makes no reference to these explicit teachings. From Mormon's records it would appear that the actual small plates of Nephi were buried in the archives, forgotten and uncatalogued until Mormon stumbles upon them in the course of his research.

---

[272] 1 Nephi 13:26-29.
[273] Words of Mormon 3

Of course, any historian would be thrilled to uncover a thousand-year-old firsthand autobiographical record of the national founder. But what strikes Mormon the most is precisely those pre-Christian prophecies that we find so incongruous. Mormon is delighted to find them, knowing that many of the prophecies have been fulfilled by his time in the fourth century CE.[274] Hence, he chose to "finish my record upon them," meaning to abridge the Nephite records consistent with them.

The Book of Mormon makes clear that the scribal line preceding Mormon preserved and updated the records but, unlike with the Jews, there is no reference to the scribes before Mormon studying Nephi's Christian writings. Prophets such as Alma are called to mission by angels or inspired by the Holy Spirit, not as a result of studying the national archives.

While there is certainly a tradition of learning in the law of Moses and the national origin story of Lehi's voyage, and even access to pre-Lehi prophets from the brass plates of Laban, there is no indication that the average Nephite was reading or aware of the prophecies in the plates of Nephi (1 Nephi through Omni in our Book of Mormon).

Indeed, by the first century before Christ's appearance, the "church" had declined to a small messianic cult, considered by the larger culture to be very noisome and annoying, as such cults often are. Belief in Christ is so insignificant that God has to send a Lamanite to

---

[274] Words of Mormon 4. In verse 6 he says he will "put them with the remainder of my record." Historians have assumed that this means that the small plates were "bound in with" the larger set of plates. However, Neville has argued, based on a close review of the events surrounding the translation and addition of the small plates to our Book of Mormon, that they were separate, and that to "put them with" meant that they were "kept close to" the larger plates. After all, king Benjamin had "put them with the other plates," (Words of Mormon verse 10) but Mormon still had to search to find them in the archives. See Neville, *Whatever Happened to the Golden Plates?*, chapter 11.

preach to the Nephites.[275] And even after the destruction preceding the dramatic appearance of Christ himself, it takes several years of preaching against great resistance to convert enough people for Christianity to impact the larger society.[276]

We recognize that this larger context does not "prove" that the explicit pre-Christian revelations recorded in the books of Nephi were not just put there by Joseph Smith. But Mormon's surprised delight informs us that he, too, recognized the unexpected clarity of Nephi's pre-Christian knowledge of Christ. Within the context of the Book of Mormon narrative, Nephi's Christian writings are plausible and consistent.

3. Jonathan Edwards in the Book of Mormon

Neville's nonbilical intertextuality research has added another dimension. Neville discovered that an unusually large amount of the non-biblical language of the Book of Mormon could be linked to the writings of the great American theologian Jonathan Edwards. As explained in more detail in *Infinite Goodness,* not only the language, but the theological concepts of Edwards are found in the Book of Mormon. While this could be seen as evidence of both composition and translation by Joseph Smith, it also points toward divine inspiration.

For example, King Benjamin declares "The natural man is an enemy to God." (Mosiah 3:19). That could be an allusion to 1 Cor. 2:14 ("the natural man received not the things of the Spirit of God") blended with James 4:4 ("whosoever therefore will be a friend of the world is the enemy of God"). But "enemy **of** God" is not the same as

---

[275] Helaman 13:1-3. One of the fascinating subtexts of Mormon's record is how he includes both the preaching of Samuel and Christ's rebuke of the Nephites for not including Samuel's teachings in their sacred records (3 Nephi 23:11-13), a subtle rebuke of the anti-Lamanite prejudice of his own society.

[276] 3 Nephi 28:18-23

"enemy **to** God," (a nonbiblical phrase used four times in the Book of Mormon). Further, the Biblical passages do not squarely fit with Benjamin's expression.

Alternatively, Benjamin's teaching can be seen as a shorthand allusion to Jonathan Edwards's sermon "Natural Men are God's Enemies," which explains in detail what constitutes the "natural man" and how such a person is an enemy to God.[277] This sermon is in the 1808 collection of Edwards' works on sale in the Palmyra print shop Joseph visited weekly.[278] Just as the Book of Mormon alludes to but never explains the "law of Moses," requiring readers to consult the Bible to understand the reference, the Book of Mormon alludes to numerous terms explained in more detail in the works of Jonathan Edwards.

For much of its history, the Book of Mormon has been used primarily as a proselyting tool. "The Book of Mormon is true; if your church does not accept it, your church is false" is a crude summary of the argument. However, there is an intellectual tradition in LDS history which suggests another way of looking at the Book of Mormon. Even in his *The Great Apostasy*, Elder James Talmage acknowledged that divine permission underlay:

> Wycliffe and Huss, Luther and Melancthon, Zwingle and Calvin, Henry VIII in his arrogant assumption of priestly authority, John Knox in Scotland, Roger Williams in America—these and a host of others built better than they knew, in that their efforts laid in part

---

[277] Neville, *Infinite Goodness*, Chapter 9; Jonathan Edwards, "Sermon III. Natural men naturally God's Enemies," in *The Works of President Edwards in Eight Volumes*, Volume VII (Worcester, MA: Isaiah Thomas, Jun., 1808), pp. 159-207 available at https://www.mobom.org/men-naturally-gods-enemies.

[278] Books on sale in the Palmyra print shop, listed in the *Palmyra Register*, September 22, 1818. Image of the newspaper is available online at http://pioneerlibrarysystem.advantage-preservation.com/viewer/?k=book%20seller&i=f&by=1818&bdd=1810&d=01011817-12311829&m=between&ord=k1&fn=palmyra_register_usa_new_york_palmyra_18180922_english_1&df=1&dt=10.

the foundation of the structure of religious freedom and liberty of conscience, - and this in preparation for the restoration of the gospel as had been divinely predicted.[279]

By 2020, this somewhat more generous view of pre-Restoration Christians has evolved to the suggestion by Elder M. Russell Ballard that they were among the "*other choice spirits* who were reserved to come forth in the fulness of times to take part in laying the foundations of the great latter-day work" (Doctrine and Covenants 138:53, emphasis added by Elder Ballard).[280]

Joseph Smith might have been indirectly influenced by the theology of Jonathan Edwards. Or Jonathan Edwards may have been guided by the Holy Spirit, as a sort of Elias, to preach and teach ideas that further plowed the ground for the Restoration through Edwards' own pious New England folk a few generations later.

Encountering 19th century American concepts in the Book of Mormon one may ask:

1. Is this unique to 1820s America, or is it also applicable to other times, places and peoples?

2. Is it discordant with the broader context of the Book of Mormon?

3. Could it be American thought being prepared by divine inspiration for the coming Restoration?

---

[279] James E. Talmage, *The Great Apostasy: Considered In The Light Of Scriptural And Secular History* (Salt Lake City, UT: Deseret News, 1909), Chapter X, para. 20, available at https://www.gutenberg.org/cache/epub/35514/pg35514.html.

[280] M. Russell Ballard, *How the Lord Prepared the World for the Restoration*, Ensign (January 2020), pp. 14 – 21, quote at p. 15, available at https://www.churchofjesuschrist.org/study/ensig15n/2020/01/how-the-lord-prepared-the-world-for-the-restoration?lang=eng. LDS attitudes toward the concept of the Great Apostasy are explored in Miranda Wilcox and John D. Young (eds), *Standing Apart: Mormon Historical Consciousness and the Concept of Apostasy* (New York: Oxford University Press, 2014).

4. Or, as we will discuss below in Chapters 5(B) and 6(C), perhaps Joseph added it as part of his mission as prophet/translator?

D. Summary – What Level of Proof?

In Chapter 1 we introduced the idea of multiple plausible hypotheses in evaluating the Book of Mormon by quoting Richard Bushman's observation "that modern readers go through the text thinking with two minds: the religious teachings of the prophets are processed with one mind, and the question about Joseph Smith's authorship is entertained in another.... Some [passages] may look very much like an insertion by the nineteenth-century Joseph."[281] The issue is further complicated if Joseph was an active participant in the translation because what may look like composition also looks like the results of translation. Language and even concepts in the text would be Joseph's handiwork whether he was translating a pre-existing source text or creating it out of his imagination.

Distinguishing the two is our challenge. In subchapter B above we gave reasons why we find translation a more persuasive explanation than composition. In subchapter C we further argued that, even if it appears that a concept is firmly linked to the 19th century, on closer analysis the text may offer plausible explanations consistent with translation rather than composition.

While believers may carry the burden of reading with two minds, skeptical readers also should read the Book asking if this might be truly an ancient source text, filtered through the mind and language of a 19th century American translator. Because it is impossible to definitively prove that Joseph wrote the Book of Mormon, readers must recognize all plausible alternatives—including Joseph's claim that he translated the plates.

---

[281] Bushman, "Reading From the Gold Plates," p. 86.

Critics may argue that plausibility does not apply to a narrative based on angels and missing golden plates and mysterious translation spectacles. Extraordinary claims require extraordinary evidence and so forth. The absence of the plates and the interpreters leaves each person with a spiritual decision as to whether to pass through the golden door of belief in the canonical account of the Book of Mormon's origins. However, that passage can be facilitated by plausible explanations for aspects of the book which might appear to come from Joseph Smith. We will now propose that one major aspect of that origin story, translation through use of the interpreters, may not be as fantastical as it once may have seemed.

5. Translation

> *And I will even venture to say that if the Book of Mormon were now to be rewritten, in many instances it would materially differ from the present translation.*
>
> Brigham Young[282]

A. The Nature of the Book of Mormon

What do we see when we look at the Book of Mormon as a document? We believe that four characteristics stand out that can be broadly, although not universally, accepted:

1. <u>Complexity</u>. It is a very complex narrative, with hundreds of names, places, characters and events, foreshadowing and back references, and elaborate descriptions of social, political and military events as well as consistent and constant exposition of religious themes and issues. And, as discussed in Chapter 4(B)(4), it deploys an elaborate narrative structure on top of the numerous narrative details using sophisticated literary forms. We are not arguing that it is the most complex book ever written, or that one man could not have written it. However, even the firmest composition advocate would have to agree that it is a very substantial work.

2. <u>19th Century Language</u>. The language is from the 19th century, from Joseph's environment. The NID research has demonstrated that words, grammar and phrases carried forward from Early Modern English were present in Joseph's immediate language world. (Actually,

---

[282] Brigham Young, "The Kingdom of God" (July 13, 1862) in *Journal of Discourses* (Liverpool, UK: George Q. Cannon, 1862) volume 9, quote at p. 311 available at https://jod.mrm.org/9/308.

all modern English retains roots from Early Modern English.) It is not impossible that some supernatural translator who preferred Early Modern English actually made the text appear on Joseph's seer stone, but the cleaner and simpler explanation is that Joseph translated the engravings on the plates by using his own lexicon drawn from his social and cultural environment.

3. <u>Ancient Language Substrate</u>. Underlying the 19th century language are many wordings, phrases, linguistic structures and descriptions of customs and rituals which are ancient, both Hebraic and others. Composition advocates generally refuse to acknowledge these, but if one starts with Sidney Sperry's pioneering work in the 1930s, there is now almost a century of scholarship on this, a massive body of work by dozens of trained scholars which cannot be simply dismissed as accidental or coincidental.

4. <u>King James Bible</u>. The Book of Mormon does draw on the King James translation of the Bible current in Joseph's time.[283]

In this chapter we will explore how translation works, and in Chapter 6 we will propose a model of the Book of Mormon's translation which can explain how it came to embody the characteristics described above.

---

[283] There are differences between the Book of Mormon texts which overlap the biblical text and the KJV, but these are generally sporadic and subsumed within the more general dependency. A comprehensive comparison can be found in Skousen, *Critical Text of the Book of Mormon, Volume 3, The History of the Text, Part Five, The King James Quotations in the Book of Mormon*. Note also that this dependency does not mean that Joseph and Oliver surreptitiously smuggled a King James Bible into the translation room to copy from. The KJV text could have been supplied by the interpreters. If the entire KJV text can fit into a technology as primitive as a modern smartphone, surely the interpreters could manage it. (See more on this point in subchapter C below.) Or it could have come from Joseph's memory. Richard Dilworth Rust and author Neville are currently working on a paper arguing that Joseph was blessed with a prodigious, perhaps even eidetic, memory.

B. The Nature of the Translation

On July 12, 1862, Brigham Young addressed the translation of scriptures at a meeting in Salt Lake City:

> When God speaks to the people, he does it in a manner to suit their circumstances and capacities. ... Should the Lord Almighty send an angel to rewrite the Bible, it would in many places be very different from what it now is. And I will even venture to say that if the Book of Mormon were now to be rewritten, in many instances it would materially differ from the present translation. According as people are willing to receive the things of God, so the heavens send forth their blessings. If the people are stiffnecked, the Lord can tell them but little.[284]

Absent the judgmental slant, Brigham's view of translation is compatible with that advocated by leading modern Bible translation scholars such as Eugene A. Nida.[285] Traditionally, Bible translations

---

[284] Brigham Young, "The Kingdom of God," quote at p. 311 (emphasis added).

[285] Eugene Nida was a towering figure in the modern history of Bible translation and translation scholarship generally. After getting a PhD in linguistics from the University of Michigan, he directed the Bible translation activities of the American Bible Society for over 40 years. When the world's Bible societies formed the United Bible Societies, he served as one of its primary consultants. He worked on hundreds of Bible translations, and traveled the world lecturing on and guiding Bible translations until his death in 2011 at the age of 96. See Philip C. Stine, Eugene Nida: Theoretician of Translation, *International Bulletin of Missionary Research*, Vol. 36, No. 1 (January 2012) pp. 38–39 available at http://www.internationalbulletin.org/issues/2012-01/2012-01-038-stine.pdf and Philip C. Stine, *Let The Words Be Written: The Lasting Influence of Eugene A. Nida* (Atlanta, GA: Society of Biblical Literature, 2004). One reviewer of the latter work wrote of Nida that he "never occupied an academic post, but he had more influence in a wide variety of academic fields than most academics can hope for in one field. This book traces his cumulative intellectual development from classics through Biblical studies, linguistics, anthropology, communication theory, semiotics, translation studies, each discipline building on the

had tried to hew closely to the original languages, which could make them difficult to understand. For example, many readers of the KJV Old Testament assume their difficulty in understanding is due to their unfamiliarity with the English of the 1600s. However, it is also due in part to the efforts of the KJV translators to track the Hebrew idiom as closely as possible.[286]

Nida developed the approach originally called "dynamic equivalence" (later "functional equivalence" became his preferred term). This approach endeavors to translate meaning more than words, to take account of how the translation will be understood and received by the receptor audience. This approach would correspond to Brigham's "circumstances and capacities," or Doctrine and Covenants 1:24 which tells us that God speaks "unto my servants in their weakness, after the manner of their language, that they might come to understanding." For Nida and his colleague Charles Taber,

> The old question: Is this a correct translation? must be answered in terms of another question, namely: For whom? Correctness must be determined by the extent to which the average reader for which a translation is intended will be likely to understand it correctly. Moreover, ... we aim to make certain that such a person is very unlikely to misunderstand it. Posing the question of correctness in this manner naturally implies that there will be different translations which can be called "correct."[287]

---

last to produce a mind of staggering intellectual breadth. ... The end result is that scholars, not only in Bible translation but in translation work generally, are deeply indebted to Nida, whether they know it or not, and whether they like it or not." David Clark, *Journal of Semitic Studies*, Volume 52, no. 1, (Spring 2007): 145–147, at p. 145 available at https://academic.oup.com/jss/article-abstract/52/1/145/1719514?redirectedFrom=fulltext .

[286] Leonard Greenspoon, *Jewish Bible Translations: Personalities, Passions, Politics, Progress* (Philadelphia: The Jewish Publication Society, 2020), pp. 142-145, 199.

[287] Eugene A. Nida and Charles R. Taber, *The Theory and Practice of Translation* (Leiden, NL: E. J. Brill for the United Bible Societies, 1969), p. 1.

Since "all languages differ in form (and that is the essence of their being different languages), then quite naturally the forms must be altered if one is to preserve the content." And to translate where the source and receptor languages are both of very different language families and cultural contexts, such as from English to Zulu, "the formal modifications must be ... extreme."[288]

At this point we would note that, although we have no knowledge of the Nephite language other than that it was based on "the learning of the Jews and the language of the Egyptians," both Hebrew and Egyptian are of language groups far removed from English and, especially in their form in the sixth century before Christ, would have been wildly different from modern English.[289]

Further, Nida and Taber note, an intelligible translation requires more than that "the words are understandable and the sentences grammatically constructed," but must also ask what "total impact the message has on the one who receives it. ... a translation of the Bible must not only provide information which people can understand but must present the information in such a way that people can feel its relevance ... and can then respond to it in action."[290]

In this approach, "renderings must be sufficiently clear that one can understand not merely what they must have meant to people in ancient times but also how they can be applied in the present-day context."[291] Joseph translated Nephi's comparable approach this way: "I did liken all scriptures unto us, that it might be for our profit and learning."[292]

This describes a very substantial task, in which the translator must not only understand the source language words in their original context,

---

[288] Nida and Taber, *The Theory and Practice of Translation*, pp. 5-6.

[289] 1 Nephi 1:2. English is an Indo-European language, Hebrew is in the Northwest Semitic language family while early Egyptian is considered to be its own branch of the Afroasiatic language family.

[290] Nida and Taber, *The Theory and Practice of Translation*, pp. 22, 24.

[291] Nida and Taber, *The Theory and Practice of Translation*, p. 26.

[292] 1 Nephi 19:23.

but also convey that understanding in a manner which the receptor audience will not only understand, but respond to. The presence of the translator cannot but loom large in such an endeavor, especially when the source and receptor languages and contexts are as distant from each other as with Joseph Smith's translation of Mormon's book.

A significant effort to understand how Joseph bridged this distance is Blake Ostler's 1987 article interpreting the Book of Mormon as "a modern expansion of an ancient source."[293] This is the idea that the text Joseph dictated was a translation of an ancient document, yet, as Ostler explains,

> Joseph Smith gave us not merely the words of the Book of Mormon prophets, but also the true meaning of the text within a nineteenth- century thought-world. The translation was not merely from one language into another but was also a transformation from one thought-world to another that expands and explains the meaning of the original text in terms that Joseph Smith and his contemporaries would understand.[294]

Ostler argues that to accomplish this Joseph inserted sometimes very extensive material which bore no relation to what was on the plates. Usually, this material addressed 19th century theological disputes. While we agree with Ostler's view of Joseph as an active participant in the translation process, as opposed to being a passive transcriber, we feel that Ostler may overstate his case in some respects.[295]

---

[293] Blake Ostler, "The Book of Mormon as a Modern Expansion of an Ancient Source."

[294] Blake Ostler, "The Book of Mormon as a Modern Expansion of an Ancient Source," p. 107.

[295] While a proper critique of Ostler's well-researched and ground-breaking thesis is beyond the scope of this book, we would quickly note the following points: (1) While his "conclusion that the Book of Mormon is pious fraud derived from

A more useful concept may perhaps be found in the Jewish translation tradition, the *targum*. The targums derived from the need to translate the Hebrew Bible into Aramaic after that language became the common language of the Jews in Babylon. The targums were a combination of "literal translations of the Hebrew text with a great deal of additional and sometimes highly creative material" to explain the text, which could range "in size from a word to several paragraphs."[296] Targums are integrated into the descriptive flow of, but remain tied to, the original text.[297] The translator elaborates in order to

---

nineteenth-century influences does not logically follow from the observation that it contains KJV quotations and is expressed in terms of a nineteenth- century world view" (Blake Ostler, "The Book of Mormon as a Modern Expansion of an Ancient Source, p. 115) actually *does* logically follow from evidence of the 19th century influences; it just does not *necessarily* follow. One could also logically conclude from that evidence the one Joseph claimed; i.e., that he translated the ancient writings into English. (2) His expansions assume (a) that because we have no evidence that a theological issue was present among Jews in the Old World after Lehi's departure it could not have arisen among the Lehite peoples centuries separated from the world of the Hebrew Bible and (b) that a theological issue debated among 19th century Americans was only present in Joseph's time. However, (aa) it is entirely possible that issues arose among the Lehites over centuries which did not present themselves to Jews living under entirely different historical circumstances on the other side of the world and (bb) that the theological debates of 19th century America were not unique to that time and place, but rather had precedents going back centuries. One could also argue the reverse – that these doctrinal issues appear in the Book of Mormon shows that they are neither impossible for an early Israelite people to apprehend or uniquely exclusive to 19th century America. (3) Finally, unfortunately like so many other LDS scholars, Ostler accepts the SITH accounts at face value without any critical analysis. In addition to the difficulties of this approach which we discussed in Chapter 2, it also leads him to a vague and untenable view of the inspiration involved in the translation, as discussed in Chapter 3(A).

[296] Paul V. M. Flesher and Bruce Chilton, *The Targums: A Critical Introduction* (Waco, TX: Baylor University Press, 2011), p. 10; Martin McNamara and Paul V. M. Flesher, *Targum*, (2014) available at https://www.oxfordbibliographies.com/view/document/obo-9780195393361/obo-9780195393361-0187.xml

[297] Flesher and Chilton, *The Targums: A Critical Introduction*, p. 40.

fully convey the significance of the text to the receptor audience, not to substitute a message wholly unrelated to the original text.

Thus, where Ostler would posit that entire discourses that sound like 19th century theological disputes were added to the Book of Mormon (albeit in his view by divine approval) which have no relationship to anything on the plates, we would suggest rather that the Book of Mormon prophets recorded on the plates were actually addressing the general topic of the supposed 19th century expansion.

However, Joseph (with divine approval) could have provided a targum elaborating on the text using 19th century theological language and concepts to show the specific relevance of the material on the plates to the current doctrinal concerns of his audience. As with the inquiries which led to the revelations now found in Sections 3, 6, 7, 11, 14, 15, 16 and 17 of the LDS Doctrine and Covenants, proposed targumic elaborations and other translation related questions were probably also submitted to the Lord through the interpreters.[298]

An example of how 19th century language would overlay the original Nephite is where the Book of Mormon relates experiences in which people are "overcome with the Spirit," "overcome because of my afflictions," "overcome that they fell to the earth," and "knew that this had overcome his natural frame." Such ecstatic spiritual experiences were characteristic of the awakenings and revivals in western New York of the Second Great Awakening (as well as the many accounts Jonathan Edwards recorded from the First Great Awakening of experiences that "overcome the bodily frame").

Naturally, we would expect a translator of the ancient record to express the experiences in terms familiar to his contemporaries. Hence the presence of English expressions that evoked such spiritual responses in Joseph's life experience, where religious revivals were

---

[298] Roberts, *History of the Church*, volume 1, pp. 21-23, 32-36, 44-46, 49-52.

among the largest mass gatherings in Joseph's world.[299]

Thus, when theological issues prominent in Joseph's time appear in the Book of Mormon, we can account for them first by recognizing that Joseph was going to use theological vocabulary of his time to translate the teachings of the Nephite prophets. Second, although perhaps not as expansive as envisioned by Ostler, such text may be targumic elaborations Joseph was inspired to add showing how the Book of Mormon's teachings specifically addressed matters of present import to his receptor audience.

While this raises the issue of what is targum (new) and what is original text (old), until we have the original Nephite text, that discussion is a pointless parlor game. The text we have came by the gift and power of God, regardless of the mixture of old and new. Targumic elaboration and the recognition that Joseph was using the religious language of his time, combined with the approaches discussed in Chapter 4(C), enable us to set aside Reverend Campbell's argument, and focus instead on the doctrinal substance of how the Book of Mormon addresses these theological issues.

This concern for the receptor audience is reflected in one final, but critical, feature of Joseph's translation. Nida and Taber observe that a Bible translation cannot ignore the existence in a receptor language of "a long literary tradition in which the Scriptures have existed for some time."[300] Of course, nothing exemplifies a long scriptural literary tradition more than the KJV.

Some sense of the pervasive influence of the KJV in the 19th century English-speaking world can come from looking not at its

---

[299] B. H. Roberts, *Studies of the Book of Mormon* (Salt Lake City, UT: Signature Books, 2nd edition, 1992), pp. 298 – 319 refers to this similarity of descriptions of conversion experiences in the Book of Mormon to those described by Jonathan Edwards and others as being an example of 19th century influence in the Book. Our response to these and many other such examples would be to ask how else Joseph was supposed to describe such common phenomena except in the language familiar to him and his receptor audience?

[300] Nida and Taber, *The Theory and Practice of Translation*, p. 31.

universal presence in America, but from the views of Jews in Britain. Professor Leonard Greenspoon writes that for well into the 1800s "when British Jews needed an English text of the Hebrew Bible, they made use of KJV."[301] When Jewish translations began to appear in the mid-1800s, one of their translators complained in a preface that:

> The Anglo-Jewish community, in common with all other religious denominations whose vernacular is the English tongue, are so wedded to the diction of the authorized version [the KJV] that every departure from its phraseology, however well-founded, seems to grate upon their ears. For this reason we have ... [used] the renderings of the Anglican translation in all those cases where it can be done without doing violence to the principle of fidelity. This is a sacrifice which we regret, but which appeared to us absolutely necessary, if we do not wish ... to bias against this Jewish translation the conservative feelings of many co-religionists in whose eyes ... the Anglican Version, despite its manifest unfitness for Jewish families and schools, is invested with a kind of semi-sacredness.[302]

If British Jews felt this way, imagine what American Christians would have thought of a purported book of scripture which disregarded the KJV. The Book of Mormon has long been criticized for, and Joseph Smith's authorship allegedly proven by, its extensive use not only of direct quotes from the KJV, but of the KJV's style and lexicon.

However, any effective translator of scripture would incorporate the KJV this way. In conforming so closely to the KJV, like any good translator of God's word, Joseph was just respecting the long-established scriptural literary tradition of the language of his receptor audience.

---

[301] Greenspoon, *Jewish Bible Translations*, p. 140.

[302] Abraham Benisch, *Jewish School and Family Bible* (1854), quoted in Greenspoon, *Jewish Bible Translations*, pp. 162-163.

C. Of Seer Stones and Interpreters, Then and Now

We have a seer stone with a chain of custody back to Joseph Smith. It is in the LDS Church's archives.[303] But anyone can see it is just a common, striated rock.

We do not have the Urim and Thummim interpreters, but we are informed by the scriptures that, unlike the rock, the interpreters were specifically prepared to assist with translation. Sacred holy instruments of heavenly design, which have existed at least since they were given to the brother of Jared untold millennia ago (see Doctrine and Covenants 17:1), they have been returned to their angelic caretakers.

However, you undoubtedly have a crude Urim and Thummim. You may even be using it to read this book.

Consider this description of an instrument:

1) Small and portable
2) visual display screen or screens
3) provides an interpretation of scanned unknown characters
4) can display other information[304]
5) communications capabilities[305]

---

[303] Joseph Smith gave it to Oliver Cowdery, whose widow gave it to Brigham Young's brother Phineas, who gave it to Brigham who left it to one of his widows, who gave it to the Church. See Richard E. Turley Jr., Robin S. Jensen and Mark Ashurst-McGee, "Joseph the Seer - What Happened to the Seer Stone?" *Ensign* (October 2015), pp. 53-54 available at https://www.churchofjesuschrist.org/study/ensign/2015/10/joseph-the-seer?lang=eng.

[304] Joseph Knight, Sr. reported that when he first received the interpreters Joseph [Smith] "seamed to think more of the glasses or the urim and thummim then he Did of the plates for said he I can see any thing they are they are Marvelus." In Vogel, *Early Mormon Documents*, volume 4, p. 15.

[305] As noted above, the interpreters were also used to receive revelations such as Sections 3, 6, 7, 11, 14, 15, 16 and 17 of the LDS Doctrine and Covenants.

Your smartphone has many of the functions of a Urim and Thummim.[306] To be clear, there are still differences:

1) The interpreters are thousands of years old, and Joseph never seemed to have power problems (and he also did not have any place to plug in if he did), so they have an amazing power source.

2) It is capable of translating unknown languages, so the Programmer has an extraordinary database to draw on.

3) It does not need to be connected to a cellular or satellite network to communicate.

4) Like the Liahona, the interpreters apparently function according to the user's state of mind, suggesting some kind of mind-technology interface capability.

Of course, it is entirely possible that the interpreters and the Liahona use technology far in advance of anything we can dream of. We leave to readers with greater technical expertise the debate as to what extent these functionalities could be replicated with current technology. Such a study would evoke the longstanding view that the Restored Gospel "includes all truth. There is no truth but what belongs to the Gospel."[307] As Elder John A. Widtsoe explained, miracles are

---

[306] Elder Dieter Uchtdorf famously preceded us by several years in comparing the Urim and Thummim to modern smartphones. See https://www.ldsliving.com/President-Uchtdorf-Shares-What-He-Believes-About-Seer-Stones/s/82469. And Elder Uchtdorf is not alone in comparing the interpreters to modern technology. In the first part of the 20th century Elder John A. Widtsoe used examples of scientific instruments which augment human senses in explaining why Joseph used the Urim and Thummim. John A. Widtsoe, "Why Did Joseph Smith, the Prophet, Need the Help of the Urim and Thumim?" in *Evidences and Reconciliations* (Salt Lake City, UT: Bookcraft, 1960, 1987), p. 91 (Section III – Revelation, article 2) available at https://www.cumorah.com/language/evidencesandreconciliations.html.

[307] Brigham Young, "Building the Temple – Mormonism Embraces All Truth" (April 8, 1867) in *Journal of Discourses* (Liverpool, UK: B. Young, Jr. 1867) volume 11, quote at p. 375, available at https://contentdm.lib.byu.edu/digital/collection/JournalOfDiscourses3/id/4384.

"done only by superior knowledge. Nothing is unnatural." Although they may "transcend our understanding" they are "in full and complete harmony with the laws of nature. For ourselves we must discover all of nature that we can. ... A miracle is simply that which we cannot understand, and at which we marvel."[308]

Even in the 19th century Orson Pratt understood the Urim and Thummim as heavenly technology, not earthly rocks, declaring that this Urim and Thummim

> was not something that existed on the earth in a natural state, it was something made by the Lord. He is a good mechanic, he understands how to make things. ... When he undertakes to do a thing, he does it in the best manner possible, and what he makes is made perfect. ... He made the Urim and Thummim, ... two crystal stones that he gave unto the brother of Jared were made by him.[309]

We infer that when God made the Urim and Thummim he designed the instrument to interpret languages.

Modern scholars' drive to equate the interpreters with the seer stone comes from an effort to understand the Restoration in the context of Joseph's environment. Such studies can help us understand a great deal about the early Saints, what they were thinking, how they wrote, and why they did what they did. Indeed, we are arguing in this book that Joseph's language and thought-world impacted his translation of the Book of Mormon. However, this thread of scholarship risks reducing the Restored Gospel to a mere product of

---

[308] John A. Widtsoe, *A Rational Theology As Taught by the Church of Jesus Christ of Latter-day Saints* (Salt Lake City, UT: General Priesthood Committee, 1915), pp. 157 – 158, (Chapter 31) available at https://www.gutenberg.org/cache/epub/35562/pg35562.html.

[309] Orson Pratt, "King Limhi's Enquiry, From The Book Of Mormon—Ammon Replies—Seership And The Urim And Thummim—The Brother Of Jared, etc." (December 9, 1877) in *Journal of Discourses* (Liverpool, UK: William Budge, 1878) volume 19, quote at p. 214, at https://contentdm.lib.byu.edu/digital/collection/JournalOfDiscourses3/id/929.

the 19th century America where it was first restored, which is how many critics seek to frame it.[310]

The seeming near obsession with the seer stone is an example of this peril. For almost 40 years, since Mark Hofmann and Michael Quinn promoted the folk magic focus in the 1980s, the proponents of the SITH narrative have been trying to push the Book of Mormon into this historical box of early 19th century superstition. Academic eagerness to embrace SITH has resulted in a failure to examine critically the SITH sources while ignoring the best and most historically solid evidence provided by Joseph and Oliver's near contemporaneous primary eyewitness testimony.

While 19th century beliefs provide context for 19th century writings, including the Book of Mormon and related materials, the Restoration transcends those beliefs. The seer stone vs. Urim and Thummim debate exemplifies the problem. To David, Emma, and Martin, it may have been just as easy to believe words appeared on an ordinary stone as to believe specially-prepared "spectacles" of mysterious provenance could assist in translation. Thus, Joseph could use the stone to demonstrate the translation without violating the commandment to never display the Urim and Thummim.

Modern technology, however, lets us distinguish between the two. No "i-Stone" technology exists, but "i-Phones" that can easily translate written languages are ubiquitous. The eminent science fiction author Arthur C. Clarke, in his Third Law, famously observed that "any

---

[310] Further, SITH advocates may not be limiting the reframing of the Restored Gospel in terms of 19th century superstitions to the beginnings of the Restoration. To urge the adoption of a new "theology of seer stones" in our times, they cite a few instances where Church leaders later in the 1800s referred to seer stones (see MacKay and Frederick, *Joseph Smith's Seer Stones*, pp. 125 – 138 and Dirkmaat and MacKay, *Let's Talk About the Translation*, p. 91). However, unless there is a secret codicil to the General Handbook of Instructions of which we are not aware, 19th century style folk magic seer stones are not part of the doctrine or practice of the Church of Jesus Christ of Latter-day Saints.

sufficiently advanced technology is indistinguishable from magic."[311] The interpreters represent an incredibly advanced technology – they are of the technology of the heavens. However, it is understandable that they may have seemed no different than magic to early 19th century rural Americans.

Imagine a classic science fiction scenario. You are part of a team of time travelers sent to different places in the early United States. You are transported to rural upstate New York in the 1820s – and you have a satellite phone (and there are satellites for it to connect to or, for fun, let's say it's the starship *Enterprise*). Not only can you make calls to your fellow time travelers far away, but your phone is programmed so it can scan a book in another (known) language and its screen will display an English translation. What are the rural 1820s New Yorkers to make of this? The closest their culture could come to it would be a folk magic seer stone. And there is little chance they could ever understand how utterly different your satellite phone is from a magic rock.

There is always a danger that contemporary people will feel superior to those of earlier times due to our advanced technology. Many people today cannot imagine how human society functioned before the existence of the internet, let alone a society with no electrical devices at all - yet somehow people survived and prospered in those conditions.

However, if we are blessed with advanced understanding, it behooves us to make use of it. The best the early Saints could make of the interpreters was to think of seer stones, especially when only Joseph, and possibly Oliver, were allowed to operate the interpreters.

---

[311] Arthur C. Clarke, *Profiles of the Future: An Inquiry into the Limits of the Possible*, (London: Victor Gollancz, 1999, originally published 1962) p. 2. Interestingly, in the 1999 edition, Clarke illustrates his law by stating that even he would have thought modern cellular communications improbable when he first wrote the book in 1962 – little wonder that people in the 1820s compared the interpreters to the seer stones used in folk magic of the time.

We must do better. That many early Saints held on to superstitious beliefs does not mean that we have to. The Lord has blessed us with the benefits of much greater understanding of what Elder Widtsoe called "the laws of nature" of which "we must discover all of nature that we can." And from our 21st century perspective the interpreters look like highly advanced technology, not magic. Meanwhile, the seer stone looks exactly like what it is – a mere rock.

It is past time for us to pull our understanding of the Restoration of all things out of this mire of 19th century superstition, not to drive it ever deeper into that mire with an invented untenable "theology of seer stones." At a 1987 general conference, shortly after the Hofmann imbroglio, Gordon B. Hinckley spoke to the "effort to ferret out every element of folk magic and the occult in the environment in which Joseph Smith lived to explain what he did and why. I have no doubt there was folk magic practiced in those days. Without question there were superstitions and the superstitious. ... [but] that there were superstitions among the people in the days of Joseph Smith is no evidence whatever that the Church came of such superstition."[312]

In 1830, both the seer stone and the Urim and Thummim interpreters seemed fantastical and bizarre, the products of folk magical beliefs. Today, the seer stone rock still looks like that. We understand the chemistry and physics of rocks, and they do not accommodate writing or translate ancient characters. However, unlike in 1830, from the perspective of 21st century technology, the interpreters described by Joseph and Oliver are completely plausible.[313]

We recognize that this way of thinking about the Restored Gospel may be novel, especially to those who have been told that it can only

---

[312] Gordon B. Hinckley, "Lord, Increase Our Faith," *Ensign* (November 1987), quote at p. 52, available at https://www.churchofjesuschrist.org/study/ensign/1987/11/lord-increase-our-faith?lang=eng. Recognizing and abandoning the early Saints' folk magic superstitions could also provide a model for leaving behind other nineteenth century detritus such as their racism and sexism.

[313] For further discussion see Lucas' presentations at https://youtu.be/N53Ju8CvFE and https://www.youtube.com/watch?v=MmuchRz1shw&t=8s

be understood in terms of the 19th century environment in which it was first was revealed. Here is another thought experiment to illustrate this new approach. You are Joseph Smith, and you have had a vision of a time when computer technology will unite and organize generations of people over centuries, and which will be so simple it could be used by children, and yet enable millions of saving ordinances to be carried out. But you have to convey this vision of future technology in a way comprehensible in your time. The following might be an apt explanation:

> I might have rendered a plainer translation to this, but it is sufficiently plain to suit my purpose as it stands. It is sufficient to know, in this case, that the earth will be smitten with a curse unless there is a welding link of some kind or other between the fathers and the children, upon some subject or other—and behold what is that subject? It is the baptism for the dead. For we without them cannot be made perfect; neither can they without us be made perfect. Neither can they nor we be made perfect without those who have died in the gospel also; for it is necessary in the ushering in of the dispensation of the fulness of times, which dispensation is now beginning to usher in, that a whole and complete and perfect union, and welding together of dispensations, and keys, and powers, and glories should take place, and be revealed from the days of Adam even to the present time. And not only this, but those things which never have been revealed from the foundation of the world, but have been kept hid from the wise and prudent, shall be revealed unto babes and sucklings in this, the dispensation of the fulness of times.[314]

Next, we must ask if the man who operated the interpreters, Joseph Smith, is plausible as a translator.

---

[314] Doctrine and Covenants 128:18.

D. Joseph Smith – Young Seeker to Prophet/Translator

Lucas knows a member of the Church who joined as an adult from a Jewish background. This brother frequently has remarked that there was one aspect of his initial study of the Restored Gospel that did, and continues to, strike him as very odd. This was the missionaries' adamant insistence that the first leader of the Church was a complete and total ignoramus.

Of course, his missionaries were simply echoing a long tradition of characterizing Joseph Smith as an unlearned farm boy who was a blank slate upon which the Lord could write. Crudely put, the dumber Joseph Smith is, the more amazing the Book of Mormon becomes. It is easy to understand why, from an apologetic and missionary perspective, such a narrative developed over time, but this image of the young Joseph is difficult to reconcile with the historical record.

For example, we know that the adult Joseph was an avid learner.[315] He procured tutors to teach him Hebrew and German, collected an extensive library, and founded the School of the Prophets, an extensive adult education program dedicated to filling the commandment to "study and learn, and become acquainted with all good books, and with languages, tongues and peoples."[316]

William McLellin was an experienced schoolteacher who started a school in Kirtland which Joseph attended during the winter of 1834. Of Joseph, McLellin said that, although "when I took him into my school he was without scientific knowledge or attainments, ... I learned the strength of his mind as to the study and principles of

---

[315] Gregory B. Wightman, "Thy mind, o man: an interpretive biography of Joseph Smith as an adult learner," (PhD dissertation, University of Idaho, 2013) and Petra Javadi-Evans, "'Knowledge Saves a Man': Joseph Smith's Devotion to Learning," in *Know Brother Joseph: New Perspectives on Joseph Smith's Life and Character*, in R. Eric Smith, Matthew C. Godfrey, Matthew J. Grow (eds.) (Salt Lake City, UT: Deseret Book, 2021), pp. 77 - 81.

[316] Doctrine and Covenants 90:15

science. Hence I think I knew him. And I here say that he had one of strongest, well balanced, penetrating, and retentive minds of any man with whom I ever formed an acquaintance, among the thousands of my observation."[317]

Joseph surrounded himself with better educated men such as Sidney Rigdon, Oliver Cowdery, W. W. Phelps and the Pratt brothers, sometimes to the chagrin of more rustic early supporters like David Whitmer.[318] At Nauvoo he encouraged lecturers to come and speak on many topics and participated in debating them.[319] He donated books to the Nauvoo Library and founded the University of the City of Nauvoo.

There is evidence that the young Joseph was not so completely different. Begin with this question: why did Joseph go to the grove to pray? The traditional narrative begins with him confused by the religious strife around him, and inspired by the promise in James 1:5 that "if any of you lack wisdom, let him ask of God ... and it shall be given him." Yet almost everyone else in Joseph's environment was also swept up in the turmoil of the Second Great Awakening, and untold millions of Christians had read the first verses of one of the major epistles of the New Testament. What was it about young Joseph Smith, Junior that sent him to the woods to ask of God?

---

[317] Quoted from a journal by McLellin first located in 2009. William Earl McLellin, *William E. McLellin's Lost Manuscript* (Salt Lake City, UT: Eborn Books, 2012) Mitchell K Schaefer (ed), p. 175 - 176. Also available at Michael De Groote, "Inside the lost McLellin notebook," *Deseret News* January 28, 2009, at https://www.deseret.com/2009/1/28/20298664/inside-the-lost-mclellin-notebook. At the time McLellin wrote the journal in 1871, he had been out of the Church for over 30 years.

[318] See Richard Lloyd Anderson, *Investigating the Book of Mormon Witnesses* (Salt Lake City, UT: Deseret Book Company, 1981) p. 69 on David's view of Sidney Rigdon.

[319] Bushman, *Rough Stone Rolling*, p. 522. An interesting example is the two-day long public discussion with the English socialist John Finch. See Bushman, *Rough Stone Rolling*, p. 502 and Roberts, *History of the Church*, volume 6, pp. 37-38.

Contrary to the traditional narrative, we propose that Joseph Smith was an active seeker of truth, prepared from a young age for his calling as translator of the Nephite plates, and that by that time he had an "intimate acquaintance with those of different denominations" including Christian theology, vocabulary and rhetoric.[320]

Of course, the narrative of Joseph as ignoramus is not without its sources. Both Joseph himself and his mother referred to him as an "unlearned youth."[321] Both used the narrative not as a comprehensive description of Joseph's background and knowledge but for dramatic effect and contrast. Joseph wrote, "I stood alone, an unlearned youth, to combat the worldly wisdom and multiplied ignorance of eighteen centuries with a new revelation." Lucy wrote, "he stood alone an unlearned youth opposed to all the casuistry and learning and ingenuity of the combined world."

In the 1879 "Last Testimony of Sister Emma," Joseph Smith III reported that his mother told him that "Joseph Smith ... could neither write nor dictate a coherent and well-worded letter; let alone dictating a book like the Book of Mormon."[322] Yet Joseph's October 1829 letter

---

[320] Joseph Smith, Jr., *History, circa Summer 1832*, available at https://www.josephsmithpapers.org/paper-summary/history-circa-summer-1832/2.

[321] Joseph Smith to James Arlington Bennett, 13 Nov. 1843, available at https://www.josephsmithpapers.org/paper-summary/letter-to-james-arlington-bennet-13-november-1843/2 and Lucy Mack Smith *History 1844 – 1845*, p. 3, book 7, available at https://www.josephsmithpapers.org/paper-summary/lucy-mack-smith-history-1844-1845/83.

[322] Joseph Smith III, "Last Testimony of Sister Emma," p. 200. While this quote has been repeated numerous times in both LDS and RLDS literature, like every other substantive statement in the 'Last Testimony," this one is contradicted by other historical evidence. In addition to the letter to Oliver noted above, Joseph's cousin George A. Smith recounted that when George's father, John Smith, saw a letter "written by Joseph himself, and this letter bore testimony of the wickedness and the fallen condition of the Christian world. My father read the letter, and I well remember the remark he made about it. "Why," said he, "he writes like a prophet." (*Journal of Discourses* volume 5, p. 103 available at https://contentdm.lib.byu.edu/digital/

to Oliver Cowdery is both coherent and well-worded.[323] Unless Joseph took a crash course in writing after he dictated the text of the Book of Mormon, the statement Joseph Smith III attributed to his mother 50 years later seems more of an apologetic effort to combat the composition theory (as well as conflating writing skills with reading and speaking skills, when they actually are quite different).

Another source is the recollections of the Smiths' neighbors. The emergence of a new religion in their midst was generally not well received by the Palmyra community. Thus, when Philastus Hurlbut went there some years after the Saints left looking for derogatory information on Joseph and his family, he found many willing interviewees. These accounts were printed in *Mormonism Unvailed*, painting the picture of Joseph as an unserious ne'er-do-well.[324]

Joseph loved to be with friends and family; indeed, he needed to be with people, and became morose when alone.[325] However, extroverts also have inner lives. Our new paradigm expands our understanding of Joseph. We do not argue that he was a bookish introvert. The amiable, garrulous Joseph was real. Our proposal is that there was also an inner Joseph who was far more aware of, and concerned with, deep religious questions than was apparent to the

---

collection/JournalOfDiscourses3/id/2273). Admittedly, Joseph's penmanship, spelling and knowledge of grammar left much to be desired. However, Emma's statement, made after Joseph III had repeatedly pestered her through several questions aiming to solicit statements usable against the Spalding theory, like her claim to have been a witness to the entire translation process, is very exaggerated. It fails to acknowledge the substantial difference between writing and speaking. And, of course, regardless of one's explanation as to how it was sourced, today few dispute that Joseph in fact did dictate the entire Book of Mormon. See the discussion in Chapter 2(B) for cautions on the use of the *"Last Testimony"* as a historical source.

[323] Joseph Smith, Jr., "Letter to Oliver Cowdery," (October 22, 1829), available at https://www.josephsmithpapers.org/paper-summary/letter-to-oliver-cowdery-22-october-1829/1. For an annotated version of the letter, see https://www.mobom.org/annotated-js-letter-to-oc.

[324] Howe, *Mormonism Unvailed*, at pp. 232-269.

[325] Bushman, *Rough Stone Rolling*, pp. 185-186, 473.

Palmyra townsfolk whose affidavits appear in *Mormonism Unvailed*. This is based in part on a new reading of long known accounts from Joseph himself and his mother. However now, thanks to the NID research, we can also see this inner Joseph in the words of the Book of Mormon.

When a gentleman visited Joseph in 1835 to inquire about the Church's doctrines and origins, Joseph began not with his First Vision when he was 14, as we do today, but rather with his "juvenile years, say from 6 years old."[326] In his 1832 history, Joseph wrote that his "goodly Parents... spared no pains to instructing me in the Christian religion."[327] We lack details to know what this instruction consisted of, but apparently it began at an early age because Joseph once declared "It is a love of libe[r]ty which inspires my soul. civil and religious liberty— were diffused into my soul by my grandfathers while they dandld me on their knees."[328]

Another indication of the Smith family attitude toward religious instruction comes from a talk by Joseph's mother in Nauvoo in which Lucy told the Saints that God "gives us our children and we are accountable. In the fear of God I warn you. I want you to take your little children and teach them in the fear of God. I want you to teach them about Joseph in Egypt and such things, and when they are four years old they will love to read their Bible. I presume there never was a family more obedient than mine."[329]

---

[326] Joseph Smith, *Journal, 1835-1836*, p. 36 – 37, available at https://www.josephsmithpapers.org/paper-summary/journal-1835-1836/37.

[327] Joseph Smith, Jr., *History, circa Summer 1832*, https://www.josephsmithpapers.org/paper-summary/history-circa-summer-1832/1

[328] Joseph Smith, Jr., *Journal, December 1842–June 1844; Book 2, 10 March 1843–14 July 1843*, p. 301, available at https://www.josephsmithpapers.org/paper-summary/journal-december-1842-june-1844-book-2-10-march-1843-14-july-1843/309.

[329] Lucy Mack Smith, "Lucy Mack Smith Speaks to the Nauvoo Saints," in Ronald W. Walker (ed) *BYU Studies* (1991) Vol. 32, nos. 1 and 2, quote at p. 278, also available at https://byustudies.byu.edu/wp-content/uploads/2020/02/32.1-2WalkerHistorians-4dd4b307-de92-4283-aee0-a0b613be247d.pdf, quote at p. 3.

That Joseph began his account at age 6 is significant because of the leg surgery around 1813 which apparently played a key role in his preparation to become a prophet.[330] Due to complications from the surgery, Joseph went with his uncle Jesse Smith to Salem, Massachusetts, for convalescence.[331] Although only seven years old at the time, Joseph was old enough to read and he was laid up with nothing else to do.

And self-education was not unknown at the time. Joseph was only just over three years older than Abraham Lincoln, who also came from a hardscrabble background to become famously well self-educated. Parley P. Pratt wrote that as a child, he always had a book. "At the age of seven years my mother gave me lessons to read in the scriptures; I read of Joseph in Egypt, -- his dreams, his servitude, his temptation and exaltation... All this inspired me with love, and with the noblest sentiments ever planted in the bosom of man."[332]

There is circumstantial evidence that Joseph read Christian materials while staying in Salem. Samuel Deane delivered a series of four sermons for young men that were collected and published as a booklet in Salem, Massachusetts, in 1774, with multiple printings.[333] Joseph's uncle Jesse was known for his strong religious beliefs[334] and would naturally give such reading material to his recuperating nephew. The booklet contains nonbiblical language that the NID research

---

[330] The surgery and circumstances around it are described in LeRoy S. Wirthlin, "Joseph Smith's Boyhood Operation: An 1813 Surgical Success," *Brigham Young University Studies,* Vol. 21, no. 2 (Spring 1981), pp. 131–154 available at https://scholarsarchive.byu.edu/cgi/viewcontent.cgi?article=2059&context=byusq

[331] Lucy Mack Smith, *History 1845*, p. 2, book 3, available at https://www.josephsmithpapers.org/paper-summary/lucy-mack-smith-history-1844-1845/32.

[332] Pratt, Parley P., *The Autobiography of Parley P. Pratt*, 1888 edition, page 19, online at https://archive.org/details/autobiographyofp00prat/page/18.

[333] Samuel Deane, Four Sermons to Young Men, from Titus II.6. preached at Falmouth (Salem, MA: Samuel and Ebenezer Hall, 1774).

[334] John W. Welch, "Jesse Smith's 1814 Protest," *BYU Studies* Vol. 33, no. 1 (1993), pp. 131-144, online at https://scholarsarchive.byu.edu/cgi/viewcontent.cgi?article=2892&context=byusq

shows to appear in the Book of Mormon, including *design, anxious, tendency, rising generation, opposite, in other words, on the other hand, garb, regulation, faculties, lay before, state of probation, everlasting damnation, soften, reluctance, look forward, ignominious, thoughtless,* and more. As indicated by this terminology, the sermons focus on themes that the Book of Mormon writers also address.

Joseph's convalescence did not conclude in Massachusetts. He wrote that after the doctors removed "a large portion of the bone from my left leg… fourteen additional pieces of bone afterwards worked out before my leg healed, during which time I was reduced so very low that my mother could carry me with ease. & after I began to get about I went on crutches till I started for the State of New York."[335]

These years of disability compromised Joseph's usefulness for farm work, leaving him more time to read and engage in what his mother Lucy Mack Smith later called "meditation and deep study." Those who know children well in their older pre-puberty years are often surprised at how bumptious noisy children can suddenly reflect on serious spiritual questions. For Joseph this tendency was accentuated by his comparative immobility, and his parents noticed even if others did not.[336]

In a patriarchal blessing Joseph, Sr. gave Joseph, Jr. in 1834, the elder Joseph said to his son "thou hast sought to know his ways,

---

[335] Joseph Smith, *History, 1838-1856*, volume A-1, Addenda, Note A (handwriting of Willard Richards) https://www.josephsmithpapers.org/paper-summary/history-1838-1856-volume-a-1-23-december-1805-30-august-1834/137

[336] On Joseph's spiritual preparation in these younger years, see Richard Lloyd Anderson, "The Early Preparation of the Prophet Joseph Smith," *Ensign* (December 2005), pp. 12-17 at https://www.churchofjesuschrist.org/study/ensign/2005/12/the-early-preparation-of-the-prophet-joseph-smith?lang=eng. Professor Anderson puts the beginning of this spiritual seeking at the age of twelve after the move to New York, but we believe that these tendencies began even earlier in New England during Joseph's prolonged convalescence. A young person's interests may shift as they grow, but the underlying personality that drives these interests is influenced by much earlier experiences.

and from thy childhood thou hast meditated much upon the great things of his law."[337] Similarly, his mother wrote that Joseph "always seemed to reflect more deeply than common persons of his age upon everything of a religious nature."[338] Writing about events after Moroni's first visit, she observed that:

> From this time forth, Joseph continued to receive instructions from the Lord; and we, to get the children together every evening for the purpose of listening while he imparted the same to the family. I presume we presented an aspect as singular, as any family that ever lived upon the face of the Earth: all seated in a circle, father, mother, sons, and daughters, and giving the most profound attention to a boy, eighteen years of age, who had never read the Bible through in his life; for he was much less inclined to the perusals of books then any of the rest of our children, but far more given to meditation and deep study.[339]

Note that books were not unavailable to the Smith family; the rest of the children read them. Perhaps Joseph was simply uninterested in the books his siblings read, but it was Joseph's different approach that Lucy commented on. Scholars usually interpret this passage to mean that Joseph was "unbookish," in contrast to his siblings who "perused" books. However, we propose an alternative reading of Lucy's comments, starting with the term *perusal*.

It is important to note that Lucy's earlier draft read "Joseph was less inclined to the **study** of books than any child we had but much

---

[337] Joseph Smith, Sr., Blessing 9 December 1834, at https://www.josephsmithpapers.org/paper-summary/blessing-from-joseph-smith-sr-9-december-1834/1

[338] Lucy Mack Smith, *History, 1844–1845*, p. 10, book 3, at https://www.josephsmithpapers.org/paper-summary/lucy-mack-smith-history-1844-1845/40

[339] Lucy Mack Smith, *History 1845*, p. 86, at https://www.josephsmithpapers.org/paper-summary/lucy-mack-smith-history-1845/93.

more given to reflection and deep study."³⁴⁰ It is unknown who edited the earlier draft and why. Here, the phrase "study of books" was replaced by "perusal of books." Perhaps the editor simply sought to avoid duplication of the word "study" in the same sentence. Perhaps Lucy realized that the first draft conveyed a misunderstanding and she wanted to make the point that Joseph did not read/study/peruse as many books as the other children, but focused on meditation and deep study of the books he did access.

At any rate, "peruse" is not a self-executing word. Webster's 1828 dictionary defines *perusal* as "the act of reading."³⁴¹ However, *peruse* is a contronym, meaning "a word that has two meanings which seem to contradict each other." It can mean "to look at or read (something) in an informal or relaxed way" or "to examine or read (something) in a very careful way."³⁴²

To clarify which meaning they intend, writers use adjectives such as "attentively" or "negligently." In a letter dated April 13, 1833, Joseph Smith wrote "Dear Broth Carter your letter to Broth Jared is just put into my hand and I have **carefully perrused** [sic] its contents, and imbrace [sic] this oppertunity [sic] to answer it."³⁴³ The adverb *carefully* would be redundant if the term had the meaning commonly ascribed to Lucy's statement.

Lucy contrasted "the perusals of books" with "meditation and deep study." This suggests she meant that the other children's perusals were more relaxed and informal than Joseph's "deep study." This connotation is consistent with her observation that Joseph had not

---

³⁴⁰ Lucy Mack Smith, *History, 1844–1845*, p. 1, book 4, at https://www.josephsmithpapers.org/paper-summary/lucy-mack-smith-history-1844-1845/43.

³⁴¹ "Perusal," *Webster's Dictionary 1828*, Online Edition at http://webstersdictionary1828.com/Dictionary/meditation.

³⁴² "Peruse," Merriam-Webster.com, accessed November 12, 2022, https://www.merriam-webster.com/words-at-play/peruse-usage.

³⁴³ Joseph Smith, Jr., "Letter to John S. Carter," (April 13, 1833), Joseph Smith Papers, Letterbook 1, (emphasis added) at https://www.josephsmithpapers.org/paper-summary/letter-to-john-s-carter-13-april-1833/1.

"read the Bible through," because "meditation and deep study" requires more detailed examination of cross-references and commentaries than merely reading it through like a novel.

To *search* the scriptures—especially when not reading it straight through—one needs a guide to passages relevant to one's interests. The Bible is not organized by topic. There was no "topical guide" in the Bibles of the day. People consulted the writings of theologians and ministers who organized and quoted Bible passages by theme. Joseph explained that his parents "spared no pains" to instruct him in the Christian religion. Presumably they would provide reading material.

In 1832 Joseph wrote in his own hand that "thus applying myself to them [i.e., the scriptures] and my intimate acquaintance with those of different denominations."[344] Traditionally, it has been thought that Joseph referred to personal relationships with members or leaders of different denominations. But he mentioned only one Methodist minister to whom he related his experience (JS-H 1:22). In his 1838 history, Joseph explains he "kept myself aloof from all these parties, though I attended their several meetings as often as occasion would permit. … but so great were the confusion and strife among the different denominations, that it was impossible for a person young as I was, and so unacquainted with men and things, to come to any certain conclusion who was right and who was wrong." (JS-H 1:8)

When Joseph referred to "my intimate acquaintance with those of different denominations," he could have meant (i) members or ministers of different denominations he personally knew in Palmyra, and/or (ii) the writings of Christian ministers and theologians he had read. It would be incongruous for Joseph to say he was both "unacquainted with men" and had "an intimate acquaintance" with ministers from whom he "kept [him]self aloof."

---

[344] Joseph Smith, Jr., *History, 1832*, available at https://www.josephsmithpapers.org/paper-summary/history-circa-summer-1832/2 (clarification added).

We propose that he was referring to Christian authors because his *History, circa Summer 1832*, like the Book of Mormon and the revelations in the Doctrine and Covenants, is replete with the vocabulary of Christian theologians such as Jonathan Edwards, James Hervey and others. As noted above, the pervasive appearance of these theologians' terminology in the Book of Mormon was an unexpected result of the NID research.[345] While the Smiths had the Bible and religious literature in their home, there is no evidence they had a large home library. How could Joseph have been exposed to such Christian authors?

First, in the early 1800s, many sermons and writings were available in inexpensive pamphlets. For example, just one publisher, the American Tract Society, printed over a million copies of Jonathan Edwards' writings.[346] Magazines like the *New York Missionary Magazine* reprinted famous sermons and even Edwards' correspondence.

Second, the words of that great theologian of the First Great Awakening would also have filled the hours of revivals of the Second Great Awakening which Joseph attended. Historian Douglas Sweeney writes that Edwards' thought thrived such that by "the early 1830s, Edwards' legacy grew so large that he might well have been dubbed 'America's evangelical.' ... In western New York especially, Edwards was read among the clergy and played a role in shaping spiritual expectations for the revival."[347] Indeed, throughout "the United States, many thousands of evangelicals honored Edwards as a founder of their

---

[345] The presence of Jonathan Edwards' language in the Book of Mormon is extensively discussed in *Infinite Goodness*. These influences can be seen in Joseph's other writings. See, for example, the annotated version of Joseph's 1832 *History* which is an appendix in *Infinite Goodness*.

[346] Joseph A. Conforti, *Jonathan Edwards, Religious Tradition, and American Culture* (Chapel Hill, NC: The University of North Carolina Press, 1995), at p. 37.

[347] Douglas A. Sweeny, "Evangelical tradition in America," in Stephen J. Stein (ed), *The Cambridge Companion to Jonathan Edwards* (New York: Cambridge University Press, 2007), pp. 220-221.

movement for revival, as well as a theological genius."[348]

Third, bookstores and libraries in western New York carried numerous Christian publications. In Palmyra, the TC Strong bookstore and printing shop, which printed the *Palmyra Register* newspaper, carried the works of many Christian writers. Among these was the popular eight-volume set of Edwards' writings published in 1808.

Orsamus Turner, a contemporary of Joseph who later wrote a history of the Palmyra area, happened to work in the TC Strong shop. He recalled that "once a week he [Joseph] would stroll into the office of the old Palmyra Register, for his father's paper." Orsamus described Joseph as a "meddling, inquisitive lounger" whose face he blackened "once and a while" with the ink balls from the printing press.[349] Although Orsamus did not mention Joseph's reading habits, the weekly visits gave Joseph ready access to the writings of Edwards and other Christian ministers.

Although Lucy claimed Joseph "had never read the Bible through in his life," Joseph wrote that his "concerns for the welfare of my immortal Soul ... led me to searching the scriptures."[350] One of

---

[348] Sweeney, "Evangelical tradition in America," p. 227. On Edwards' influence on the Second Great Awakening generally, see Sweeney, "Evangelical tradition in America," pp. 218-229; Mark Noll, "Edwards' Theology after Edwards," in Sany Hyun Lee (ed), *The Princeton Companion to Jonathan Edwards* (Princeton, NJ: Princeton University Press, 2005), pp. 296-304; George M. Marsden, *Jonathan Edwards: A Life* (New Haven, CT: Yale University Press, 2003), pp. 8-9, 499; and Conforti, *Jonathan Edwards, Religious Tradition, and American Culture*, pp. 36-61.

[349] Orsamus Turner, *History of the Pioneer Settlement* (Rochester, NY 1851), p. 214. Available online at https://archive.org/details/historyofpioneer00turn/page/214. Turner also recounted that Joseph was active in their young men's debating society and was "a very passable exhorter" at revival meetings. Although Turner was as dismissive of Joseph as other Palmyra residents, these facts suggest that Joseph was more intellectually engaged in the opportunities available to him than portrayed in the Hurlbut affidavits.

[350] In his *History, circa Summer 1832*, Joseph describes some of the specifics of his Bible reading following the First Vision which he "pondered ... in my heart." In her

Joseph's Palmyra acquaintances, Pomeroy Tucker, although hostile, wrote that as Joseph "advanced in reading and knowledge, he assumed a spiritual or religious turn of mind, and frequently perused the Bible, becoming quite familiar with portions thereof, both of the Old and New Testaments."[351]

Joseph's familiarity with the Bible enabled him to detect that Moroni quoted Malachi "with a little variation from the way it reads in our Bibles."[352] In his 1838 history, Joseph quoted Moroni's version of the passages exactly. During the first night when Moroni appeared to Joseph, Moroni "quoted also the fourth or last chapter of [Malachi], though with a little variation from the way it reads in our Bibles.... He quoted also the third chapter of Acts, twenty-second and twenty-third verses, precisely as they stand in our New Testament." (JS-H 1:36, 40). To recognize the variation with such precision, Joseph must have known those passages by heart.

Reviewing Joseph's exposure to the Bible and heavy use of biblical language in even the earliest records, historian Philip Barlow concludes that it seems probable that as early as his teen years Joseph "had been ... well exposed to the KJV, that his language and thought patterns had been colored by it, and that ... when Deity did come, Smith heard him speak in both biblical and Bible-like language."[353]

Autobiography, Lucy Smith wrote that her son told her that "I will take my Bible and go out into the woods and learn more in two hours than you could if you were to go to meeting two years." Lucy Mack Smith, *History 1844 – 1845*, p. 8, book 4, available at https://www.josephsmithpapers.org/paper-summary/lucy-mack-smith-history-1844-1845/50.

[351] Pomeroy Tucker, *Origin, Rise, and Progress of Mormonism: Biography of Its Founders and History of Its Church* (New York: D. Appleton, 1867), quote at p. 17, available at https://archive.org/details/originriseprogre00tuck/page/n23/mode/2up. Also see https://www.josephsmithpapers.org/paper-summary/history-circa-summer-1832/3, p. 3 and fn. 17.

[352] Joseph Smith – History 1:36.

[353] Barlow, *Mormons and the Bible*, pp. 10 – 25, quote at p. 15.

We conclude our argument that Joseph was actually familiar with the religious language and issues of his day when he translated the Book of Mormon by calling a hostile witness. A hostile witness is a qualified witness who is opposed to your side, often someone who has already testified on behalf of the opposing side, who nonetheless under oath concedes points helpful to your side. Hostile witness testimony can be among the most effective evidence in a trial.

Our hostile witness is the Reverend Alexander Campbell. In Chapter 4(C) we discussed his charge that the Book of Mormon dealt with every issue "discussed in N. York for the last ten years. He decides all the great controversies – infant baptism, ordination, the trinity, regeneration, repentance, justification, the fall of man, the atonement, transubstantiation, fasting, penance, church government, religious experience, the call to the ministry, the general resurrection, eternal punishment, who may baptize, and even the question of freemasonry, republican government, and the rights of man. All these topics are repeatedly alluded to."

Campbell's charge remains to this day one of the most potent arguments that Joseph composed the Book of Mormon. When one of Campbell's chief lieutenants, Sidney Rigdon, converted to the new faith, Campbell undertook a three-week preaching tour of Ohio to try to keep others from leaving his churches for this new Church of Christ (the LDS Church's original name). This included a long meeting with Rigdon, where neither succeeded in convincing the other.[354]

Campbell's hostility toward the Book of Mormon arose from his status as one of the leading American evangelists of the time.[355] His critique was generally accurate. Any reader of the Book of Mormon

---

[354] Eva Jean Wrather, *Alexander Campbell: Adventurer in Freedom – a literary biography* (Ft. Worth, TX: TCU Press, 2009), volume 3, pp. 24-29.

[355] Richard J. Cherok, *Debating God: Alexander Campbell's Challenge to Skepticism in Antebellum America* (Abilene, TX: Abilene University Christian Press, 2008), pp. 16-22, 157; S. Morris Eames, *The Philosophy of Alexander Campbell* (Bethany, WV: Bethany College, 1966).

can confirm that much (but not all) of Campbell's list of topics is addressed in the text.

The Joseph Smith as ignoramus paradigm offers little defense to Campbell's charge. What defense is it that, while these were live topics in Joseph's day, he was too ignorant to discuss them? The Book of Mormon itself, with its sophisticated analyses of many theological questions employing the very language and concepts used in these debates, refutes this defense. That Joseph was actually as knowledgeable in these questions as Reverend Campbell unwittingly attests provides an avenue to understanding why the Book of Mormon is the way it is.

Of course, one can always say that God inspired Lehi or Abinadi over two millennia ago, or some supernatural translator, who for some inexplicable reason insisted on using Early Modern English, to lay out true doctrine in the language and conceptual world-view of 1820s America. That is one of multiple working hypotheses. Another is the hypothesis that an American translator of the late 1820s used the language and concepts of his time to express the truths engraved by ancient prophets, with occasional inspired targumic elaborations to customize those teachings for his audience. Each reader can consider which of these hypotheses best explains and reconciles the evidence.

There is one other aspect of Joseph's preparation worth noting. Reverend Nida wrote that "creative translators are the best examples of the fact that interlingual communication is essentially a special skill that does not necessarily depend on long years of training, …. In many respects creative translating is like a portrait painting and artistic musical performance" which look to non-academic skills.[356] "Many people assume that translating requires considerable training in linguistics. But that is not true. Some of the best translators have no training whatsoever in linguistics, although some introduction to linguistics can" be helpful. "The essential skill of translators is being

---

[356] Nida, *Contexts in Translating*, p. 4.

able to understand correctly the meaning of a source text. ... Linguists analyze texts, but translators must understand texts."[357]

And understanding texts and rendering them effectively in another language also is a talent unrelated to academic training. Indeed, particularly in the domain of translation of scripture, Nida and Taber observe that "too much knowledge of the subject matter can be a deterrent to effective translation."[358]

> If the study of theology tended to stimulate a person's imagination, perhaps he would be more capable of dealing with new and creative situations, but for the most part theological studies concentrate on proving the given truth, rather than on dealing with multiple hypotheses. Accordingly, neither in the area of communication to the uninitiated nor in the handling of the subject matter is there much emphasis upon the creative and imaginative aspects of communicating Christian truth. It is perhaps for these reasons that theologically trained persons have special problems in learning how to translate.[359]

Joseph's early preparation armed him with a mental language bank--a lexicon--that enabled him to deliver an English translation of the ancient Nephite text that fit squarely within the Christian tradition. But coming from outside the Christian establishment, he was unhampered by the indoctrination, groupthink and prejudices which would have come from more formal education.

Joseph as a young seeker creates a new paradigm to replace that of the farm boy who was either virtuous and hard-working or a ne'er-do-well, depending on the source, but deeply ignorant in either scenario. To be clear, we are not suggesting that Joseph was some precocious junior theologian. He was not reading Jonathan Edwards when he was eight years old (that kind of exposure only came later in his teenage

---

[357] Nida, *Contexts in Translating*, p. 10.
[358] Nida and Taber, *The Theory and Practice of Translation*, p. 99.
[359] Nida and Taber, *The Theory and Practice of Translation*, p. 100.

years and early twenties in New York). However, we believe the historical record shows that he was literate (he could read even if his writing skills like penmanship, spelling and grammar were unformed), he was exposed to, aware of, and concerned with the religious issues and literature of his time, and he read the Bible seriously.

Under this new view, we have a Joseph who, aided by extensive self-education, starting with his long childhood convalescence, was well equipped to study out in his mind the best way to express in English the meaning of the Nephite text engraved on the plates that he read by means of the interpreters. Joseph was uniquely prepared to translate the plates in language which could be both understood and acted upon by his contemporaries. He was, in other words, as he always claimed, a real translator.

6. How the Book of Mormon Was Translated – A Theory

> *... a translation of the Bible must not only provide information which people can understand, but must present the message in such a way that people can feel its relevance ... and can then respond to it in action.*
>
> Eugene A. Nida[360]

We can now pull these elements together and present a theory as to how the Book of Mormon was translated. The reader can judge whether the canonical account claiming that Joseph Smith translated the Book of Mormon is persuasive.

Joseph never left any specific description himself as to how the translation process worked, beyond saying that he copied and translated characters off the plates months before beginning to dictate the translation. We look to the scriptures cited in Chapter 1(A) and the accounts that corroborate those scriptures including Oliver's firsthand account, along with Lucy's close-to-firsthand accounts (see Appendix B).[361] The rest is extrapolation. And could be wrong, or incomplete.

---

[360] Nida and Taber, *The Theory and Practice of Translation*, p. 24.

[361] We note that, while we are advancing some more specific proposals about the translation process, our overall approach is hardly new, and indeed would have been normative before the recent rise of scholarship prioritizing the SITH accounts and transcription explanation over the canonical account. See, for example, McConkie and Ostler, "The Process of Translating the Book of Mormon" and Richard Lloyd Anderson, "By the Gift and Power of God," *Ensign* (September 1977), pp. 78 - 85 available at https://www.churchofjesuschrist.org/study/ensign/1977/09/by-the-gift-and-power-of-god?lang=eng. Professor Anderson argued that: (1) David Whitmer's accounts should not be taken at face value, as he was not a firsthand witness of the translation and they reflect his rigid perfectionist view of scripture,

However, we believe that this theory best incorporates the available evidence and best accounts for the actual text of the Book of Mormon.

A. The Plates

The analysis begins with Moroni's explanation: "He said there was a book deposited, written upon gold plates..." (JS-H 1:33). The Book of Mormon starts with, and comes from, the plates Moroni deposited in the Hill Cumorah. The plates, created and preserved at great effort, were engraved in a language unknown in Joseph's or our time.

Previous generations of Latter-day Saints took the plates as the source of the Book of Mormon for granted. That is no longer the case because many modern LDS scholars claim instead that Joseph did not use the plates to produce the Book of Mormon. In their view, the entire text came from the stone in the hat (SITH).

Consequently, readers must choose whether or not to believe that Joseph used the plates. In our view, based on the evidence we have laid out in this book and Appendix B, Joseph did translate the engravings on the plates.

---

which is rebutted by Joseph's numerous edits in later editions and errors in the Original Manuscript, (2) despite references to the stone in the hat from Emma Smith and Martin Harris, he gives greater weight to Joseph and Oliver's statements that the translation was from the plates using the interpreters, (3) under inspiration Joseph exercised considerable discretion in the wording of the translation and (4) as confirmed by inspiration, the Book of Mormon does directly follow the KJV. An excellent summary of the history of various models for the process of translating the Book of Mormon can be found in John-Charles Duffy, "The 'Book of Mormon Translation' Essay in Historical Context." We note that, while our proposal falls within what Duffy labels the "composed-translation" approach which prevailed for most of the twentieth century from B. H. Roberts through Richard Lloyd Anderson, we believe our proposed model advances that approach by, among other points, (1) accounting for ancient linguistic structures relied on for "read-translation" approaches, (2) explaining why God would have used such a complicated process, and (3) using insights from modern translation scholarship and technology to offer a more precise description of the possible translation process.

B. The Interpreters

Moroni told Joseph Smith "that there were two stones in silver bows—and these stones, fastened to a breastplate, constituted what is called the Urim and Thummim—deposited with the plates; and the possession and use of these stones were what constituted "seers" in ancient or former times; and that God had prepared them for the purpose of translating the book." (JS—History 1:35)

Less than a year before his death, Joseph re-emphasized his role as translator when he explained that "by the gift and power of God I translated the Book of Mormon from hieroglyphics, the knowledge of which was lost to the world."[362]

According to Moroni, "none other people knoweth our language" so the Lord "hath prepared means for the interpretation thereof."[363] The Lord explained to the brother of Jared,

> 22 And behold, when ye shall come unto me, ye shall write them and shall seal them up, that no one can interpret them; for ye shall write them in a language that they cannot be read.
>
> 23 And behold, these two stones will I give unto thee, and ye shall seal them up also with the things which ye shall write.
>
> 24 For behold, the language which ye shall write I have confounded; wherefore I will cause in my own due time that these stones shall magnify to the eyes of men these things which ye shall write.[364]

---

[362] Joseph Smith to James Arlington Bennett, 13 Nov. 1843, in Roberts, *History of the Church*, volume 6, p. 74, also available at https://www.josephsmithpapers.org/paper-summary/letter-to-james-arlington-bennet-13-november-1843/2.

[363] Mormon 9:34

[364] Ether 3:22–24

The interpreters instrument was often described as "spectacles," but Joseph and possibly Oliver (who was authorized to try to translate, although he was unsuccessful) were likely the only persons to actually see them used.[365] After the translation was completed, David Whitmer and Martin Harris may have seen them during their Three Witnesses experience. Martin described them as being larger than spectacles, and that the stones were translucent rather than clear.[366]

Other descriptions by non-witnesses were hearsay, assumptions, or speculation. We therefore cannot say if they could actually be worn on the bridge of the nose (even a nose as large as Joseph's), were used hands-free by being held by the rod that attached them to the breastplate described in the canonical account, or were detached from the breastplate and hand held to scan them over the plates.

A translator must first understand the original writing and then deliver that understanding in the target language (in this case, English) by making choices about how to express the interpretation. Joseph described such a two-step process. First, he copied the characters and isolated individual characters and "by means of" the Urim and Thummim he translated, or interpreted, them.[367]

---

[365] John Whitmer's statement as a scribe that Joseph dictated the text while using the breastplate and Urim and Thummim leaves it unclear whether he observed the instruments directly, through a screen or curtain, or did not see them at all but relied on his own inferences or something Joseph said.

[366] Interview with Martin Harris in *Tiffany's Monthly* (1859 New York), available at: http://www.utlm.org/onlineresources/sermons_talks_interviews/harrisintervie wtiffanysmonthly.htm. This interview may be mostly hearsay, leaving us to speculate whether Martin actually saw them or merely reported what others had said. David Whitmer's account is in Edward Stevenson to the editor, November 30, 1881, *Deseret Evening News*, December 13, 1881, at p. 4. However, Zenas Gurley wrote that David admitted to him that David never actually saw the interpreters except in a "heavenly vision." Gurley, "The Book of Mormon," at p. 453 available at https://hdl.handle.net/2027/nyp.33433075797161.

[367] Joseph Smith – History 1:62. While Joseph was engaged in this step of the process, Martin Harris took one of these copies of characters on an extended trip

Ether 3:24 says that the interpreters would "magnify to the eyes of men these things." This could be understood literally, as making the small characters larger for viewing, as well as metaphorically as increasing the user's understanding of their meaning. The extant records suggest that Joseph did not copy out the entire Book of Mormon in this way. There would be no point in copying duplicate words, of which the text has many. Rather, it would appear that this was part of his initial study process to familiarize himself with the characters he was going to translate.[368] Only after he had studied the characters for a while did he begin dictating to Martin Harris.

---

through New York and Pennsylvania to show them to learned individuals. It was in the course of this trip that he visited Professor Charles Anthon in New York City, as recounted in Joseph Smith – History 1:63-65. See Richard E. Bennett, "Read This I Pray Thee": Martin Harris and the Three Wise Men of the East," *Journal of Mormon History*: Vol. 36, no. 1 (Winter 2010), pp. 178-216, available at https://digital commons.usu.edu/cgi/viewcontent.cgi?article=1052&context=mormonhistory and Michael Hubbard MacKay, "'Git Them Translated': Translating the Characters on the Gold Plates," in *Approaching Antiquity: Joseph Smith and the Ancient World*, Lincoln H. Blumell, Matthew J. Grey, and Andrew H. Hedges (eds) (Provo, UT: Religious Studies Center; Salt Lake City: Deseret Book, 2015), pp. 83–116, available at https://rsc.byu.edu/approaching-antiquity-joseph-smith-ancient-world/git-them-translated-translating-characters-gold. It has been suggested that the purpose of this trip was variously (1) for Martin to get personal assurances of the project, (2) to secure testimonials to promote the work, (3) to find publishers and/or (4) to find a reputable scholar who would perform the translation for Joseph. These are not mutually exclusive, and more than one may have motivated Martin's trip. What is significant for the history of the Church is that Martin returned from his trip determined to continue to support Joseph's efforts, which ultimately led to Martin financing the first printing of the Book of Mormon.

[368] According to Joseph Fielding Smith, although prevented by his circumstance from starting the actual translation Joseph "was busy studying the characters and making himself familiar with them and the use of the Urim and Thummim. He had a great deal more to do than merely to sit down and with the use of the instrument prepared for that purpose translate the characters on the plates. Nothing worthwhile comes to us merely for the asking. All knowledge and skill are obtained by consistent and determined study and practice, and so the Prophet found it to be the case in the

The unresolved question is, how did the Urim and Thummim work? Without the instrument available for examination, there can be no definitive answer. And at first view, there are two lines of evidence which appear contradictory. However, we would like to suggest a hypothesis which may account for all the available evidence in both lines of evidence.

Although many speculated about the operation of the interpreters, only the actual translation team—Joseph and possibly Oliver—could speak from firsthand experience. Neither left a formal description of the operation of the interpreters.

However, an 1831 article claimed to relate Oliver's testimony in a trial that Joseph "found with the plates, from which he translated his book, two transparent stones, resembling glass, set in silver bows. That by looking through these, he was able to read in English, the reformed Egyptian characters, which were engraved on the plates."[369]

And in 1848, as he was returning to the Church, Oliver discussed the subject with Samuel W. Richards. Years later Richards left an account of how he remembered Oliver describing the use of the Urim and Thummim. According to Richards, Oliver said the translation was "done by holding the translators over the words of the written record," upon which "the translation appears distinctly in the instrument, which had been touched by the finger of God and dedicated and consecrated for the purpose of translating languages."[370]

---

translating of the Book of Mormon." Joseph Fielding Smith, *Doctrines of Salvation*, volume 3, p. 216 available at https://archive.org/details/Doctrines-of-Salvation-volume-3-joseph-fielding-smith/page/n127/mode/2up.

[369] A. W. Benton, "Mormonites," *Evangelical Magazine and Gospel Advocate* (Utica, NY), vol. 2, no. 15 (Apr. 19, 1831), available at https://www.mrm.org/mormonites.

[370] Samuel Whitney Richards, from a handwritten record made in 1907 and now in the LDS Church archives. Reprinted in John. W. Welch (ed.), *Opening the Heavens: Accounts of Divine Manifestations 1820-1844* (Provo and Salt Lake City, UT: BYU Press/Deseret Book, 2005), p. 144. Richards' information from Oliver was not passing or casual, as Oliver spent three weeks snowbound with the Richards family in Iowa as

In both of these cases, it is not clear whether Oliver spoke as an eyewitness, inferred what he thought Joseph saw, or was reporting what Joseph told him.[371] Regardless, Oliver's testimony is the closest we will come to an accurate account of what Joseph experienced. The key point is that Joseph was using the interpreters instrument to interact with the engravings on the plates. He was not merely reading words off a stone in a hat, unconnected with the plates.

There are other witnesses who purported to describe what Joseph saw. Of course, all these statements are limited by the constraint that none said they looked through the translation instrument themselves (as always with the possible exception of Oliver Cowdery). And these

---

Oliver was coming back into the Church. The late date of the actual writing down of the account (1907 vs. 1848) would be a concern in evaluating the account. However, we note that Richards was an attorney who served for many years as a judge, which makes it likely that he would have been careful and precise in setting down his recollections even after 60 years. See Orson F. Whitney, *History of Utah* (Salt Lake City, UT: G.Q. Cannon and Sons Co., 1892), pp. 323-325, available at https://archive.org/details/bub_gb_C0cOAAAAIAAJ/page/n319/mode/2up and Faulring, "The Return of Oliver Cowdery," at p. 150.

[371] Another account suggests Oliver did not use the Urim and Thummim when he tried to translate. "A few days after these men appeared again, a few of us went to see them and Cowdery was requested to state how the plates were found, which he did. He stated that Smith looked onto or through the transparent stones to translate what was on the plates. I then asked him if he had ever looked through the stones to see what he could see in them; his reply was that he was not permitted to look into them. I asked him who debarred him from looking into them; he remained sometime in silence, then said that he had so much confidence in his friend Smith, who told him that he must not look into them, that he did not presume to do so lest he should tempt God and be struck dead." One problem with this account is the dating, because it was published ten years after the purported date of the interview. Another problem is the way it closely follows Martin Harris' famous account, raising the possibility that the reporter conflated two or more accounts. In Milton V. Backman, Jr., "A Non-Mormon View of the Birth of Mormonism in Ohio," *BYU Studies* Vol. 12, no. 3 (1972), quoting Josiah Jones, "History of the Mormonites," dated 1831 but published in *The Evangelist* (June 1841), available at https://byustudies.byu.edu/wp-content/uploads/2020/01/12.3BackmanNon-Mormon.pdf.

accounts differ on the central question of whether the instrument was the interpreters or the seer stone.

Nonetheless, they all do agree that Joseph was seeing English. For example, in 1836 a non-LDS resident of Kirtland, Truman Coe, gave a description, which he said was given by Joseph himself, that the "manner of translation was as wonderful as the discovery. By putting his finger on one of the characters and imploring divine aid, then looking through the Urim and Thummim, he would see the import written in plain English on a screen placed before him."[372]

It would seem from all these witness statements that Joseph was seeing the exact text in English. And, as discussed in Chapters 1 and 2, many today argue that that is exactly what happened. Two very influential, but also very late, accounts from the 1880s come from David Whitmer and from Edward Stevenson's memories of what Martin Harris told him. (As discussed in Chapters 2(C) and (D), both of these sources are problematic.) According to Stevenson's decade-old recollection of Martin's decades old recollections, the seer stone would not display the next sentence of the translation until he had written the current sentence correctly.[373]

In David Whitmer's account, only one "character at a time would appear, and under it was the interpretation in English. Brother Joseph would read off the English to Oliver Cowdery, who was his principal scribe, and when it was written down and repeated to Brother Joseph

---

[372] Truman Coe in *Ohio Observer* (Hudson, Ohio, 11 August 1836), reprinted in Milton V. Backman, Jr., "Truman Coe's 1836 Description of Mormonism," *BYU Studies Quarterly* (1977) Vol. 17, no. 3, quote at p. 351, available at https://scholarsarchive.byu.edu/byusq/vol17/iss3/9.

[373] Edward Stevenson, "One of the Three Witnesses," *Deseret News* (December 28, 1881), p. 763 at https://newspapers.lib.utah.edu/details?id=2634097&q=seer+stone+harris&year_start=1870&year_end=1882&facet_type=%22article%22&facet_paper=%22Deseret+News%22. Of course, since Martin did not directly know what Joseph was seeing in the translation instrument, it is possible that it was Joseph rather than the instrument who was deciding not to continue until Martin copied the text correctly.

to see if it was correct, then it would disappear, and another character with the interpretation would appear."³⁷⁴

These late accounts should be put into their larger historical context and, as we have discussed previously (see Chapter 3(C)), that context is the need to refute the Spalding theory. Just as the SITH accounts of Joseph translating in public view counteract the Spalding theory claim he was reading from Spalding's manuscript behind his "vail," so would accounts implying a non-discretionary word-for-word transcription refute the idea that there was any human agency involved in the text, be it Joseph, Sidney Rigdon, Solomon Spalding's manuscript or otherwise.

Thus, although neither Martin or David knew firsthand what Joseph was seeing, they both assumed that Joseph had no intellectual input into the Book of Mormon. Rather he was just reading word-for-word an English language text presumably actually translated by someone else, or produced by the seer stone itself. Here again, we see the danger of apologetic efforts, in the service of refuting criticisms, going too far to opposite extremes in ignoring the factual record.

As with the SITH accounts, which ignore Joseph and Oliver's firsthand witness that the translation was accomplished entirely with the interpreters, the difficulty with this view is that we have at least

---

³⁷⁴ David Whitmer, *An Address to All Believers in Christ*, p. 12. Professor Stephen Ricks has observed that David Whitmer's explanation "suggests a simple one-for-one equivalency of words in the original language of the Book of Mormon and in English. This is scarcely likely in two closely related modern languages, much less in an ancient and modern language from two different language families. ... A word-for-word rendering, as David Whitmer's statement seems to imply, would have resulted in a syntactic and semantic puree." Professor Ricks instead found the Oliver Cowdery description conveyed by Samuel W. Richards quoted above, where the Urim and Thummim were scanned over the plates, more plausible as it "need not imply a word-for-word rendering, but simply a close link between the words of the original and those of the translation." Stephen D. Ricks, "Translation of the Book of Mormon: Interpreting the Evidence," *Journal of Book of Mormon Studies* (1993) Vol. 2, no. 2, pp. 201–206, quotes at pp. 203-204, available at https://doi.org/10.2307/44758930.

parts of the Original Manuscript (unfortunately much of it was destroyed or seriously damaged by water seepage when it was put into the cornerstone of a building in Nauvoo), and it is full of errors and bad grammar. On top of this, as noted in Chapter 3(E)(4), Joseph freely revised subsequent editions. Ever since critics have asked how the most correct book on earth could require hundreds of corrections? And finally, as noted in Chapter 3(E)(5)-(7), the Book's language seems to be that of a Bible-literate and religiously aware, but very modestly educated, early 19th century backwoods American, not the Almighty Lord of all.

Students of the history have argued about how to reconcile Joseph receiving a divinely sourced English text with the abundant faults evident in the Original Manuscript and the way that Joseph treated the text as something he could continue to exercise creative control over. Some have advanced the idea that all the witnesses who said Joseph saw English were wrong. Instead, they argue that Joseph only received visions, ideas and concepts rather than specific English words, despite the attestation of numerous witnesses that Joseph saw English. They also point to the ever-enigmatic Doctrine and Covenants 9:8 implying that Joseph had to study something out in his mind (but what?).[375]

This dispute divides SITH proponents. Strict transcriptionists argue that Joseph was reading word-for-word someone else's translation (see Chapter 2(A)), while those with what we call shamanist explanations say it was not words on the seer stone but visions, ideas and concepts in Joseph's head (see Chapter 3(A)). Untethered to the plates-and-interpreters translation narrative taught by Joseph and

---

[375] A good summary of these conflicting views is provided in Don Bradley, "Written by the Finger of God?: Claims and Controversies of Book of Mormon Translation," *Sunstone* (December 2010) at pp. 23 – 27, also available at https://sunstone.org/written-by-the-finger-of-god-claims-and-controversies-of-book-of-mormon-translation/ (updated October 17, 2011).

Oliver, the SITH narrative has led to a proliferation of contradictory models for the production of the Book of Mormon.[376]

We propose a translation model which we believe resolves these apparently conflicting lines of evidence. We suggest that the interpreters did display English, as all the witnesses said, but that the text displayed on the two "stone" screens was not a complete, final interpretation of the engravings. Instead, the interpreters provided a literalistic English rendition of the Nephite characters. In some cases, it may have been transliterated phonetic spellings of proper names and foreign words untranslated in the Nephite text such as *cureloms*.

The isolated meanings for each character given by the interpreters would rarely transfer directly word-for-word into contemporary English. Even the Title Page, which Joseph said was a literal translation, includes English pronouns and conjunctives to make the text flow coherently.

Carrying on the analogy to modern technology from Chapter 5(C), software on our smartphones can already "look" at foreign language characters and instantly display them in English. In that sense, the software literally "translates" the characters, but does not interpret the meaning in a fully useful way.

The interpreters' "stones" may have been crystalline matrices operated by qubit circuitry embedded in the silver-colored rims or the crystals themselves, perhaps powered by a body-machine interface channeled through the breastplate, but the actual technology may still be entirely beyond us.

The important comparison is that the English read-out displayed on the interpreters' double screens was not a final translation. It was left to Joseph to render the close-to-Nephite literal English presentation displayed on the interpreters into English which would

---

[376] Dirkmaat and MacKay, *Let's Talk About the Translation*, pp. 62-102. These authors present their approach as historically based, but their model, like all the SITH-based models, simply cite some historical sources while rejecting (or ignoring) others.

be meaningful to modern readers, a deliberative process that involved myriad word and grammar choices he had to study out in his mind using his own learning and linguistic resources. Further, as with any literary work, the translator continued to refine his work as his spiritual understanding and language skills grew.

C. The Interpretation

We assume that God was perfectly capable of providing a finished text in modern English. Theoretically, he could have had Mormon and Moroni engrave the text in English in the first place. Or, the interpreters could have supplied a finished English text, as contemplated by the transcription explanations.

But according to Doctrine and Covenants 9:8, the translator had to next study it out in his mind, and the NID research shows that the Book of Mormon is in fact sourced from Joseph's linguistic environment. We suggest that the "study" consisted of determining how to best express in English the specific character interpretations conveyed to Joseph by means of the Urim and Thummim, which provided a primarily literal rendering of the Nephite text.

Many Latter-day Saints are familiar with more than one language, whether from foreign language missions, being immigrants, studying other languages in school (almost universal outside the US), or otherwise living in bilingual or multilingual environments. One does not have to be a professional translator or interpreter to understand that even closely related languages cannot be translated word-for-word and be understandable. Any translation requires the translator to make choices among the many ways one can express in a language something from another language. This was Joseph's challenge as a translator.

A helpful illustration to understand Joseph's task is the Rosetta Stone. Discovered by French military forces in 1799, it is a stone tablet with a royal decree written in Egyptian hieroglyphics, the more phonetic Egyptian demotic script, and ancient Greek. Working from the Greek text, Jean-François Champollion was able to decipher the Egyptian scripts, publishing his results in 1822. The following comparison of word-for-word translation of some of the demotic Egyptian with a modern English rendering shows the differences.[377] (We use the demotic script rather than the hieroglyphs or Greek because some, including Hugh Nibley and Sidney Sperry, have suggested that the script used for the plates of Nephi was an early form of demotic Egyptian.[378])

Demotic Egyptian (interpreted word-for-word):

and he happen while her recognize that the in Egypt give for the emerging god for that be beautiful the one of the benefactions according the that in law of do he and they write the order in stela of stone hard in writing of words of god writing of letter writing of the Greek and they give that stand he in the temple first the temple second the temple third beside the image of pharaoh living eternally.

Modern English:

(thus) shall it be known that those who are in Egypt honor the God who appears, whose goodness is perfect as is right to do. They

---

[377] http://rosettastone.hieroglyphic-texts.net/sections/section-57/ and http://rosettastone.hieroglyphic-texts.net/sections/section-58/. These are taken from the Rosetta Stone Online project maintained jointly by Excellence Cluster Topoi and the Institut für Archäologie, Humboldt-Universität zu Berlin. http://rosettastone.hieroglyphic-texts.net/

[378] Hugh W. Nibley, *Since Cumorah*, pp. 167-168; Sperry, "The Book of Mormon as Translation English" https://scholarsarchive.byu.edu/cgi/viewcontent.cgi?article=1106&context=jbms, pp. 210-211. Some have attempted to translate the few lines of characters in what is referred to as the "Anthon transcript" (although it is questioned whether that was the document Martin Harris showed to Charles Anthon) assuming they are demotic Egyptian. See, for example, Jerry D. Grover, Jr., "Translation Of The "Caractors" Document," available at http://bmslr.org/translation-of-the-caractors-document/, although we should note that Grover argues that the "Caractors" are closer to hieratic Egyptian than demotic.

shall write the decree on a stela of hard stone in the script of the words of god, the script of documents and the script of the Ionians and set it up in the first-rank temples, the second-rank temples and the third-rank temples, in the vicinity of the divine image of Pharaoh living forever.

Another sense of what Joseph got from the interpreters can be seen in the Book of Mormon's Title Page. As we noted previously, Joseph said the Title Page was a "literal translation taken from the last leaf on the left hand side of the collection, or book of plates."[379] Only the first and last lines of the Title Page are complete English sentences. A good case can be made that the last line is an emendation by Joseph Smith, acknowledging his own faults and mistakes as well as any Mormon or Moroni alluded to. This leaves a string of descriptive phrases unlike the rest of the text.

A close-to-literal rendering, while challenging to work with, would have helped resolve Joseph's principal shortcoming as a translator, which is that he was not fluent in the source language. While we cannot know how literal the read-out from the interpreters would have been, such a rendering could have given Joseph a sense of the original meaning of the Nephite text he was to translate. Short of a vision, it would be as close as Joseph could come to actually hearing Nephi, Mormon or the dozens of other authors speaking in their own words.

For Nida clarity "in understanding the source text is the key to successful translating into a receptor language. Translators do not translate language, but texts. ... The essential skill of translators is being able to understand correctly the meaning of a source text."[380] Language is more than just the dictionary meanings of its words. The words of a text must be understood within their broader rhetorical context such as "repetition of words and phrases (for emphasis),

---

[379] History of Joseph Smith," *Times and Seasons* 3(1842), p. 943, available at https://www.josephsmithpapers.org/paper-summary/times-and-seasons-15-october-1842/1; also Roberts, *History of the Church,* volume 1, p. 71.

[380] Nida, *Contexts in Translating*, pp. 3, 10.

embedding of one idea within another, the incorporation of parenthetical information ..., back-flashes and forward-flashes ..., parallelism and chiasm (the order abcabc in contrast with abccba) ..., rhythm ..., highlighting ..., purposeful deletion"[381] and so on, all of which are found in the Book of Mormon.[382] Such "stylistic features of a source text ... so often reveal the subtle associative (connotative) values being communicated by the writer."[383]

Nida notes word-for-word Bible translations as useful to give "readers a 'feeling' of how ancient Hebrew speakers might have understood the text."[384] Of special interest in the context of the Book of Mormon translation is Nida's strong recommendation that translation be orally dictated if possible.[385]

Such a close-to-literal read-out would not only have enabled Joseph to understand the Nephite writers' broader contextual meaning, but also account for how these complex literary and narrative forms and structures, discussed in Chapter 4(B)(4), flowed through into the English text along with the many Hebraisms and other ancient linguistic forms discussed in Chapter 4(B)(5).

The English text Joseph was seeing would correspond very closely to how the text was expressed in the original Nephite, including literary and poetic phrasings, parallelistic formatting, grammatical formations and overarching narrative structures. Joseph would have to adjust these considerably to make the text comprehensible in modern English, but starting from this literalistic base assured that much of the art of the Nephite authors could also carry through into Joseph's English translation.[386]

---

[381] Nida, *Contexts in Translating*, pp. 78 - 79.
[382] See for example Hardy, *Understanding the Book of Mormon*, pp. 97 - 111.
[383] Nida, *Contexts in Translating*, pp. 104.
[384] Nida, *Contexts in Translating*, p. 92.
[385] Nida, *Contexts in Translating*, p. 42.
[386] See the references in subchapters 4(B)(4) and 4(B)(5). For the most recent summary of these points, see Parry, *Preserved in Translation*, including the bibliography at pp. 149-163.

Why would God would entrust a man, and one as ill-educated as Joseph, with such a mammoth and important task? To answer this, we must consider the nature of translation. There are certain inherent limits in translating human language. There are over a hundred full translations of the Christian Bible (Old and New Testaments) into English, plus numerous other partial translations and translations only of the Hebrew Bible, all drawing on substantially similar original sources, but each rendering the original words differently in English – more than a hundred different ways to say the same thing.[387]

The translator must ask her or himself how close does one stay to the source language (what Nida called "formal equivalence") as opposed to getting the meaning across in the receptor language (Nida's "functional equivalence")? Will the receptor audience need some inspired targumic elaboration to clearly see the messages intellectually, emotionally and culturally? There is no right or wrong answer, not even rules for getting it right. This is why the results from even the most advanced AI translation software must in the end go to a human translator.[388]

Choosing among alternatives is a deliberative process, as explained in Doctrine and Covenants 9:8 ("study it out in your mind"). And, as we noted in Chapter 5(D), it is a task which Reverend Nida described as requiring an ability to deal "with new and creative situations, … [and] multiple hypotheses [and] … the creative and imaginative aspects of communicating Christian truth."[389]

As Nida argued, simply coming up with grammatically coherent English sentences was not enough. Indeed, that was probably not the main part of the task. Joseph had to decide how his contemporaries would take what the Nephite writers were saying. In a book of over 500 pages, all approaches, whether a close to literal formal equivalence,

---

[387] https://en.wikipedia.org/wiki/List_of_English_Bible_translations
[388] Demetrius Williams, "Using AI to Crack Ancient Languages," available at https://www.translatemedia.com/us/blog-usa/using-ai-crack-ancient-languages/
[389] Nida and Taber, *The Theory and Practice of Translation*, p. 100.

more freely using the language of the time to achieve functional equivalence, or targumic elaboration to apply the text directly to current debates, would have been appropriate in different parts of the book, as confirmed by the Holy Spirit.[390]

And, the translation had to be put into a style which was close enough to the KJV that Joseph's audience would accept the writing as properly scriptural sounding. As with the Jewish Britons, any other style would likely have grated on the ears of Americans of his time.

Here Joseph drew on his lifetime of self-education in the language and thinking of his time and place. His mental language bank provided vocabulary and phrases which his contemporaries would understand, and his familiarity with the Bible and the religious teachings of the Christian groups he knew would help him to make the Nephite prophets' words relevant to Joseph's people.

D. Verification

After all this Doctrine and Covenants 9:8 says that the translator must then ask the Lord if the work is right. If "it is right I will cause that your bosom shall burn within you." If not, verse 9 says there will be a "stupor of thought," and it's back to the drawing board.

And this was work. Many have made note of how quickly the translation went. Instead of the widely accepted three-month time frame, we favor David Whitmer's eight-month time frame as the best fit with the known facts. Joseph told his mother that he had begun translating in the fall of 1828 after Moroni had returned the plates and

---

[390] Brant Gardner wrestles with distinguishing what parts of the Book of Mormon might be formally or functionally equivalent. However, because he accepts the SITH narrative, his interpretation is unnecessarily complicated because he must add a category for "conceptual equivalence" to accommodate what we call the "shamanist" ideas of translation which arise from the SITH narrative. Gardner, *The Gift and Power*, pp. 157 – 192, 241 – 247, 279 – 283.

the Urim and Thummim.[391] The manuscript evidence shows that Joseph resumed the translation with the Book of Mosiah, and there is evidence that Joseph had translated all, or most of, Mosiah before Oliver arrived in Harmony in April 1829. This means it took Joseph and Oliver two full months to produce Alma through Moroni before they left for Fayette.

If Joseph merely read words off the stone, he could have read that entire text in much less time. The only time Joseph dictated rapidly was during the demonstration in the Whitmer home when three scribes took turns because they tired. That exception proves the rule, that the translation was normally a difficult, time-consuming process.

No wonder David Whitmer described the translation as long hard work, telling E. C. Briggs that Joseph and Oliver "worked hard, early and late, while translating the plates. It was slow work, and they could only write a few pages a day."[392]

We suggest that the Book of Mormon translation is a prime example, perhaps the example *par excellence*, of how God works with humanity. As we saw in Chapter 3(E)(2), the Judeo-Christian concept of scriptural revelation is a dialogue between the Lord and His prophets and people. God giving a word-for-word text for

---

[391] Compare John W. Welch, "The Miraculous Translation of the Book of Mormon," in *Opening the Heavens*, pp. 76-213, available online at https://archive.bookofmormoncentral.org/content/miraculous-translation-book-mormon and Neville, *A Man That Can Translate*, chapter 1.

[392] E. C. Briggs, letter dated June 4, 1884 to *The Saints Herald*, volume 31, No. 25, June 21, 1884, at p. 396, available at http://www.sidneyrigdon.com/dbroadhu/ia/sain1882.htm#062184. Although he was not a scribe and therefore only a secondhand hearsay witness to the actual translation process, David was in his family home while the later translation was happening, and thus would be a firsthand witness as to the length of Joseph and Oliver's workdays, and how they appeared as a result of their labors. We also note that Briggs presented this as a direct quote from David (and we have no reason to doubt Briggs' report) but says David said Joseph and Oliver were "translating the plates," which contradicts David's claim that Joseph was no longer was using the plates during the later translation work at the Whitmer home.

transcription would have eliminated the human side of that dialogue. The prototype in our time is the First Vision. God talked to Joseph because the human first asked a question. Our input is needed as well as God's. Otherwise, we would not grow. The back-and-forth is the means by which God educates us. This is how if people "humble themselves before me, and have faith in me, then I will make weak things become strong unto them."[393]

E. Both Loose and Tight Control

In addition to doing detailed work on the earliest manuscripts of the Book of Mormon, Royal Skousen has studied the production of the Book of Mormon. Based on the SITH narrative he advocates, Skousen introduced the concepts of tight control and loose control to describe approaches to how the Book of Mormon was produced. (A third category, iron-clad control, has received less use.)[394]

By loose control, Skousen means that Joseph only received ideas which he put into his own language. Tight control means Joseph received an exact text in English.[395] Although there are many variations, these roughly correspond to our categories of transcription (Chapter 2(A)) and shamanist explanations (Chapter 3(A)).

Jana Riess has summarized the advantages of each approach. Tight control can explain the Hebraic derivation of proper nouns in the Book of Mormon and other Hebraisms and complex linguistic and cultural features. However, loose control can better explain

---

[393] Ether 12:27

[394] We discussed his SITH-based Early Modern English hypothesis in Chapter 2(G).

[395] Skousen, "Translating and Printing the Book of Mormon," pp. 78-79, 98-100, available at https://criticaltext.byustudies.byu.edu/translating-and-printing-book-mormon

anachronisms, poor grammar, KJV insertions, and verbal missteps.[396]

This artificial dichotomy between tight and loose control can be collapsed by returning to the canonical translation narrative. In our model, the formally equivalent text Joseph received from the interpreters gave him the Hebraic forms and other ancient features. He then restated the text in functionally equivalent English resulting in the features ascribed to a loose translation.

F. The Nature of the Book of Mormon's Translation

Our approach is inductive - we work back from the text to see what description of the translation consistent with the historical record would result in the Book of Mormon that we have. In Chapter 5(A) we reviewed four basic characteristics of the Book of Mormon as a document. Let's now review these characteristics in light of the last two chapters to see if we can better understand why the Book of Mormon is the way it is.

1. <u>Complex narrative</u>. The complexity of the narrative militates against composition, nor is it compatible with a shamanist explanation in which Joseph sees some panoramic vision or receives generalized spiritual impressions. This level of detail and precision could only have come from closely tracking a text written by someone else with much more time to assemble and organize the narrative. This can be readily explained if Joseph was translating directly from the plates. It could also be explained by a tight control transcription process where Joseph was simply receiving word-for-word someone else's translation.

2. <u>Language from Joseph's environment</u>. Yet, a transcription scenario seems unlikely when we confront the reality that the language of the Book of Mormon is all sourced from Joseph's environment and thought-world. Although he lived a century after Joseph, we believe

---

[396] Jana Riess, "Critique of 'Linguistic Translation,'" (Faith Matters conference May 16, 2017) at https://www.youtube.com/watch?v=Tslzdq08qeQ

that the Reverend Dr. Eugene Nida's concept of functional equivalence is widely apparent in Joseph's translation. Joseph was translating not only using the vocabulary of his time, but expressing and framing the ancient prophets' words in a way which would have real meaning for his receptor audience. And the many mistakes in the original manuscript and changes in later editions show that Joseph was an actively engaged translator, charged with the task of both realizing and continually refining the translated text.

3. <u>Ancient language artifacts</u>. That the Book of Mormon reflects its translator's environment is the main argument for composition. However, composition cannot explain the substrata of ancient concepts and linguistic phrases and forms which underlie the English text. We have proposed that, although his overall product reflects a functional equivalence approach of translating meaning rather than words, Joseph received the text from the interpreters in a more literalistic form, closer to what Nida called formal equivalence. This enabled Joseph to come as close as possible to understanding the original Nephite text. The concepts of formal and functional equivalence are a continuum, not binaries, and receiving a more literal English translation from the interpreters gave Joseph the option of also reflecting in his translation language which was closer to the original Nephite phrasing, narrative structure and literary forms.

4. <u>Use of the King James Version of the Bible</u>. The core of Eugene Nida's philosophy of Bible translation was respect for the receiving audience. Given the profound reverence which Joseph's world held for the KJV, it was logical for Joseph to use that venerable text except where the Nephite text or the Spirit gave a substantive variation.

Only translation, as opposed to transcription or composition, can fully explain the Book of Mormon we have. And we believe the Lord's work through Joseph to produce this translation reflects the most profound respect and love for us, its intended receptor audience.

7. Why Does This Matter?

Which commandments were given to Joseph Smith, Jun., who was called of God, and ordained an apostle of Jesus Christ, to be the first elder of this church; and to Oliver Cowdery, who was also called of God, an apostle of Jesus Christ, to be the second elder of this church, and ordained under his hand; ...

and gave him power from on high, by the means which were before prepared, to translate the Book of Mormon; which contains a record of a fallen people, and the fulness of the gospel of Jesus Christ to the Gentiles and to the Jews also; ...

proving to the world that the holy scriptures are true, and that God does inspire men and call them to his holy work in this age and generation, as well as in generations of old; thereby showing that he is the same God yesterday, today, and forever. Amen.

Doctrine and Covenants 20:2-3, 8-9, 11-12

Did Joseph Smith compose the Book of Mormon? Those who believe in the historicity and divinity of the Book can answer this way: yes and no.

No, in the sense that it was not his *original* composition. He did not imagine or invent it.

But yes, in the sense that, like all translators, he conveyed the meaning and structure of the original text on the plates in his own language (English), using his own lexicon, thought patterns and artistry.

Translators are "authors of constrained representations" of the original work.[397]

Joseph was specially prepared by the Lord to accomplish the translation. Starting with his long childhood convalescence from surgery due a leg disease, he became a religious seeker and pursued a course of self-education and reflection which prepared him for his service as translator of the Book of Mormon, a service which we believe he rendered rather well. Nevertheless, Joseph's translation was unique in that:

(1) he had the assistance of an incredibly advanced ancient technology called the interpreters, and

(2) he had the guidance of the Holy Spirit that confirmed the accuracy of his translation.

Some who believe in the Book of Mormon disagree with all of the foregoing except the last point. They note that we do not need gold plates or interpreters to receive personal revelation. Indeed, Joseph himself evolved away from depending on the Urim and Thummim. These argue that direct inspiration, or a pretty rock, were sufficient. Others, sometimes less openly, accept the Book of Mormon as inspired, but consider it to be wholly Joseph's product, a pious fiction.[398] Such an understanding would not be compatible with the translation narrative, tied as it is to working from real physical objects.

---

[397] Katerina Bantinaki, "The literary translator as author: A philosophical assessment of the idea," available at https://www.researchgate.net/publication/336268361_The_literary_translator_as_author_A_philosophical_assessment_of_the_idea

[398] The most concise exposition of this view is probably Anthony A. Hutchinson, "The Word of God is Enough: The Book of Mormon as Nineteenth-Century Scripture" in Brent Lee Metcalfe (ed), *New Approaches to the Book of Mormon: Explorations in Critical Methodology* (Salt Lake City, UT: Signature Books, 1993), pp. 1-19 available at http://signaturebookslibrary.org/the-book-of-mormon/

However, it is entirely possible under the SITH narrative, since no one can say what was really going on inside Joseph's hat.

We recognize the available historical evidence supports multiple working hypotheses, but choosing among those hypotheses requires consideration not only of evidence but of the implications of each choice. For those who consider the Book of Mormon to be inspired, but also no more than Joseph's fervent imaginings, or the folk magic ephemera of the SITH narrative, we offer the following observations.

A. Privileging the SITH accounts undermines Joseph Smith's credibility

The Book of Mormon is central to the divinity of Joseph Smith's prophetic ministry and the Restoration. Gordon B. Hinckley declared that:

> If the Book of Mormon is true, Joseph Smith was a Prophet of God, for he was the instrument in the hands of God in bringing to light this testimony of the divinity of our Lord. ... If the Book of Mormon is true, the Church is true, for the same authority under which this sacred record came to light is present and manifest among us today. It is a restoration of the Church set up by the Savior ...[399]

As Richard Bushman has pointed out, many people in Joseph's time had visions of Jesus.[400] It was launching his ministry by declaring himself a translator that set Joseph apart.[401] And, as we hope we have

---

[399] Gordon B. Hinckley, "The Power of the Book of Mormon," *Ensign* (June 1988), p. 2 – 6, quote at p. 6, also available at https://www.churchofjesuschrist.org/study/ensign/1988/06/the-power-of-the-book-of-mormon?lang=eng.

[400] Richard L. Bushman, "The Visionary World of Joseph Smith," *BYU Studies* (1997-1998) Vol 37, no. 1, pp. 138-204 https://byustudies.byu.edu/article/the-visionary-world-of-joseph-smith/

[401] Richard L. Bushman, "Joseph Smith as Translator," in Bryan Waterman (ed), *The Prophet Puzzle* (Salt Lake City, UT: Signature Books, 1999), pp. 69-86.

shown in this book, Joseph and his primary scribe, Oliver Cowdery, the major eyewitnesses to the creation of the Book of Mormon we have today, consistently stated that the Book was produced by translating the plates using the interpreters. Neither ever mentioned the use of a stone in a hat, or any other method of generating the Book. Unlike with the disparate accounts of the First Vision, which was not originally central to the Restoration message, Joseph and Oliver's accounts of the coming forth of the Book of Mormon were consistent and unequivocal.

The SITH accounts conflict with Joseph's account as found in the Pearl of Great Price and elsewhere. In Chapter 2, we argued that the SITH accounts were largely secondary, vague and unreliable and in Chapter 2(F) that they could be plausibly explained as originating with Joseph's efforts to provide a demonstration of the translation without violating the divine injunction to not show the plates and interpreters (or possibly misunderstandings arising from instances where the interpreters were used for non-translation revelations). We have shown how these demonstrations were inflated and exaggerated over the decades in misguided attempts to rebut the Spalding theory.

The SITH accounts are part of the historical record, but they can now be explained in a way that corroborates the claims of Joseph and Oliver. The alternative—promoting the SITH narratives at face value—makes Joseph the unreliable witness, and critics have understandably seized on them to denigrate Joseph's credibility. From a faithful perspective, privileging the SITH accounts is not a vaccine, it is the disease.[402] Most importantly, as we have argued in the previous

---

[402] We refer here to the argument that exposing LDS students and audiences to the seer stone narrative will "inoculate" them from being shaken when they encounter this information from hostile sources. However, as we have argued in this book, the seer stone narrative is based on unreliable sources and ignores or questions the testimony of Joseph and Oliver, the two primary eyewitnesses. And many scholars' presentation of the seer stone narrative has gone beyond merely providing information to active advocacy. This can only give credibility to the critics' use of

three chapters, Joseph's account is the most plausible explanation of the Book of Mormon's origins.

B. The Book of Mormon is quantitatively different than any other revelation

The current LDS edition of the Book of Mormon is 530 printed pages long. If the lost manuscript was included, it would probably be well over 700 printed pages.[403] In contrast, even Joseph's longest revelations are shorter by orders of magnitude. Doctrine and Covenants Section 76 is seven printed pages, Section 84 is eight printed pages, and Section 88 is ten, but the latter is an amalgamation of several different revelations. The Books of Moses and Abraham are longer but were produced incrementally over many months and largely follow the biblical narrative, albeit with supplementary material.[404]

With its myriad names, timelines, events, places, cultural facts and teachings, the Book of Mormon far surpasses any other revelation we know of in sheer size and volume. And the Book of Mormon was produced at the beginning of Joseph's prophetic ministry, when he was least experienced in receiving revelation. The vast majority of revelation Latter-day Saints receive are confirmations on single focused issues, even as momentous as ending plural marriage or extending the priesthood to all races, not thousand-year histories of entire civilizations. No, the Book of Mormon is a special case, and

---

the seer stone narrative to undermine faith, and open the door for believers to accept critics' other attacks on the authenticity of the Book of Mormon and other teachings of the Restored Gospel.

[403] Despite the title of his book and the traditional count, Don Bradley argues that there were well over 200 pages in the lost manuscript. Don Bradley, *The Lost 116 Pages: Reconstructing the Book of Mormon's Missing Stories* (Salt Lake City, UT: Greg Kofford Books, 2019), pp. 83-103.

[404] Based on Ether 1:3-4, Neville thinks the first few chapters of the Book of Moses may have come from plates Joseph accessed in the repository in the Hill Cumorah.

should not, cannot, be analogized to other revelations, even though all ultimately come from the Lord.

C. The Book of Mormon is materially different than any other revelation

By now the reader certainly realizes that we prefer the canonical account of how the Book of Mormon came forth, as found in the Pearl of Great Price, over the new priority given by many scholars to the SITH accounts. However, at least among those who accept the Pearl of Great Price as scripture, there must be some nominal acknowledgement of the existence of the plates and interpreters, even if they reject the rest of the canonical account and use the SITH accounts to claim neither the plates or the interpreters were ever actually used in the translation process of the Book of Mormon we have today.

As we noted in Chapter 3(E), the plates and the interpreters are central to the Book of Mormon story. For a thousand years Nephite scribes maintained and built their national archive, somehow preserving it through wars and apostasies. In the end, Mormon, in the midst of a war for national survival, struggled to create a record summarizing the lessons to be learned from his people's long history.

This involved not only painstaking labor to inscribe his account on metal plates, but taking time from his pressing military duties to research through archives, all of which may have been maintained in a scribal writing form which, after a thousand years, was very different from the colloquial Nephite of his time.[405] Then Moroni had to go

---

[405] Jerry Grover has suggested that the language may have changed so much in the course of the Nephite millennium that Mormon and/or his scribal predecessors had to use the interpreters to understand the earliest writings in the archives.

through untold struggles to safely secure the plates and interpreters in the Hill Cumorah.[406]

Then comes the saga of Joseph's receipt of the Book of Mormon. Four years tutelage under Moroni, the dangers, near misses and suffering involved in securing and protecting the plates and accompanying interpreters.

And the interpreters have their own saga, serving prophets in the Americas from at least the time of the brother of Jared, somehow preserved over thousands of years of Jaredite history, then passing into the service of King Mosiah, and presumably his successors. They were the objects of prophecy and revelation, kept secure by Moroni and then Joseph Smith along with the plates to be used, according to the canonical account, to translate the plates. They were, in the words of Samuel W. Richards, "touched by the finger of God and dedicated and consecrated for the purpose of translating languages."[407] These were objects so sacred that no one could view them without divine authorization, and are now in the care of heavenly guardians.

No other revelation is tied so closely to special sacred material objects like this. There is no point to all this epic struggle over millennia if these ancient sacred physical objects could be replaced by a little rock. There is a magisterial grandeur to these ancient holy objects. A rock in a hat has no such grandeur.

D. The plates and interpreters ground the Book of Mormon in the real world.

At the beginning of this book, we quote an interview with Leo Tolstoy where he says he preferred a religion whose sacred book is dug

---

[406] We note that many SITH supporters are also advocates of a Mesoamerican setting for the Book of Mormon. For them one must add that Moroni would have had to travel across an entire continent with the plates and other objects to reach what would become the home of the Joseph Smith family in upstate New York.

[407] Samuel Whitney Richards in John. W. Welch (ed), *Opening the Heavens*, p. 144.

out of the earth rather than pretending to be let down from heaven. We cannot say definitively what the novelist meant by that. But Tolstoy's statement touches on a core aspect of the Book of Mormon. It presents itself as real. It is not an inspiring fiction or pious fraud. We are to understand that the Lehites and Jaredites are real, their history real (in so far as their archival records were accurate) and, most importantly, that the resurrected Jesus really did appear to early Americans.

These physical objects, the plates and the interpreters, ground the Book of Mormon in reality. Expunging the plates and interpreters reduces the Book of Mormon to being just another inspirational work of vague origins. Of course, we no longer have these sacred objects, so a leap of faith is still required to pass through the golden door to belief in the Book's authenticity. But the plates and interpreters are powerful symbols of the reality of the Book and the history it tells.

There are many inspiring books "let down from heaven," to use Tolstoy's phrase. These books are not rooted in any physical reality but rather came directly to the mind of their giver. The Quran is a prime example, but one could include the Bhagavad Gita, the books of the Buddha and Bahá'u'lláh, as well as the works of innumerable visionaries in Christian traditions.[408] None present themselves as grounded in concrete reality like the Book of Mormon with its plates and interpreters. Without the latter we have to fall back on what we call the shamanist explanation (see Chapter 3(A)). Then, to a modern observer, the Book of Mormon becomes indistinguishable from these other works of vague spiritual origins.

But this may suit many just fine. There has long been a tension among followers of the Restoration between a desire for respectability and its embarrassing, goofy origins story of angels, gold plates and magic translation spectacles. As one commentator has observed,

---

[408] See the probably very over-inclusive list at https://en.wikipedia.org/wiki/List_of_Christian_mystics. Interestingly, Brigham Young and James Strang make the list, but Joseph Smith does not.

"imagining the translation of the Book of Mormon as an outpouring of pure revelation is quite agreeable to the educated faithful, as it confers a welcome religious respectability on the Restoration. Joseph Smith would thus fit more neatly into the long history of prophets and mystics, and it lessens unpleasant tension with notions of what religious inspiration should look like. Those with a secular outlook, for their part, are frequently prepared to consider the Book of Mormon as a work of tremendous genius and creativity. Given the minimal conceptual gap between divine illumination and creative genius, the more we treat the Book of Mormon as an ethereal and spontaneous outpouring of inspiration" the less the Book of Mormon is "appalling to our modern, educated sensibilities."[409]

We leave to each one the choice as to whether it is sufficient that the Book of Mormon count as but one of many inspirational writings, or if its unique materiality confronts us with the word of God.

E. The Book of Mormon's physical and historical reality is central to its mission

This decision whether the Book of Mormon is to sit with other uplifting writings, whether fictional or of some indeterminate immaterial source, or rather relates authentic history that actually happened to real people, goes to the core of its power.[410] Uprooted

---

[409] Jonathan Green, "Use of the gold plates in Book of Mormon translation accounts," (November 30, 2020) at https://www.timesandseasons.org/harchive/2020/11/use-of-the-gold-plates-in-book-of-mormon-translation-accounts/. To be clear, Green opposes the trend he so eloquently describes.

[410] "There is something strange about accepting the moral or religious content of a book while rejecting the truthfulness of its authors' declarations, predictions, and statements. This approach not only rejects the concepts of faith and revelation that the Book of Mormon explains and advocates, but it is also not even good scholarship." Dallin H. Oaks, "The Historicity of the Book of Mormon," in *Historicity and the Latter-day Saint Scriptures*, Paul Y. Hoskisson (ed), (Provo, UT: Religious

from its physical grounding in the plates and interpreters, it drifts into nether realms where we do not know what it really is – inchoate if beneficent preachments, or really the hard-edged warnings of a true prophet of God who really lived, declaring that "Jesus Christ has shown you unto me, and I know your doing ... that ye do walk in the pride of your hearts ... unto envying, and strifes, and malice, and persecutions, and all manner of iniquities, ... For behold you do love money, and your substance ... more than you love the poor and needy, the sick and the afflicted."[411]

Can a Book of Mormon so deracinated, a Book of Mormon cut off from any materiality, really make us feel the reality of these warnings from the mighty warrior/prophet Moroni, son of Mormon? And how did Moroni, son of Mormon, entrust these writings to Joseph Smith, Junior? He gave Joseph exquisitely engraved plates of gold and crystal interpreters of divine creation, of a technology probably so advanced that we perhaps cannot even begin to imagine its workings. That is what Moroni, son of Mormon, gave Joseph, son of Joseph – not a dumb brown rock.

Lucas has been blessed from time to time to serve as teacher of adult Sunday School in the LDS Church. Some time ago he began a year cycle of studying the Book of Mormon by citing a newspaper article. He initially thought it simply a way to engage the class once at the beginning of the year. However, week after week, each text assigned for reading related to the current news, seemingly ripped from the day's headlines. By the year's end, it was as though the *New York Times* had unknowingly taught the Book of Mormon's overarching relevance to our modern world.

Do we see discord – family, ethnic, civil, national, international? Do we suffer from doubt or discouragement – personal, civilizational

---

Studies Center, Brigham Young University, 2001), pp. 237–48, quote at p. 241, available at https://rsc.byu.edu/historicity-latter-day-saint-scriptures/historicity-book-mormon.

[411] Mormon 8:35 – 37.

or spiritual? Do we seek justice – individual, racial, social, economic or political? Do we long for understanding, hope or solace in the midst of trial, troubles and tragedy? De we wonder how to truly serve others and our Savior? Did Mormon, son of Mormon, Nephi, son of Lehi, and Moroni, son of Mormon, miss anything?

And almost two centuries since its appearance, we continue to learn from the Book of Mormon. For example, there is much of war in the Book, but only recently a Protestant Bible scholar showed us that the exact center of the Book of Mormon (by page and word count) is the story of the Anti-Nephi-Lehies, who would surrender their lives rather than resort to bloodshed.[412] How much do we still have to learn from this holy book, which so utterly surpasses its 19th century origins, whose destiny is to warn and bless our entire modern world?

F. The Book of Mormon as fulfillment of Christian aspirations

The ongoing decline of religion in many parts of the world, including the United States, is well documented.[413] Equally well documented is that these trends are larger the younger the age group surveyed.[414] It also appears that these trends are reflected among Latter-day Saints.[415] This latter trend is driven in part by the use by

---

[412] Thomas, *A Pentecostal Reads The Book of Mormon*, pp. 255 – 261. Lucas has argued that Mormon, son of Mormon, was a descendent of Anti-Nephi-Lehies. See https://bycommonconsent.com/2016/11/27/mormon-was-a-lamanite/.

[413] Pew Research Center, "In U.S., Decline of Christianity Continues at Rapid Pace" (October 17, 2019), available at https://www.pewforum.org/2019/10/17/in-u-s-decline-of-christianity-continues-at-rapid-pace/.

[414] Pew Research Center, "Religious Landscape Survey" (2021), available at https://www.pewforum.org/religious-andscape-study/generational-cohort/.

[415] Jana Riess, *The Next Mormons: How Millennials Are Changing the LDS Church* (New York: Oxford University Press, 2019), pp. 4-7. Her survey found that only half of LDS Millennials believe that the Book of Mormon is a literal historical account (p.19).

dissidents of the replacement by the SITH accounts of the canonical narrative to dishearten members who had believed the canonical account was reliable.

Reframing the interpreters as high technology and Joseph Smith as a nerd is not revisionist history. It is an accurate description in modern terms of what we can see in the historical record. Perhaps this reframe will help people today to better relate to the origin story of the Book of Mormon, and to try an experiment upon its words.[416]

What we do know is that the world needs the Book of Mormon, and it needs it in all its glory, translated by a well-prepared prophet from the gold plates with the interpreters through the gift and power of God. It needs the Book of Mormon not only to confirm the divinity of Christ, but also for its thousand-year examination of the challenge of living as a Christian in a fallen world.

The world needs the Book of Mormon to fulfill the hopes of Christians who share the faith of Jonathan Edwards that the Christian Church will yet accomplish its mission. As Edwards once wrote,

> Sometimes Mr. Smith and I walked there together, to converse of the things of God; and our conversation used much to turn on the advancement of Christ's kingdom in the world, and the glorious things that God would accomplish for his church in the latter days.[417]

As the Book of Mormon fulfills its purposes, the time truly shall come "when the knowledge of a Savior shall spread throughout every nation, kindred, tongue, and people." (Mosiah 3:20)

---

[416] Alma 32:27

[417] *The Works of President Edwards in Eight Volumes,* Volume I (Worcester, MA: Isaiah Thomas, Jun., 1808), quote at p. 39.

REFERENCES CITED

References to the Bible, Book of Mormon, Doctrine and Covenants and Pearl of Great Price use the 1981 LDS Church editions. References to Joseph Smith's writings are to the online editions produced by the Joseph Smith Papers project sponsored by the LDS Church. Note that, while Joseph did write some of the documents himself, others were written by secretaries and clerks under his direction. See the Historical Introductions to the various documents at the online citations for detailed discussion of the nature of each of the Joseph Smith documents.

"A Witness to the Book of Mormon," *Des Moines Iowa State Register*, August 28, 1870; in Vogel, *Early Mormon Documents*, volume 2, p. 330 and at http://www.sidneyrigdon.com/dbroadhu/IA/misciow2.htm

Anderson, Richard Lloyd, "Reuben Miller, Recorder of Oliver Cowdery's Reaffirmations," *BYU Studies Quarterly* (1968) Vol. 8, no. 3, pp. 277 – 293 at https://scholarsarchive.byu.edu/byusq/vol8/iss3/5

Anderson, Richard Lloyd, "The House Where the Church Was Organized," *Improvement Era* 73 (April 1970) pp. 16-25 at https://catalog.churchofjesuschrist.org/assets/af8e45bb-cf4a-43f4-8fb8-18a2f094d283/0/0.

Anderson, Richard Lloyd, "By the Gift and Power of God," *Ensign* (September 1977), pp. 78-85 at https://www.churchofjesuschrist.org/study/ensign/1977/09/by-the-gift-and-power-of-god?lang=eng

Anderson, Richard Lloyd, *Investigating the Book of Mormon Witnesses* (Salt Lake City, UT: Deseret Book Company, 1981)

Anderson, Richard Lloyd, "David Whitmer Interviews: A Restoration Witness" (book review), *Journal of Mormon History* (Spring 1994), vol. 20, no. 1, pp. 186–193 at http://digitalcommons.usu.edu/cgi/viewcontent.cgi?article=1022&context=mormonhistory

Anderson, Richard Lloyd, "The Early Preparation of the Prophet Joseph Smith," *Ensign* (December 2005), pp. 12-17 at https://www.churchofjesuschrist.org/study/ensign/2005/12/the-early-preparation-of-the-prophet-joseph-smith?lang=eng

Anderson, Richard Lloyd, "A Scholar as a Witness: A Conversation with Richard Lloyd Anderson, Interview by Kay and Joseph F. Darowski," *Mormon Historical Studies* 7 (Spring Fall 2006), pp. 50-82 at https://ensignpeakfoundation.org/mormon-historical-studies-spring-fall-2006-vol-7-no-1-2

Arrington, Leonard J., *Reflections of a Mormon Historian: Leonard J. Arrington on the New Mormon History*, Reid L. Neilson and Ronald W. Walker (eds) (Norman, OK: The Arthur H. Clark Company, 2006)

Ashurst-McGee, Mark, "Foreword" in Michael Hubbard MacKay and Nicholas J. Frederick, *Joseph Smith's Seer Stones* (Salt Lake City, UT: Deseret Book Company and Provo, UT: Brigham Young University Religious Studies Center, 2016)

Aston, Warren P. and Michaela Knoth Aston, *In the Footsteps of Lehi: New Evidence for Lehi's Journey across Arabia to Bountiful* (Salt Lake City, UT: Deseret Book Company, 1994)

Augustine of Hippo, *Concerning the City of God Against the Pagans*, Book 3, chapter 17, at https://www.gutenberg.org/files/45304/45304-h/45304-h.htm#Page_114.

Backman, Milton V., Jr., "A Non-Mormon View of the Birth of Mormonism in Ohio," *BYU Studies* (1972) Vol. 12, No. 3, pp. 1-4 at https://byustudies.byu.edu/wp-content/uploads/2020/01/12.3BackmanNon-Mormon.pdf

Ballard, M. Russell, "How the Lord Prepared the World for the Restoration," *Ensign* (January 2020), pp. 14 – 21, at https://www.churchofjesuschrist.org/study/ensig15n/2020/01/how-the-lord-prepared-the-world-for-the-restoration?lang=eng

Bantinaki, Katerina, "The literary translator as author: A philosophical assessment of the idea," at https://www.researchgate.net/publication/336268361_The_literary_translator_as_author_A_philosophical_assessment_of_the_idea

Barlow, Philip L., *Mormons and the Bible: The Place of the Latter-day Saints in American Religion* (New York: Oxford University Press, 1991, Updated Edition 2013)

Becerra, Daniel, Amy Easton-Flake, Nicholas J. Frederick and Joseph M. Spencer, *Book of Mormon Studies: An Introduction and Guide* (Provo, UT: Brigham Young University Religious Studies Center and Salt Lake City, UT: Deseret Book, 2022)

Bennett, Richard E., "Read This I Pray Thee": Martin Harris and the Three Wise Men of the East," *Journal of Mormon History*: Vol. 36, no. 1 (Winter 2010), pp. 178-216) at https://digitalcommons.usu.edu/cgi/viewcontent.cgi?article=1052&context=mormonhistory

Benton, A. W., "Mormonites," *Evangelical Magazine and Gospel Advocate* (Utica, NY), vol. 2, no. 15 (Apr. 19, 1831) at https://www.mrm.org/mormonites

Black, Susan Easton and Larry C. Porter, *Martin Harris: Uncompromising Witness of the Book of Mormon* (Provo, UT: BYU Studies, 2018)

Blair, William W., *The Saints Herald*, Vol. 35, No. 9, March 3, 1888, pp. 129-130, at https://www.google.com/books/edition/Saints_Herald/vJD0EOEmJyYC?hl=en&gbpv=1&dq=%22saints+herald%22+%22march+3,+1888%22&pg=PA129&printsec=frontcover

Bloom, Harold, *The American Religion: The Emergence of the Post-Christian Nation* (New York: Simon Schuster, 1992)

"The Book of Mormon," *The Chicago Daily Tribune*, Vol. XLV Thursday, December 17, 1885, at https://en.wikisource.org/wiki/Chicago_Daily_Tribune,_December_17,_1885

Bradley, Don, "Written by the Finger of God?: Claims and Controversies of Book of Mormon Translation," *Sunstone* (December 2010), pp. 20-29 at https://sunstone.org/written-by-the-finger-of-god-claims-and-controversies-of-book-of-mormon-translation/ (updated October 17, 2011)

Bradley, Don, *The Lost 116 Pages: Reconstructing the Book of Mormon's Missing Stories* (Salt Lake City, UT: Greg Kofford Books, 2019)

Briggs, E. C., letter dated June 4, 1884 to *The Saints Herald*, Volume 31, No. 25, June 21, 1884, pp. 396-397, at http://www.sidneyrigdon.com/dbroadhu/ia/sain1882.htm#062184

Brodie, Fawn McKay, *No Man Knows My History: The Life of Joseph Smith the Mormon Prophet* (New York: Alfred A. Knopf, 1945)

Brown, S. Kent and Peter Johnson (eds), *Journey of Faith* (Provo, UT: The Neal A. Maxwell Institute for Religious Scholarship, 2006)

Brown, Samuel Morris, *Joseph Smith's Translation* (New York: Oxford University Press 2020)

Bushman, Richard L., *Joseph Smith and the Beginnings of Mormonism* (Urbana, IL: University of Illinois Press, 1984)

Bushman, Richard L., "The Mysteries of Mormonism," *Journal of the Early Republic* 15 (Autumn 1995), vol. 3, pp. 501-508

Bushman, Richard L., "The Visionary World of Joseph Smith," *BYU Studies* (1997-1998) Vol 37, no. 1, pp. 138-204 at https://byustudies.byu.edu/article/the-visionary-world-of-joseph-smith/

Bushman, Richard L., "Joseph Smith as Translator," in Bryan Waterman (ed), *The Prophet Puzzle* (Salt Lake City, UT: Signature Books, 1999), pp. 69-86.

Bushman, Richard Lyman, *Joseph Smith: Rough Stone Rolling: A cultural biography of Mormonism's founder* (New York: Alfred A. Knopf, 2005)

Bushman, Richard Lyman, "Reading From the Gold Plates," in Blair G. Van Dyke, Brian D. Birch and Boyd J. Petersen (eds) *The Expanded Canon: Perspectives on Mormonism & Sacred Texts* (Salt Lake City, UT: Greg Kofford Books, 2018)

Bushman, Richard Lyman, "Nephi's Project: The Gold Plates as Book History," in Michael Hubbard MacKay, Mark Ashurst-McGee and Brian M. Hauglid (eds) *Producing Ancient Scripture: Joseph Smith's Translation Projects in the Development of Mormon Christianity* (Salt Lake City, UT: The University of Utah Press, 2020), pp 187-204

C (anonymous), "Are They of Israel," *Millennial Star*, No. 3, Vol. LXIX (49), Jan. 17, 1887, p. 37

Callister, Tad R., *A Case for the Book of Mormon* (Salt Lake City, UT: Deseret Book, 2019)

Campbell, Alexander, "Delusions: An Analysis of the Book of Mormon: With an Examination of Its Internal and External Evidences, and a Refutation of Its Pretences to Divine Authority," *The Millennial Harbinger*, February 7, 1831 at https://archive.org/details/delusionsanalysi01camp

Carmack, Noel A., "Joseph Smith, Captain Kidd Lore, and Treasure-Seeking," *Dialogue: A Journal of Mormon Thought*, Vol. 46, No. 3 (Fall 2013), at https://www.dialoguejournal.com/wp-content/uploads/sbi/articles/Dialogue_V46N03_412b.pdf

Cherok, Richard J., *Debating God: Alexander Campbell's Challenge to Skepticism in Antebellum America* (Abilene, TX: Abilene University Christian Press, 2008)

Clark, David, "Review of *Let the Word Be Written*," *Journal of Semitic Studies*, Volume 52, no. 1, (Spring 2007) pp. 145–147 at https://academic.oup.com/jss/article-abstract/52/1/145/1719514?redirectedFrom=fulltext

Clark, John A., *Gleanings by the way*, (Philadelphia: W.J. & J.K. Simon, 1842), at https://archive.org/details/gleaningsbyway00clarrich/page/230/mode/2up.

Clarke, Arthur C., *Profiles of the Future: An Inquiry into the Limits of the Possible*, (London: Victor Gollancz, 1999, originally published 1962)

Clements, MaryAnn, "Before the Urim & Thummim: Pre-1833 Newspaper Accounts of the Book of Mormon Translation," (January 26, 2023) at https://wheatandtares.org/2023/01/26/before-the-urim-thummim-pre-1833-newspaper-accounts-of-book-of-mormon-translation/

Coe, Truman in *Ohio Observer* (Hudson, Ohio, 11 August 1836), in Milton V. Backman, Jr., "Truman Coe's 1836 Description of Mormonism," *BYU Studies Quarterly* (1977) Vol. 17, no. 3, pp. 347-355 at https://scholarsarchive.byu.edu/byusq/vol17/iss3/9

Conforti, Joseph A., *Jonathan Edwards, Religious Tradition, and American Culture* (Chapel Hill, NC: The University of North Carolina Press, 1995)

Cowdery, Oliver, "Letter I," *Latter Day Saints' Messenger and Advocate*, Vol. 1, No. 1, October 1834, at https://contentdm.lib.byu.edu/digital/collection/NCMP1820-1846/id/7160

Cowdery, Oliver, "Letter IV," at https://www.josephsmithpapers.org/paper-summary/history-1834-1836/60

Cowdery, Oliver "Letter VII," at http://www.josephsmithpapers.org/paper-summary/history-1834-1836/83

Cowdery, Wayne L., Howard A. Davis and Arthur Vanick, "'Manuscript Found' and the Moroni Myth: The Importance of Being Honest, A Reply to the Matthew Roper-BYU/FARMS review of 'Who Really Wrote The Book of Mormon?—The Spalding Enigma'," pp. 26-33, at https://www.whatismormonism.com/SPALDING_ENIGMA_ROPER_REBUTTAL.pdf

Davis, William L., *Visions in a Seer Stone: Joseph Smith and the Making of the Book of Mormon* (Chapel Hill, NC: University of North Carolina Press, 2020)

Deane, Samuel, *Four Sermons to Young Men, from Titus II.6. preached at Falmouth* (Salem, MA: Samuel and Ebenezer Hall, 1774)

DeGroote, Michael, "Inside the lost McLellin notebook," *Deseret News* January 28, 2009, at https://www.deseret.com/2009/1/28/20298664/inside-the-lost-mclellin-notebook

Dehlin, John, *Mormon Stories* (podcasts) at https://www.mormonstories.org/episodes/top-25-most-important-episodes/ and https://www.mormonstories.org/truth-claims/the-books/the-book-of-mormon/book-of-mormon-authorship-translation-timeline/

Dirkmaat, Gerrit J. and Michael Hubbard MacKay, *Let's Talk About the Translation of the Book of Mormon* (Salt Lake City, UT: Deseret Book, 2023)

Donofrio, Thomas E., "Early American Influences on the Book of Mormon – Part II Book of Mormon Historical Influences," at http://www.mormonthink.com/influences.htm#part2 (accessed November 12, 2022)

Duffy, John-Charles, "The 'Book of Mormon Translation' Essay in Historical Context," in Matthew L. Harris and Newell G. Bringhurst (eds), *The LDS Gospel Topics Series: A Scholarly Engagement* (Salt Lake City, UT: Signature Books, 2020), pp. 97–130

Duke, James T., *The Literary Masterpiece Called the Book of Mormon* (Springville, UT: Cedar Fort, Inc., 2003)

Eames, S. Morris, *The Philosophy of Alexander Campbell* (Bethany, WV: Bethany College, 1966)

Edmond, David, *An Oration delivered at Ridgfield on the Fourth of July* (Danbury, CT: Dougles & Nichols, 1799)

Edwards, Jonathan, "Personal Narrative," in Chapter II "Extracts from his Private Writings" in *The Works of President Edwards in Eight Volumes*, Volume I (Worcester, MA: Isaiah Thomas, Jun., 1808), pp. 13-47

Edwards, Jonathan, "Sermon III. Men naturally God's Enemies," in *The Works of President Edwards in Eight Volumes*, Volume VII (Worcester, MA: Isaiah Thomas, Jun., 1808), pp. 159-207 at https://www.mobom.org/men-naturally-gods-enemies

Edwards, Jonathan, "Some Thoughts Concerning the Revival of Religion in New England," (1742) in David Turley (ed) *American Religion: Literary Sources and Documents* (London and New York: Routledge, 1998, 2019), pp. 145-153 at https://books.google.com/books?id=DwwLEAAAQBAJ&pg=PA145&lpg=PA135&dq=American+Religion+literary+souces+turley&source=bl&ots=J_tcorGlCV&sig=ACfU3U37gXgym_jXVU29BKXlf075RL7z_g&hl=en&sa=X&ved=2ahUKEwjs4qj56az6AhWblIkEHXllB_kQ6AF6BAgXEAM#v=onepage&q=American%20Religion%20literary%20souces%20turley&f=false

Edwards, Paul M., *Our Legacy of Faith: A Brief History of the Reorganized Church of Jesus Christ of Latter Day Saints* (Independence, MO: Herald House, 1991)

Excellence Cluster Topoi and the Institut für Archäologie, Humboldt-Universität zu Berlin, *The Rosetta Stone online*, at http://rosettastone.hieroglyphic-texts.net/

Faulring, Scott H., "The Return of Oliver Cowdery," in Stephen D. Ricks, Donald W. Parry and Andrew H. Hedges (eds) *The Disciple as Witness: Essays on Latter-day Saint History and Doctrine in Honor of Richard Lloyd Anderson* (Provo, UT: The Foundation for Ancient Research and Mormon Studies, 2000), pp. 117 – 173

Flesher, Paul V. M. and Bruce Chilton, *The Targums: A Critical Introduction* (Waco, TX: Baylor University Press, 2011)

Gardner, Brant A., *The Gift and Power: Translating the Book of Mormon* (Salt Lake City, UT: Greg Kofford Books, 2011)

Givens, Terryl L., *By the Hand of Mormon: The American Scripture that Launched a New World Religion* (New York: Oxford University Press, 2002)

Godfrey, Kenneth W., "David Whitmer and the Shaping of Latter-day Saint History," in Stephen D. Ricks, Donald W. Parry and Andrew H. Hedges (eds) *The Disciple as Witness: Essays on Latter-day Saint History and Doctrine in Honor of Richard Lloyd Anderson* (Provo, UT: The Foundation for Ancient Research and Mormon Studies, 2000), pp. 223 – 256 at https://scholarsarchive.byu.edu/cgi/viewcontent.cgi?filename=9&article=1083&context=mi&type=additional

"Golden Bible," *The Gem: A Semi-Monthly Literary and Miscellaneous Journal* (Rochester, NY: 5 September 1829), p. 70, at https://contentdm.lib.byu.edu/digital/collection/BOMP/id/161

"Golden Bible," *The Palmyra Freeman* (Palmyra, NY: 31 August 1829) at https://contentdm.lib.byu.edu/digital/collection/BOMP/id/4381

Gospel Topics, "Book of Mormon Translation," at https://www.churchofjesuschrist.org/study/manual/gospel-topics-essays/book-of-mormon-translation?lang=eng

Green, Jonathan, "Of early modern English and the Book of Mormon," (April 1, 2019) at https://www.timesandseasons.org/index.php/2019/04/of-early-modern-english-and-the-book-of-mormon/

Green, Jonathan, "Use of the gold plates in Book of Mormon translation accounts," (November 30, 2020) at https://www.timesandseasons.org/harchive/2020/11/use-of-the-gold-plates-in-book-of-mormon-translation-accounts/

Greenspoon, Leonard, *Jewish Bible Translations: Personalities, Passions, Politics, Progress* (Philadelphia: The Jewish Publication Society, 2020)

Grover, Jerry D., Jr., "Translation Of The "Caractors" Document," at http://bmslr.org/translation-of-the-caractors-document/

Grunder, Rick, *Mormon Parallels* (2014) available at http://www.rickgrunder.com/parallels.htm

Gurley, Zenas H. Jr., "The Book of Mormon," *Autumn Leaves* (1892), Vol. 5, pp. 451 - 454, at https://hdl.handle.net/2027/nyp.33433075797161 and https://babel.hathitrust.org/cgi/pt?id=nyp.33433075797161&view=1up&seq=485&skin=2021

Hales, Brian C., "Joseph Smith: Monogamist or Polygamist?" *Interpreter: A Journal of Latter-day Saint Faith and Scholarship* 25 (2017), pp. 117-156, at https://journal.interpreterfoundation.org/joseph-smith-monogamist-or-polygamist/

Hales, Brian C., "Automatic Writing and the Book of Mormon: An Update," *Dialogue*, Vol. 52, No. 2, (Summer 2019), at https://www.dialoguejournal.com/wp-content/uploads/sbi/articles/Dialogue_V52N02_1.pdf

Hales, Brian C., "Naturalistic Explanations of the Origin of the Book of Mormon: A Longitudinal Study," *BYU Studies* (2019), Vol 58, no. 3, pp. 105-148, at https://byustudies.byu.edu/article/naturalistic-explanations-of-the-origin-of-the-book-of-mormon-a-longitudinal-study/

Hamblin, William J., "That Old Black Magic," in *Review of Books on the Book of Mormon 1989–2011*: Vol. 12 (2000): No. 2, at https://scholarsarchive.byu.edu/msr/vol12/iss2/17

Hardy, Grant, *Understanding the Book of Mormon: A Reader's Guide* (New York: Oxford University Press, 2010)

Hardy, Grant, "The Book of Mormon Translation Process," *BYU Studies* (2021), Vol 60, no. 3, pp. 203 – 211, at https://byustudies.byu.edu/article/the-book-of-mormon-translation-process/

Harper, Steve C., *First Vision: Memory and Mormon Origins* (New York: Oxford University Press, 2019)

Harris, Franklin S., Jr., *The Book of Mormon: Messages and Evidences* (Salt Lake City, UT: The Church of Jesus Christ of Latter-day Saints, Deseret News Press, 1953)

Hart, James H., "About the Book of Mormon," *Deseret Evening News* (Salt Lake City), March 25, 1884 at https://newspapers.lib.utah.edu/ark:/87278/s6d22s6w/2648947

Hilton, Lynn M. and Hope A. Hilton, *Discovering Lehi: New Evidence of Lehi and Nephi in Arabia* (Springville, UT: Cedar Fort, Inc, 1996)

Hinckley, Gordon B., "Lord, Increase Our Faith," *Ensign* (November 1987), pp. 51-54 at https://www.churchofjesuschrist.org/study/ensign/1987/11/lord-increase-our-faith?lang=eng

Hinckley, Gordon B., "The Power of the Book of Mormon," *Ensign* (June 1988), pp. 2-6 at https://www.churchofjesuschrist.org/study/ensign/1988/06/the-power-of-the-book-of-mormon?lang=eng

Hoskisson, Paul Y., "Book of Mormon Names," *Encyclopedia of Mormonism* (New York: Macmillan Publishing Company, 1992) Vol. 1, pp. 186-187 at https://eom.byu.edu/index.php/Book_of_Mormon_Names

Howard, Richard P., "The Changing RLDS Response to Mormon Polygamy: A Preliminary Analysis," *The John Whitmer Historical Association Journal*, vol. 3 (1983), pp. 14-29, at https://www.jstor.org/stable/43200716

Howard, Richard P., *The Church Through the Years*, (Independence, MO: Herald Publishing House, 1992, 2 volumes)

Howe, Daniel Walker, *What Hath God Wrought: The Transformation of America 1815-1848* (Oxford History of the United States, New York: Oxford University Press, 2007)

Howe, Eber B., *Mormonism Unvailed, or, A Faithful Account of That Singular Imposition and Delusion, From its Rise to the Present Time* (Painesville, OH: Printed and published by the author, 1834), at https://archive.org/details/mormonismunvaile00howe

Hunt, Gilbert J., *The Late War, between the United States and Great Britain, from June, 1812, to February, 1815* (New York: Daniel D. Smith, 1819, originally published 1816) at https://archive.org/details/latewarbetweenun00inhunt

Hutchinson, Anthony A., "The Word of God is Enough: The Book of Mormon as Nineteenth-Century Scripture" in Brent Lee Metcalfe (ed), *New Approaches to the Book of Mormon: Explorations in Critical Methodology* (Salt Lake City, UT: Signature

Books, 1993), pp. 1-19 at http://signaturebookslibrary.org/the-book-of-mormon/

Javadi-Evans, Petra, "'Knowledge Saves a Man': Joseph Smith's Devotion to Learning," in R. Eric Smith, Matthew C. Godfrey, Matthew J. Grow (eds.) *Know Brother Joseph: New Perspectives on Joseph Smith's Life and Character* (Salt Lake City, UT: Deseret Book, 2021), pp. 77-81

Jenson, Andrew (editor and publisher), "Church Encyclopedia, Book 1," in *The Historical Record*, Salt Lake City, Utah (1889), pp. 219-234, at https://archive.org/details/churchencyclopae58jens/page/218/mode/2up

Jenson, Andrew, *Latter-day Saint biographical encyclopedia: a compilation of biographical sketches of prominent men and women in the Church of Jesus Christ of Latter-day Saints* (Salt Lake City, UT: The Andrew Jenson History Co., 1901) at https://archive.org/details/latterdaysaintbi01bjens/mode/2up

Johnson, Chris and Duane Johnson, "A Comparison of the Book of Mormon and The Late War Between the United States and Great Britain," (March. 9, 2014), published at http://wordtree.org/thelatewar/ (accessed November 12, 2022)

"Joseph the Seer's Plural Marriages," *Deseret Evening News*, October 22, 1879, p. 13 at https://newspapers.lib.utah.edu/details?id=2663429

Kneeland, Abner, "Questions proposed to the Mormonite Preachers and their answers obtained before the whole assembly at Julien Hall, Sunday Evening, August 5, 1832," *Boston Investigator* (August 10, 1832), Vol. 2, No. 20, at http://www.sidneyrigdon.com/dbroadhu/NE/miscne01.htm#081032

Larsen, Val, "In His Footsteps: Ammon$_1$ and Ammon$_2$," *Interpreter: A Journal of Latter-day Saint Faith and Scholarship* 3 (2013), pp. 85-113 at https://journal.interpreterfoundation.org/in-his-footsteps-ammon-and-ammon/

Launius, Roger D., *Joseph Smith III: Pragmatic Prophet* (Urbana and Chicago, IL: University of Illinois Press, 1988)

Levin, Mark R., *Unfreedom of the Press* (New York: Simon & Schuster, 2019)

Lucas, James W., "Mormon Was A Lamanite" (November 27, 2016) at https://bycommonconsent.com/2016/11/27/mormon-was-a-lamanite/

MacKay, Michael Hubbard, "The Secular Binary of Joseph Smith's Translations," *Dialogue*, Vol. 54, No. 3, (Fall 2021), pp. 1-40, at https://www.dialoguejournal.com/articles/the-secular-binary-of-joseph-smiths-translations/#pdf-wrap)

MacKay, Michael Hubbard, "'Git Them Translated': Translating the Characters on the Gold Plates," in Lincoln H. Blumell, Matthew J. Grey, and Andrew H. Hedges (eds), *Approaching Antiquity: Joseph Smith and the Ancient World*, (Provo, UT: Religious Studies Center; Salt Lake City, UT: Deseret Book, 2015), pp. 83–116, at https://rsc.byu.edu/approaching-antiquity-joseph-smith-ancient-world/git-them-ranslated-translating-characters-gold

MacKay, Michael Hubbard and Gerrit J. Dirkmaat, *From Darkness unto Light: Joseph Smith's Translation and Publication of the Book of Mormon* (Salt Lake City, UT: Deseret Book Company and Provo, UT: Brigham Young University Religious Studies Center, 2015)

MacKay, Michael Hubbard and Nicholas J. Frederick, *Joseph Smith's Seer Stones* (Salt Lake City, UT: Deseret Book Company and Provo, UT: Brigham Young University Religious Studies Center, 2016)

MacKay, Michael Hubbard, Mark Ashurst-McGee and Brian M. Hauglid (eds) *Producing Ancient Scripture: Joseph Smith's Translation Projects in the Development of Mormon Christianity* (Salt Lake City, UT: The University of Utah Press, 2020)

Marquardt, H. Michael, "David Whitmer: His Evolving Beliefs and Recollections," in Newell G. Bringhurst and John C. Hamer (eds) *Scattering of the Saints: Schism within Mormonism* (Independence, MO: John Whitmer Books, 2007), pp. 46–77

Marsden, George M., *Jonathan Edwards: A Life* (New Haven, CT: Yale University Press, 2003)

"Martin Harris – One of the Witnesses of the Book of Mormon," *Deseret Evening News* (September 7. 1870) p. 3 at https://contentdm.lib.byu.edu/digital/collection/desnews2/id/43437/rec/36

McConkie, Joseph Fielding and Crag J. Ostler, "The Process of Translating the Book of Mormon," in *Revelations of the Restoration: A Commentary on the Doctrine and Covenants and Other Modern Revelation* (Salt Lake City, UT: Deseret Book, 2000), pp.

89-98, at https://emp.byui.edu/satterfieldb/Rel121/Process%20of%20Translating%20the%20BofM.pdf

McDowell, Josh, *The New Evidence That Demands A Verdict* (Nashville, TN: Thomas Nelson, 1999)

McGuire, Benjamin L, "Finding Parallels: Some Cautions and Criticisms," *Interpreter: A Journal of Latter-day Saint Faith and Scholarship* 5 (2013) pp. 1-59, at https://journal.interpreterfoundation.org/finding-parallels-some-cautions-and-criticisms-part-one/

McLellin, William E. to "My Dear Friends" (February 1870) Community of Christ archives, Joseph Smith III transcript file 1 pp. 123-124

McLellin, William Earl, *William E. McLellin's Lost Manuscript* (Salt Lake City, UT: Eborn Books, 2012), Mitchell K Schaefer (ed)

McNamara, Martin and Paul V. M. Flesher, *Targum*, (2014) at https://www.oxfordbibliographies.com/view/document/obo-9780195393361/obo-9780195393361-0187.xml

Merriam-Webster Dictionary, "Does Peruse Mean "to Skim" or "to Read Carefully"? at https://www.merriam-webster.com/words-at-play/peruse-usage

Metcalfe, Brent Lee, "Apologetic and Critical Assumptions about Book of Mormon Historicity," *Dialogue* 26/3 (1993) pp. 153-184 at https://www.dialoguejournal.com/wp-content/uploads/sbi/articles/Dialogue_V26N03_163.pdf

Miller, Reuben, *Journal 1848*, at https://catalog.churchofjesuschrist.org/assets/22222322-f4fe-41e3-aa86-bfc54b94df92/0/0

Mindich, David, *Just the Facts: How "Objectivity" Came to Define American Journalism* (New York: NYU Press, 1998)

"Mormonites," *The Sun*, August 18, 1831, at http://www.sidneyrigdon.com/dbroadhu/PA/Phil1830.htm#081831

Mouritsen, Paul, "Secret Combinations and Flaxen Cords: Anti-Masonic Rhetoric and the Book of Mormon," *Journal of Book of Mormon Studies*: Vol. 12: No. 1 (2003), pp. 65-118 at https://scholarsarchive.byu.edu/jbms/vol12/iss1/9

Nelson, Russell M., "Revelation for the Church, Revelation for Our Lives," *Ensign* (May 2018), p. 93-96, also at https://www.churchofjesuschrist.org/study/general-conference/2018/04/revelation-for-the-church-revelation-for-our-lives?lang=eng

Neville, Jonathan, *Whatever Happened to the Golden Plates?* (Salt Lake City, UT: Digital Legend, 2016)

Neville, Jonathan, *A Man That Can Translate: Joseph Smith and the Nephite Interpreters* (Salt Lake City, UT: Digital Legend, 2020, 2nd edition)

Neville, Jonathan, *Between These Hills: A Case for the New York Cumorah* (Salt Lake City, UT: Digital Legend, 2021)

Neville, Jonathan, *Infinite Goodness: Joseph Smith, Jonathan Edwards and the Book of Mormon* (Salt Lake City, UT: Digital Legends, 2021)

Neville, Jonathan, "Analysis: The Gospel Topics Essay on Book of Mormon Translation" (September 1, 2022) at http://www.ldshistoricalnarratives.com/2022/09/analysis-gospel-topics-essay-on-book_of.html

Newell, Linda King and Valeen Tippetts Avery, *Mormon Enigma* (Champaign, IL: University of Illinois Press, 2nd edition 1994)

Nibley, Hugh W., *Since Cumorah: The Book of Mormon in the Modern World* (Salt Lake City, UT: Deseret Book, 1967)

Nicholson, Roger, "The Spectacles, the Stone, the Hat, and the Book: A Twenty-first Century Believer's View of the Book of Mormon Translation" in *Interpreter: A Journal of Latter-day Saint Faith and Scholarship* 5 (2013) pp. 121-190 at https://journal.interpreterfoundation.org/the-spectacles-the-stone-the-hat-and-the-book-a-twenty-first-century-believers-view-of-the-book-of-mormon-translation/#rf30-2896

Nida, Eugene A. and Charles R. Taber, *The Theory and Practice of Translation* (Leiden, NL: E. J. Brill for the United Bible Societies, 1969)

Nida, Eugene A., *Contexts in Translating* (Philadelphia, PA: John Benjamins Publishing Company, 2001)

Noll, Mark, "Edwards' Theology after Edwards," in Sany Hyun Lee (ed), *The Princeton Companion to Jonathan Edwards* (Princeton, NJ: Princeton University Press, 2005), pp. 296-304

Oaks, Dallin H., "The Historicity of the Book of Mormon," in *Historicity and the Latter-day Saint Scriptures*, Paul Y. Hoskisson (ed), (Provo, UT: Religious Studies Center, Brigham Young University, 2001), pp. 237–48, at https://rsc.byu.edu/historicity-latter-day-saint-scriptures/historicity-book-mormon

Ostler, Blake T. "The Book of Mormon as a Modern Expansion of an Ancient Source," *Dialogue: A Journal of Mormon Thought* 20, no. 1 (Spring 1987), pp. 66-123, at https://www.dialoguejournal.com/wp-content/uploads/sbi/articles/Dialogue_V20N01_68.pdf, updated April 26, 2005, at https://www.timesandseasons.org/harchive/2005/04/updating-the-expansion-theory/

Ostler, Craig James, "Book of Mormon Translation Instrument Descriptions: Interpreters, Urim & Thummim and Seer Stones," (FIRM Foundation conference April 2020) at https://www.bookofmormonevidence.org/streaming/videos/bom/dr-craig-j-ostler-book-of-mormon-translation-instrument-descriptions-interpreters-urim-thummim-and-seer-stones/

Palmer, David, *In Search of Cumorah: New Evidences for the Book of Mormon from Ancient Mexico* (Bountiful, UT: Horizon Publishers, 1981, 2005)

Palmer, Grant H., *An Insider's View of Mormon Origins* (Salt Lake City, UT: Signature Books, 2002)

Parry, Donald W., *Poetic Parallelisms in the Book of Mormon* (Provo, UT: Maxwell Institute Publications. 2007) at https://scholarsarchive.byu.edu/mi/61/

Parry, Donald W., *Preserved in Translation: Hebrew and Other Ancient Literary Forms in the Book of Mormon, (Salt Lake City and Provo, UT:* Deseret Book and BYU Religious Studies Center, 2020)

Pearson, Lee H., "David Whitmer: Man of Contradictions – An Analysis of Statements by David Whitmer on Translation of the Book of Mormon" (February

10, 2019), at https://josephsmithfoundation.org/papers/an-analysis-of-statements-by-david-whitmer-on-translation-of-the-book-of-mormon/

Pew Research Center, "In U.S., Decline of Christianity Continues at Rapid Pace" (October 17, 2019), at https://www.pewforum.org/2019/10/17/in-u-s-decline-of-christianity-continues-at-rapid-pace/

Pew Research Center, "Religious Landscape Survey" (2021), at https://www.pewforum.org/religious-andscape-study/generational-cohort/

Potter, George and Richard Wellington, *Lehi in the Wilderness: 81 new documented evidences that the Book of Mormon is a true history* (Springville, UT: Cedar Fort, Inc., 2003)

Pratt, Orson, "King Limhi's Enquiry, From The Book Of Mormon—Ammon Replies—Seership And The Urim And Thummim—The Brother Of Jared—Hyrum Smith's Enquiry—What Is A Generation—The Immense Number Of Records To Be Revealed" (December 9, 1877) in *Journal of Discourses* (Liverpool, UK: William Budge, 1878) volume 19, pp. 204-219, at https://contentdm.lib.byu.edu/digital/collection/JournalOfDiscourses3/id/939

Pratt, Parley P., *The Autobiography of Parley Parker Pratt, one of the twelve apostles of the Church of Jesus Christ of Latter-day Saints : embracing his life, ministry and travels, with extracts, in prose and verse, from his miscellaneous writings*, (Chicago, IL: Law, King & Law, 1888) at https://archive.org/details/autobiographyofp00prat/page/n3/mode/2up

President Uchtdorf Shares What He Believes About Seer Stones," *LDS Living* (June 21, 2016) at https://www.ldsliving.com/president-uchtdorf-shares-what-he-believes-about-seer-stones/s/82469

Quinn, D. Michael, *Early Mormonism and The Magic World View* (Salt Lake City, UT: Signature Books, 1998, 2nd edition)

Reeder, Jennifer, *First: The Life and Faith of Emma Smith* (Salt Lake City, UT: Deseret Book, 2021)

Reynolds, Noel B. (ed), *Book of Mormon Authorship: New Light on Ancient Origins* (Provo, UT: Brigham Young University, 1982)

Reynolds, Noel B., "Lehi's Arabian Journey Updated" in Noel B. Reynolds (ed) *Book of Mormon Authorship Revisited: The Evidence for Ancient Origins* (Provo, UT: Foundation for Ancient Research and Mormon Studies, 1997), pp. 379-389

Ricks, Stephen D., *Joseph Smith's Translation of the Book of Mormon* (Provo, UT: FARMS, 1986), at http://farms.byu.edu/display.php?table=transcripts&id=10

Ricks, Stephen D., "King, Coronation and Covenant in Mosiah 1-6" in John L. Sorenson and Melvin J. Thorne (eds), *Rediscovering the Book of Mormon* (Provo, UT: FARMS, 1991), pp. 209-219

Ricks, Stephen D., "Translation of the Book of Mormon: Interpreting the Evidence," *Journal of Book of Mormon Studies* (1993) Vol. 2, no. 2, pp. 201–206, at https://doi.org/10.2307/44758930

Riess, Jana, "Critique of 'Linguistic Translation,'" (Faith Matters conference May 16, 2017) at https://www.youtube.com/watch?v=Tslzdq08qeQ

Riess, Jana, *The Next Mormons: How Millennials Are Changing the LDS Church* (New York: Oxford University Press, 2019)

Roberts, B. H. (ed), *Comprehensive History of the Church of Jesus Christ of Latter-day Saints* (Salt Lake City, UT: Deseret Book Company, 1930), at https://byustudies.byu.edu/further-study/history-of-the-church/

Roberts, B. H., *Defense of the Faith and the Saints* (Salt Lake City, UT: Deseret News, 1907) volume 1, at http://www.solomonspalding.com/docs2/1907RobA.htm

Roberts, B. H., *New Witness for God* (Salt Lake City, UT: Deseret News, 1909) volume 2, at https://babel.hathitrust.org/cgi/pt?id=uc1.31210001369782&view=1up&seq=9&skin=2021

Roberts, B. H., *Studies of the Book of Mormon* (Salt Lake City, UT: Signature Books, 2nd edition, 1992)

Rust, Richard Dilworth, "Joseph Smith's Prodigious Memory and the Translation of the Book of Mormon," forthcoming, copy in possession of authors

Rust, Richard Dilworth, *Feasting on the Word: The Literary Testimony of the Book of Mormon*, (Salt Lake City and Provo, UT: Deseret Book and FARMS, 1997)

Rust, Richard Dilworth, "The Book of Mormon as Epic," *AML Annual 1998*, Lavina Fieldling Anderson (ed), pp. 24-30

"Sabbath Meetings" *Desert Evening News*, (September 5, 1870), p. 2 at https://news.google.com/newspapers?nid=Aul-kAQHnToC&dat=18700905&printsec=frontpage&hl=en

Sallust (Gaius Sallustius Crispus), *Historiae Fragmenta*, 1:12, at https://www.goodreads.com/quotes/8254253-frequent-mobs-seditions-and-at-last-civil-wars-became-common

Schudson, Michael, *Discovering the News: A Social History of American Newspapers* (New York: Basic Books, 1978)

Schudson, Michael, "Questioning Authority: A History of the News Interview in American Journalism 1860-1930s," *Media Culture and Society* (1994), Vol 16, no. 4, pp. 565–587

Skousen, Royal, "John Gilbert's 1892 Account of the 1830 Printing of the Book of Mormon," in *The Disciple as Witness: Essays on Latter-day Saint History and Doctrine in Honor of Richard Lloyd Anderson*. (Provo, UT: FARMS, 2000) at https://criticaltext.byustudies.byu.edu/john-gilberts-1892-account-1830-printing-book-mormon-0

Skousen, Royal, "Translating and Printing the Book of Mormon" in John W. Welch and Larry E. Morris (eds), *Oliver Cowdery: Scribe, Elder, Witness* (Provo, UT: Neal A. Maxwell Institute for Religious Scholarship, 2006), pp. 75-116, at https://criticaltext.byustudies.byu.edu/translating-and-printing-book-mormon

Skousen, Royal, "Changes in the Book of Mormon," *Interpreter: A Journal of Latter-day Saint Faith and Scholarship* (2014), Vol. 11, pp. 161-176 at https://journal.interpreterfoundation.org/changes-in-the-book-of-mormon/

Skousen, Royal, *The History of the Text of the Book of Mormon—Parts 3 - 5—The Nature of the Original Language* (Provo, UT: BYU Studies, 2018)

Skousen, Royal, *Critical Text of the Book of Mormon, Volume 3, The History of the Text, Part Five, The King James Quotations in the Book of Mormon* (Provo, UT: FARMS and BYU Studies, 2019)

Citations

Smith, George A., "Joseph Smith's Family – Details of George A. Smith's Own Experience, &c.," (August 2, 1857) in *Journal of Discourses* (Liverpool, UK: Asa Calkin, 1858) volume 5, pp. 101-111 at https://contentdm.lib.byu.edu/digital/collection/JournalOfDiscourses3/id/2275

Smith, Joseph Fielding, *Doctrines of Salvation* (Bruce R. McConkie compiler, Salt Lake City, UT: Bookcraft, 1956)

Smith, Joseph, Jr., "Letter to Oliver Cowdery," (October 22, 1829) at https://www.josephsmithpapers.org/paper-summary/letter-to-oliver-cowdery-22-october-1829/1

Smith, Joseph, Jr., *History circa Summer 1832*, at https://www.josephsmithpapers.org/paper-summary/history-circa-summer-1832/1

Smith, Joseph, Jr., "Letter to John S. Carter," (April 13, 1833), Joseph Smith Papers, Letterbook 1, at https://www.josephsmithpapers.org/paper-summary/letter-to-john-s-carter-13-april-1833/1

Smith, Joseph, Jr., *History 1834 – 1836*, at http://www.josephsmithpapers.org/paper-summary/history-1834-1836

Smith, Joseph, Jr., *Journal 1835 – 1836*, at https://www.josephsmithpapers.org/paper-summary/journal-1835-1836/1

Smith, Joseph, Jr., *Elders' Journal* (Far West, MO: July 1838) at https://www.josephsmithpapers.org/paper-summary/elders-journal-july-1838/10

Smith, Joseph, Jr., *History, circa June 1839–circa 1841* at https://www.josephsmithpapers.org/paper-summary/history-circa-june-1839-circa-1841-draft-2/10

Smith, Joseph, Jr., *History, circa 1841,* (fair copy) at https://www.josephsmithpapers.org/paper-summary/history-circa-1841-fair-copy/1

Smith, Joseph, Jr., "Church History," *Times and Seasons* (1 March 1842) vol. 3, no. 9, pp. 703–710 (Wentworth letter) at https://www.josephsmithpapers.org/paper-summary/church-history-1-march-1842/1

Smith, Joseph, Jr., "History of Joseph Smith," *Times and Seasons* (15 April 1842), at https://www.josephsmithpapers.org/paper-summary/times-and-seasons-15-april-1842/3

Smith, Joseph, Jr., *Journal, December 1842–June 1844; Book 2, 10 March 1843–14 July 1843*, at https://www.josephsmithpapers.org/paper-summary/journal-december-1842-june-1844-book-2-10-march-1843-14-july-1843/3

Smith, Joseph, Jr., "Letter to James Arlington Bennet," (November 13, 1843) at https://www.josephsmithpapers.org/paper-summary/letter-to-james-arlington-bennet-13-november-1843/1

Smith, Joseph, Jr., *History, 1838–1856, volume A-1 [23 December 1805–30 August 1834]* at https://www.josephsmithpapers.org/paper-summary/history-1838-1856-volume-a-1-23-december-1805-30-august-1834/1

Smith, Joseph, Sr., Blessing 9 December 1834, at https://www.josephsmithpapers.org/paper-summary/blessing-from-joseph-smith-sr-9-december-1834/1

Smith, Joseph III to James T. Cobb, (February 14, 1879) Community of Christ archives, Joseph Smith III transcript file 5 pp. 478-480 and in Vogel, *Early Mormon Documents*, volume 1, p. 544

Smith, Joseph III to William Smith, (May 6, 1879) Community of Christ archives, Joseph Smith III transcript file 5 pp. 547-548

Smith, Joseph III, "Last Testimony of Sister Emma," *The Saints Herald*, volume 26, No. 19, October. 1, 1879, at https://archive.org/stream/TheSaintsHerald_Volume_26_1879/the%20saints%20herald%20volume%2026%201879#page/n287/mode/2up and http://www.latterdaytruth.org/pdf/100193.pdf

Smith, Joseph III, "David Whitmer Reviewed," *The Saints Herald*, volume 33, No. 45, November 13, 1886, pp. 704-708, at https://www.google.com/books/edition/Saints_Herald/qmqsXWe1xFAC?gbpv=1&bsq=704

Smith, Lucy Mack, "Lucy Mack Smith Speaks to the Nauvoo Saints," Ronald W. Walker (ed) *BYU Studies* (1991) Vol. 32, nos. 1 and 2, pp. 276-284 at https://byustudies.byu.edu/wp-content/uploads/2020/02/32.1-2WalkerHistorians-4dd4b307-de92-4283-aee0-a0b613be247d.pdf

Smith, Lucy Mack, *History 1845* (fair copy), at https://www.josephsmithpapers.org/paper-summary/lucy-mack-smith-history-1845/1 and *History, 1844 – 1845* (original copy) at https://www.josephsmithpapers.org/paper-summary/lucy-mack-smith-history-1844-1845/1

Smith, Merina, Revelation. *Resistance and Mormon Polygamy: The Introduction of and Implementation of the Principle 1830-1853* (Logan, UT: Utah State University Press, 2013)

Smith, Thomas Wood, "Origin of the Mormon Bible," *Fall River (MA) Herald*, 28 March 1879; reprinted in *The Saints' Herald* 26 (15 April 1879), pp. 127-128 at https://archive.org/stream/TheSaintsHerald_Volume_26_1879/the%20saints%20herald%20volume%2026%201879#page/n125/mode/2up

Sorenson, John L., *Mormon's Codex: An Ancient American Book* (Salt Lake City, UT: Deseret Book, 2013)

Sowers, Kenneth, Jr., "The Mystery and History of the Urim and Thummim," in Maurice L. Draper and A. Bruce Lindgren (eds), *Restoration Studies II* (Independence, MO: The Temple School, 1983), pp. 75–79

Spencer, Stan, "Seers and Stones: The Translation of the Book of Mormon as Divine Visions of an Old-Time Seer," *Interpreter: A Journal of Latter-day Saint Faith and Scholarship* 24 (2017), pp. 27-98, at https://journal.interpreterfoundation.org/seers-and-stones-the-translation-of-the-book-of-mormon-as-divine-visions-of-an-old-time-seer/

Sperry, Sidney B., "The Book of Mormon as Translation English." *Improvement Era* 38 (March 1935): 141, 187-88 (reprinted in *Journal of Book of Mormon Studies* 4/1/1995): 209–17 at https://scholarsarchive.byu.edu/cgi/viewcontent.cgi?article=1106&context=jbms)

Sperry, Sidney B., "Hebrew Idioms in the Book of Mormon" *Improvement Era* 57 (October 1954): 703, 728-29, at https://scholarsarchive.byu.edu/jbms/vol4/iss1/24

Stevenson, Edward, *Book 2: Typescript journals (1871 August 13 - 1882 October 22)*, volumes 12 – 17 at https://catalog.churchofjesuschrist.org/assets/b2a3c8cc-3f2f-4563-91ed-7f43a1259907/0/0

Stevenson, Edward to the editor, *Deseret News* (dated November 30, 1881, printed December 13, 1881), p. 4

Stevenson, Edward, "One of the Three Witnesses: Incidents in the Life of Martin Harris," *Deseret News* (dated November 30, 1881, printed December 28, 1881) pp. 762-763 at https://newspapers.lib.utah.edu/details?id=2634097 and at https://newspapers.lib.utah.edu/details?id=2634097&q=seer+stone+harris&year_start=1870&year_end=1882&facet_type=%22article%22&facet_paper=%22Deseret+News%22

Stevenson, Edward, *Book 4: Typescript journals (1886 January 14 - 1887 August 20)*, volumes 24 - 29 at https://catalog.churchofjesuschrist.org/assets/bc546251-522d-430a-a259-964bd8bde02f/0/0

Stevenson, Edward, *Reminiscences of Joseph, the Prophet, and the coming forth of the Book of Mormon* (Salt Lake City, UT, published by the author, 1893) at https://catalog.churchofjesuschrist.org/assets/665af85e-da18-4a2b-a5f5-2b4bbd033797/0/0

Stine, Philip C., *Let The Words Be Written: The Lasting Influence of Eugene A. Nida* (Atlanta, GA: Society of Biblical Literature, 2004)

Stine, Philip C., "Eugene Nida: Theoretician of Translation," *International Bulletin of Missionary Research*, Vol. 36, No. 1 (January 2012) pp. 38–39 at http://www.internationalbulletin.org/issues/2012-01/2012-01-038-stine.pdf

Stoddard, L Hannah and James F. Stoddard III, *Seer Stone v. Urim & Thummim: Book of Mormon Translation on Trial* (Salem, UT: Joseph Smith Foundation, 2019)

Strong, T. C., "Book Seller and Printer," *Palmyra Register* (September 22, 1818) at http://pioneerlibrarysystem.advantage-preservation.com/viewer/?k=book%20seller&i=f&by=1818&bdd=1810&d=01011817-12311829&m=between&ord=k1&fn=palmyra_register_usa_new_york_palmyra_18180922_english_1&df=1&dt=10

Sweeny, Douglas A., "Evangelical tradition in America," in Stephen J. Stein (ed), *The Cambridge Companion to Jonathan Edwards* (New York: Cambridge University Press, 2007), pp. 217-238

Talmage, James E., *The Great Apostasy: Considered In The Light Of Scriptural And Secular History* (Salt Lake City, UT: Deseret News, 1909) at https://www.gutenberg.org/cache/epub/35514/pg35514.html

Taylor, Alan, "The Early Republic's Supernatural Economy: Treasure Seeking in the American Northeast, 1780-1830," *American Quarterly*, Vol. 38, No. 1 (Spring 1986), pp. 6-34 at http://inside.sfuhs.org/dept/history/US_History_reader/Chapter3/The%20Early%20Republics%20Supernatural%20Economy%20Treasure%20Seeking%20in%20the%20American%20Northeast,%201780%201830.pdf

Terry, Roger, "The Book of Mormon Translation Puzzle," *Journal of Book of Mormon Studies*: Vol. 23: No. 1 (2014), Article 10, at: https://scholarsarchive.byu.edu/jbms/vol23/iss1/10

Thomas, John Christopher, *A Pentecostal Reads The Book of Mormon: A Literary and Theological Introduction* (Cleveland, TN: CPT Press, 2016)

Tiffany, Joel, "Interview with Martin Harris," *Tiffany's Monthly* (1859 New York) pp. 163-170 at: http://www.utlm.org/onlineresources/sermons_talks_interviews/harrisinterviewtiffanysmonthly.htm

Traughber, J. L., Jr., "Testimony of David Whitmer," *The Saints' Herald* 26 (November 15, 1879) p. 341 and in Vogel, *Early Mormon Documents*, volume 5, p. 58

Tucker, Pomeroy, *Origin, Rise, and Progress of Mormonism: Biography of Its Founders and History of Its Church* (New York: D. Appleton, 1867) at https://archive.org/details/originriseprogre00tuck/page/n23/mode/2up

Turley, Richard E., Jr., *Victims: the LDS Church and the Mark Hofmann case* (Champaign, IL: University of Illinois Press, 1992; Salt Lake City, UT: Digital Legends 2nd edition, 2021).

Turley, Richard E. Jr., Robin S. Jensen and Mark Ashurst-McGee, "Joseph the Seer - What Happened to the Seer Stone?" *Ensign* (October 2015), pp. 53-54 at https://www.churchofjesuschrist.org/study/ensign/2015/10/joseph-the-seer?lang=eng

Turner, Orsamus, *History of the Pioneer Settlement* (Rochester, NY: 1851) at https://archive.org/details/historyofpioneer00turn

Tvedtnes, John A., "King Benjamin and the Feast of Tabernacles" in John M. Lundquist and Stephen D. Ricks (eds), *By Study and Also by Faith: Essays in Honor of*

Hugh W. Nibley (Salt Lake City and Provo, UT: Deseret Book and FARMS, 1990), vol 2, pp 197–236

Tvedtnes, John A., "The Hebrew Background of the Book of Mormon" in John L. Sorenson and Melvin J. Thorne (eds), *Rediscovering the Book of Mormon* (Provo, UT: FARMS, 1991), pp. 77-91

Van Wagoner, Richard and Steve Walker, "Joseph Smith - The Gift of Seeing" *Dialogue* (Summer 1982) Vol. 15, No. 2, pp. 49-68 at https://www.dialoguejournal.com/wp-content/uploads/sbi/articles/Dialogue_V15N02_50.pdf

Vogel, Dan (ed), *Early Mormon Documents* (Salt Lake City, UT: Signature Books, 1996)

Vogel, Dan, "Mormonism's 'Anti-Masonick Bible,'" *The John Whitmer Historical Association Journal* 9 (1989) at https://www.jstor.org/stable/43200831

Walker, S. F., "Synopsis of a Discourse by Zenas H. Gurley," *The Saints Herald* (December 15, 1879, vol 26, issue 24), pp. 369 – 371, at https://archive.org/details/TheSaintsHerald_Volume_26_1879/page/n369/mode/2up

Wallace, Lewis Raven, *The View From Somewhere: Undoing the Myth of Journalistic Objectivity* (Chicago, IL: The University of Chicago Press, 2019)

Webster, Noah, *An American Dictionary of the English Language*, (New Haven, CT: 1828) at http://webstersdictionary1828.com/

Wilcox, Miranda and John D. Young (eds), *Standing Apart: Mormon Historical Consciousness and the Concept of Apostacy* (New York: Oxford University Press, 2014)

Welch, John W., "Jesse Smith's 1814 Protest," *BYU Studies* (1993) Vol. 33, no. 1, pp. 131-144 at https://scholarsarchive.byu.edu/cgi/viewcontent.cgi?article=2892&context=byusq

Welch, John W., "Was There a Library in Harmony, Pennsylvania?" *Insights: An Ancient Window* (January 1994):2

Welch, John W., "How Much Was Known about Chiasmus in 1829 When the Book of Mormon Was Translated?," *Review of Books on the Book of Mormon 1989–2011*: Vol. 15 : No. 1 (2003), at https://scholarsarchive.byu.edu/msr/vol15/iss1/7

Welch, John W. (ed), *Opening the Heavens: Accounts of Divine Manifestations* 1820-1844 (Provo and Salt Lake City, UT: BYU Press/Deseret Book, 2005)

White, Andrew D., "Walks and Talks with Tolstoy," *McClure's Magazine*, volume 16 (April 1901) (at https://babel.hathitrust.org/cgi/pt?id=uc1.b000540672&view=1up&seq=535&skin=2021) and *Autobiography* (New York: The Century Co., 1905), Volume II

Whitmer, David, *An Address to All Believers in Christ* (Richmond, MO, 1887) at https://archive.org/details/addresstoallbeli00whit/mode/2up

Whitney, Orson F., "Samuel W. Richards," in *History of Utah* (Salt Lake City, UT: G. Q. Cannon and Sons Co., 1892), pp. 323-325, at https://archive.org/details/bub_gb_C0cOAAAAIAAJ/page/n319/mode/2up

Widtsoe, John A., *A Rational Theology As Taught by the Church of Jesus Christ of Latter-day Saints* (Salt Lake City, UT: General Priesthood Committee, 1915) at https://www.gutenberg.org/cache/epub/35562/pg35562.html

Widtsoe, John A., "Why Did Joseph Smith, the Prophet, Need the Help of the Urim and Thummim?" in *Evidences and Reconciliations* (Salt Lake City, UT: Bookcraft, 1960, 1987), Section III – Revelation, article 2 at https://www.cumorah.com/language/evidencesandreconciliations.html

Wightman, Gregory B., "Thy mind, o man: an interpretive biography of Joseph Smith as an adult learner," (PhD dissertation, University of Idaho, 2013)

Williams, Demetrius, "Using AI to Crack Ancient Languages," at https://www.translatemedia.com/us/blog-usa/using-ai-crack-ancient-languages/

Wirthlin, LeRoy S., "Joseph Smith's Boyhood Operation: An 1813 Surgical Success," *Brigham Young University Studies,* Vol. 21, no. 2 (Spring 1981), pp. 131–154 at https://scholarsarchive.byu.edu/cgi/viewcontent.cgi?article=2059&context=byusq

Wrather, Eva Jean, *Alexander Campbell: Adventurer in Freedom – a literary biography* (Ft. Worth, TX: TCU Press, 2009)

Young, Brigham, "The Kingdom of God" (July 13, 1862) in *Journal of Discourses* (Liverpool, UK: George Q. Cannon, 1862) volume 9, pp. 308-317 at https://jod.mrm.org/9/308

Young, Brigham, October 7, 1866, "Brigham Young Addresses, 1865—69," 5:116—19, Brigham Young Papers, LDS Church Library

Young, Brigham, "Building the Temple – Mormonism Embraces All Truth" (April 8, 1867) in *Journal of Discourses* (Liverpool, UK: B. Young, Jr. 1867) volume 11, pp. 371-375, at https://contentdm.lib.byu.edu/digital/collection/JournalOfDiscourses3/id/4388

Appendix A. Three Explanations for the Book of Mormon

Explanations of the origin of the Book of Mormon fall within one or more of three approaches: transcription, composition, and translation.

In the following table, unshaded boxes involve divine intervention. Dark shaded boxes involve no divine intervention. Light shaded boxes involve supernatural intervention that may or may not originate with the divine.

The transcription approaches are described and discussed in Chapters 1(C), 2(A), 2(G), 3(A) and 3(E).

Composition is the subject of Chapters 4 and 1(B).

Translation is introduced in Chapters 1(A) and 4(B). The nature of the translation approach is detailed in Chapter 5 and our specific proposed model of the translation process is laid out in Chapter 6.

TABLE 4 - BOOK OF MORMON ORIGIN THEORIES

Book of Mormon origin theories			
All theories can range from loose, tight, or iron-clad control			
Used the plates		Did not use the plates	
Curtain	No Curtain	Curtain	No Curtain (catalyst)
Translation. Joseph studied the characters, copied them, and translated them into English by means of the U&T that came with the plates, studying it out in his mind, using his own lexicon	**Translation.** Joseph learned the characters engraved on the plates and translated from behind the curtain, but also conducted one or more demonstrations using the seer stone in the hat	**Composition.** Joseph read the Spalding manuscript, supplemented with Rigdon's Christian sermons, except when conducting demonstrations	**Transcription.** In the presence of witnesses, Joseph read words that appeared on a seer stone (and/or the spectacles) that he placed in a hat, with the plates serving as a catalyst to the process
Transcription. Joseph looked on the plates with the U&T and dictated exact words from the U&T		**Composition.** Joseph and/or others composed the text, wrote it out, and read the manuscript	**Transcription.** Joseph read words that he saw in vision as he looked at a seer stone in a hat
			Transcription. Joseph dictated words that came into his mind
			Composition. Joseph recited a text he composed using memory clues or simple notes

Appendix B. Joseph and Oliver on the Translation (+ Lucy)

<u>Joseph Smith, Jr.</u> (translator and prophet)

1. Joseph Smith
1828. Martin Harris returned again to my house about the twelfth of April, eighteen hundred and twenty eight, and commenced writing for me, while I translated from the plates, which we continued until the fourteenth of June following, by which time he had written one hundred and sixteen pages of manuscript on foolscap paper. Some time after Mr. Harris had begun to write for me he began to teaze me to give him liberty to carry the writings home and shew them, and desired of me that I would enquire of the Lord through the Urim and Thummim if he might not do so. I did enquire, and the answer was that he must not… in the mean time while Martin Harris was gone with the writings, I went to visit my father's family at Manchester. I continued there for a short season and then returned to my place in Pennsylvania. Immediately after my return home I was walking out a little distance when behold the former heavenly messenger appeared and handed to me the Urim and Thummim again, (for it had been taken from me in consequence of my having wearied the Lord in asking for the privilege of letting Martin Harris take the writings which he lost by transgression,) and I enquired of the Lord through them and obtained the following revelation:

[D&C 3] Revelation to Joseph Smith, Jr. given July, 1828, concerning certain manuscripts on the first part of the book of Mormon, which had been taken from the possession of Martin Harris.

3 [current verse 8]. Behold, you have been intrusted with these things, but how strict were your commandments; and remember, also, the promises which were made to you…

5 [current verse 12]. And when thou deliveredst up that which God had given thee sight and power to translate, thou deliveredst up that which was sacred, into the hands of a wicked man…and this is the reason that thou hast lost thy privileges for a season, for thou

hast suffered the counsel of thy director to be trampled upon from the beginning.

6 [current verse 16]. Nevertheless my work shall go forth, for, inasmuch as the knowledge of a Saviour has come unto the world, through the testimony of the Jews, even so shall the knowledge of a Saviour come unto my people... and for this very purpose are these plates preserved which contain these records, that the promises of the Lord might be fulfilled, which he made to his people;

Also published in the *Times and Seasons* at https://www.josephsmithpapers.org/paper-summary/times-and-seasons-16-may-1842/4

2. Joseph Smith

March 1829 [D&C 5]. ... as my servant Martin Harris has desired a witness at my hand, that you, my servant Joseph Smith, jr. have got the plates of which you have testified and borne record that you have received of me... I the Lord am God, and have given these things unto you, my servant Joseph Smith, jr. and have commanded you that you shall stand as a witness of these things, and I have caused you that you should enter into a covenant with me that you should not show them except to those persons to whom I command you; and you have no power over them except I grant it unto you. And you have a gift to translate the plates; and this is the first gift that I bestowed upon you...

Verily I say unto you, that wo shall come unto the inhabitants of the earth if they will not hearken unto my words: for hereafter you shall be ordained and go forth and deliver my words unto the children of men. Behold if they will not believe my words, they would not believe you, my servant Joseph, if it were possible that you could show them all these things which I have committed unto you....

3 Behold verily, I say unto you, I have reserved those things which I have entrusted unto you, my servant Joseph, for a wise purpose in me, and it shall be made known unto future generations; but this generation shall have my word through you; in addition to your testimony the testimony of three of my servants, whom I shall call and

Appendix B

ordain, unto whom I will show these things: and they shall go forth with my words that are given through you, yea, they shall know of a surety that these things are true: for from heaven will I declare it unto them: I will give them power that they may behold and view these things as they are; and to none else will I grant this power, to receive this same testimony, among this generation, in this, the beginning of the rising up, and the coming forth of my church out of the wilderness—clear as the moon and fair as the sun, and terrible as an army with banners. And the testimony of three witnesses will I send forth of my word;

4 And now I command you, my servant Joseph, to repent and walk more uprightly before me, and yield to the persuasions of men no more...

5 ...if he [Harris] will bow down before me, and humble himself in mighty prayer and faith, in the sincerity of his heart, then will I grant unto him a view of the things which he desires to see. And then he shall say unto the people of this generation, behold I have seen the things which the Lord has shown unto Joseph Smith, jr. and I know of a surety that they are true, for I have seen them: for they have been shown unto me by the power of God and not of man.

And I the Lord command him, my servant Martin Harris, that he shall say no more unto them concerning these things, except he shall say I have seen them, and they have been shown unto me by the power of God: and these are the words which he shall say. But if he deny this he will break the covenant which he has before covenanted with me, and behold he is condemned. And now except he humble himself and acknowledge unto me the things that he has done which are wrong, and covenant with me that he will keep my commandments, and exercise faith in me, behold, I say unto him, he shall have no such views; for I will grant unto him no views of the things which I have spoken. And if this be the case I command you, my servant Joseph, that you shall say unto him, that he shall do no more, nor trouble me any more concerning this matter.

6 And if this be the case, behold I say unto thee Joseph, when thou hast translated a few more pages thou shalt stop for a season, even until I command thee again: then thou mayest translate again. And except thou do this, behold thou shalt have no more gift, and I will take away the things which I have intrusted with thee.

https://www.josephsmithpapers.org/paper-summary/doctrine-and-covenants-1835/166

3. Joseph Smith

April 1829. [D&C 6] Introduction: Revelation given to Joseph Smith the Prophet and Oliver Cowdery, at Harmony, Pennsylvania, April 1829. Oliver Cowdery began his labors as scribe in the translation of the Book of Mormon, April 7, 1829. He had already received a divine manifestation of the truth of the Prophet's testimony respecting the plates on which was engraved the Book of Mormon record. The Prophet inquired of the Lord through the Urim and Thummim and received this response.

… 10 Behold thou hast a gift, and blessed art thou because of thy gift. Remember it is sacred and cometh from above—

11 And if thou wilt inquire, thou shalt know mysteries which are great and marvelous; therefore thou shalt exercise thy gift, that thou mayest find out mysteries, that thou mayest bring many to the knowledge of the truth, yea, convince them of the error of their ways.

12 Make not thy gift known unto any save it be those who are of thy faith. Trifle not with sacred things.

15 Behold, thou knowest that thou hast inquired of me and I did enlighten thy mind; and now I tell thee these things that thou mayest know that thou hast been enlightened by the Spirit of truth;

16 Yea, I tell thee, that thou mayest know that there is none else save God that knowest thy thoughts and the intents of thy heart.

17 I tell thee these things as a witness unto thee—that the words or the work which thou hast been writing are true.

25 And, behold, I grant unto you a gift, if you desire of me, to translate, even as my servant Joseph.

26 Verily, verily, I say unto you, that there are records which contain much of my gospel, which have been kept back because of the wickedness of the people;

27 And now I command you, that if you have good desires—a desire to lay up treasures for yourself in heaven—then shall you assist in bringing to light, with your gift, those parts of my scriptures which have been hidden because of iniquity.

28 And now, behold, I give unto you, and also unto my servant Joseph, the keys of this gift, which shall bring to light this ministry; and in the mouth of two or three witnesses shall every word be established.

https://www.lds.org/scriptures/dc-testament/dc/6?lang=eng

4. Joseph Smith

April 1829. [D&C 7] Introduction: Revelation given to Joseph Smith the Prophet and Oliver Cowdery, at Harmony, Pennsylvania, April 1829, when they inquired through the Urim and Thummim as to whether John, the beloved disciple, tarried in the flesh or had died. The revelation is a translated version of the record made on parchment by John and hidden up by himself.

https://www.lds.org/scriptures/dc-testament/dc/7?lang=eng

5. Joseph Smith

April 1829. [D&C 8] A Revelation to Oliver [Cowdery] he being desirous to know whether the Lord would grant him the gift of Translation given in Harmony Susquehannah Pennsylvania.

Oliver Verily Verily I say unto you that as Shuredly as the Lord liveth which is your God & your Redeemer even so shure shall ye receive a knowledge of whatsoever things ye shall ask with an honest heart believeing that ye Shall receive, a knowledge concerning the engraveings of old Records which are ancient which contain those parts of my Scriptures of which hath been spoken by the manifestation of my Spirit yea

Behold I will tell you in your mind & in your heart by the Holy Ghost which Shall come upon you & which shall dwell in your heart now

Behold this is the spirit of Revelation Behold this is the spirit by which Moses brought the children of Israel through the red Sea on dry ground

therefore this is thy gift apply unto it & blessed art thou for [it] shall deliver you out of the hands of your enemies when if it were not so they would sley thee & bring thy soul to distruction

O remember these words & keep my commandments, remember this is thy gift

---

A. [Revelation Book 1] now this is not all for thou hast another gift which is the gift of working with the sprout

Behold it hath told you things

Behold there is no other power save God that can cause this thing of Nature to work in your hands for it is the work of God & therefore whatsoever ye shall ask to tell you by that means that will he grant unto you that ye shall know

B. [Book of Commandments 1835] Now this is not all, for you have another gift, which is the gift of working with the rod: behold it has told you things:

behold there is no other power save God, that can cause this rod of nature, to work in your hands, for it is the work of God; and therefore whatsoever you shall ask me to tell you by that means, that will I grant unto you, that you shall know.

C. [Doctrine and Covenants, current] 6 Now this is not all thy gift; for you have another gift, which is the gift of Aaron; behold, it has told you many things;

7 Behold, there is no other power, save the power of God, that can cause this gift of Aaron to be with you.

8 Therefore, doubt not, for it is the gift of God; and you shall hold it in your hands, and do marvelous works; and no power shall be able to take it away out of your hands, for it is the work of God.

9 And, therefore, whatsoever you shall ask me to tell you by that means, that will I grant unto you, and you shall have knowledge concerning it.

remember that without faith ye can do nothing trifle not with these things

do not ask for that which ye had not ought ask that ye may know the mysteries of God & that ye may Translate [and receive knowledge from] all those ancient Records which have been hid up which are Sacred & according to your faith shall it be done unto you

Behold it is I that have spoken it & I am the same which spake unto you from the begining amen

Revelation Book 1: https://www.josephsmithpapers.org/paper-summary/revelation-book-1/6

Book of Commandments: https://www.josephsmithpapers.org/paper-summary/book-of-commandments-1833/23

Doctrine and Covenants: https://www.lds.org/scriptures/dc-testament/dc/8?lang=eng

6. Joseph Smith

April 1829. [D&C 9] A Revelation to Oliver [Cowdery] he was disrous [desirous] to know the reason why he could not Translate <&> thus said the Lord unto him

Recd. in harmony Susquehannah County Pennsylvania

Behol[d] I say unto you my Son that because ye did not Translate according to that which ye desired of me & did commence again to write for my servent Joseph, even so I would that ye Should continue until ye have finished this Record which I have entrusted unto you & then Behold other Records have I that I will give unto you power that ye may assist to Translate

be patient my Son for it is wisdom in me & it is not expedient that ye should translate at this time Behold this is the work which ye are called to do is to write for my Servent & Behold it is because that ye did not continue as ye commenced when ye commenced to Translate that I have taken away this privilege from you

do not murmer my Son for it is wisdom in me that I have dealt with you after this manner Behold ye have not understood ye have

Supposed that I would give it unto you when ye took no thought save it was to ask me but Behold I say unto you that ye must study it out in your mind then ye must ask me if it be right & if it is right I will cause that your bosom shall burn within you therefore ye shall feel that it is right but if it be not right ye shall have no such feelings but ye shall have stupor of thought that shall cause you to forget the thing which is wrong there ye cannot write that which is sacred save it be given unto you [end of page, continuing with D&C] from me.

10 Now, if you had known this you could have translated; nevertheless, it is not expedient that you should translate now.

11 Behold, it was expedient when you commenced; but you feared, and the time is past, and it is not expedient now;

12 For, do you not behold that I have given unto my servant Joseph sufficient strength, whereby it is made up? And neither of you have I condemned.

13 Do this thing which I have commanded you, and you shall prosper. Be faithful, and yield to no temptation.

14 Stand fast in the work wherewith I have called you, and a hair of your head shall not be lost, and you shall be lifted up at the last day. Amen.

Revelation Book 1: https://www.josephsmithpapers.org/paper-summary/revelation-book-1/8

D&C: https://www.lds.org/scriptures/dc-testament/dc/9?lang=eng

7. Joseph Smith
Summer 1828-May 1829 [D&C 10].

1 Now, behold, I say unto you, that because you delivered up those writings which you had power given unto you to translate by the means of the Urim and Thummim, into the hands of a wicked man, you have lost them.

2 And you also lost your gift at the same time, and your mind became darkened.

3 Nevertheless, it is now restored unto you again; therefore see that you are faithful and continue on unto the finishing of the remainder of the work of translation as you have begun.

Appendix B

4 Do not run faster or labor more than you have strength and means provided to enable you to translate; but be diligent unto the end...

7 And for this cause I said that he is a wicked man, for he has sought to take away the things wherewith you have been entrusted; and he has also sought to destroy your gift....

15 For behold, he has put it into their hearts to get thee to tempt the Lord thy God, in asking to translate it over again.

16 And then, behold, they say and think in their hearts—We will see if God has given him power to translate; if so, he will also give him power again;

17 And if God giveth him power again, or if he translates again, or, in other words, if he bringeth forth the same words, behold, we have the same with us, and we have altered them;

18 Therefore they will not agree, and we will say that he has lied in his words, and that he has no gift, and that he has no power...

29 Now, behold, they have altered these words, because Satan saith unto them: He hath deceived you—and thus he flattereth them away to do iniquity, to get thee to tempt the Lord thy God.

30 Behold, I say unto you, that you shall not translate again those words which have gone forth out of your hands;

31 For, behold, they shall not accomplish their evil designs in lying against those words. For, behold, if you should bring forth the same words they will say that you have lied and that you have pretended to translate, but that you have contradicted yourself.

32 And, behold, they will publish this, and Satan will harden the hearts of the people to stir them up to anger against you, that they will not believe my words...

38 And now, verily I say unto you, that an account of those things that you have written, which have gone out of your hands, is engraven upon the plates of Nephi;

39 Yea, and you remember it was said in those writings that a more particular account was given of these things upon the plates of Nephi.

40 And now, because the account which is engraven upon the plates of Nephi is more particular concerning the things which, in my wisdom, I would bring to the knowledge of the people in this account—

41 Therefore, you shall translate the engravings which are on the plates of Nephi, down even till you come to the reign of king Benjamin, or until you come to that which you have translated, which you have retained;

42 And behold, you shall publish it as the record of Nephi; and thus I will confound those who have altered my words....

44 Behold, they have only got a part, or an abridgment of the account of Nephi.

45 Behold, there are many things engraven upon the plates of Nephi which do throw greater views upon my gospel; therefore, it is wisdom in me that you should translate this first part of the engravings of Nephi, and send forth in this work.

46 And, behold, all the remainder of this work does contain all those parts of my gospel which my holy prophets, yea, and also my disciples, desired in their prayers should come forth unto this people.

47 And I said unto them, that it should be granted unto them according to their faith in their prayers;

48 Yea, and this was their faith—that my gospel, which I gave unto them that they might preach in their days, might come unto their brethren the Lamanites, and also all that had become Lamanites because of their dissensions.

49 Now, this is not all—their faith in their prayers was that this gospel should be made known also, if it were possible that other nations should possess this land;

50 And thus they did leave a blessing upon this land in their prayers, that whosoever should believe in this gospel in this land might have eternal life;

51 Yea, that it might be free unto all of whatsoever nation, kindred, tongue, or people they may be.

52 And now, behold, according to their faith in their prayers will I bring this part of my gospel to the knowledge of my people. Behold, I do not bring it to destroy that which they have received, but to build it up....

62 Yea, and I will also bring to light my gospel which was ministered unto them, and, behold, they shall not deny that which you have received, but they shall build it up, and shall bring to light the true points of my doctrine, yea, and the only doctrine which is in me.

63 And this I do that I may establish my gospel, that there may not be so much contention; yea, Satan doth stir up the hearts of the people to contention concerning the points of my doctrine; and in these things they do err, for they do wrest the scriptures and do not understand them.

https://www.lds.org/scriptures/dc-testament/dc/10?lang=eng

Appendix B

8. Joseph Smith
1829-June.

[D&C 14-16] Introduction. [D&C 14] and the two following (sections 15 and 16) were given in answer to an inquiry through the Urim and Thummim.

[D&C 17] Introduction. Revelation given through Joseph Smith the Prophet to Oliver Cowdery, David Whitmer, and Martin Harris, at Fayette, New York, June 1829, prior to their viewing the engraved plates that contained the Book of Mormon record. Joseph and his scribe, Oliver Cowdery, had learned from the translation of the Book of Mormon plates that three special witnesses would be designated (see Ether 5:2–4; 2 Nephi 11:3; 27:12). Oliver Cowdery, David Whitmer, and Martin Harris were moved upon by an inspired desire to be the three special witnesses. The Prophet inquired of the Lord, and this revelation was given in answer through the Urim and Thummim.

1 Behold, I say unto you, that you must rely upon my word, which if you do with full purpose of heart, you shall have a view of the plates, and also of the breastplate, the sword of Laban, the Urim and Thummim, which were given to the brother of Jared upon the mount, when he talked with the Lord face to face, and the miraculous directors which were given to Lehi while in the wilderness, on the borders of the Red Sea.

2 And it is by your faith that you shall obtain a view of them, even by that faith which was had by the prophets of old...

5 And ye shall testify that you have seen them, even as my servant Joseph Smith, Jun., has seen them; for it is by my power that he has seen them, and it is because he had faith.

6 And he has translated the book, even that part which I have commanded him, and as your Lord and your God liveth it is true.

https://www.lds.org/scriptures/dc-testament/dc/17.1?lang=eng&clang=eng#p1

9. Joseph Smith

1829. I would inform you that I translated, by the gift and power of God, and caused to be written, one hundred and sixteen pages, the which I took from the Book of Lehi, which was an account abridged from the plates of Lehi, by the hand of Mormon;

(Preface to the Book of Mormon, circa August 1829) at https://www.josephsmithpapers.org/paper-summary/preface-to-book-of-mormon-circa-august-1829/1)

10. Joseph Smith

1830-April [D&C 20:8-11] 8 And gave him power from on high, by the means which were before prepared, to translate the Book of Mormon; 9 Which contains a record of a fallen people, and the fulness of the gospel of Jesus Christ to the Gentiles and to the Jews also; 10 Which was given by inspiration, and is confirmed to others by the ministering of angels, and is declared unto the world by them—11 Proving to the world that the holy scriptures are true, and that God does inspire men and call them to his holy work in this age and generation, as well as in generations of old;.

11. Joseph Smith

1832. [Martin Harris] returned to me [from New York] and gave them to <me to> translate and I said [I] cannot for I am not learned but the Lord had prepared spectacles for to read the Book therefore I commenced translating the characters and thus the Prop[h]icy of Isaiah was fulfilled. (History, circa Summer 1832)

https://www.josephsmithpapers.org/paper-summary/history-circa-summer-1832/5

12. Joseph Smith

1833. The Book of Mormon is a record of the forefathers of our western tribes of Indians; having been found through the ministration of an holy angel, and translated into our own language by the gift and power of God. (Letter to Noah C. Saxton, 4 January 1833) https://www.josephsmithpapers.org/paper-summary/letter-to-noah-c-saxton-4-january-1833/4

13. Joseph Smith

1835. [The Angel told me] that the Urim and Thumim, was hid up with the record, and that God would give me power to translate it, with the assistance of this instrument....

The Angel told me, that the reason why I could not obtain the plates at this time [1823], was because I was under transgression, but to come again in one year from that time. I did so but did not obtain them, also the third and the fourth year the last of which time I obtained them, and translated them into <the> english language by the gift and power of God and have been preaching it ever since. (Interview, 9 November 1835)

https://www.josephsmithpapers.org/paper-summary/conversations-with-robert-matthews-9-11-november-1835/4 and https://www.josephsmithpapers.org/paper-summary/history-1834-1836/125

14. Joseph Smith

1838. How, and where did you obtain the book of Mormon?

Moroni, the person who deposited the plates, from whence the book of Mormon was translated, in a hill in Manchester, Ontario County, New York, being dead; and raised again therefrom, appeared unto me, and told me where they were, and gave me directions how to obtain them. I obtained them, and the Urim and Thummim with them, by the means of which, I translated the plates; and thus came the Book of Mormon. (*Elders' Journal*, July 1838)

https://www.josephsmithpapers.org/paper-summary/elders-journal-july-1838/10

15. Joseph Smith

1839 – 1841. [The messenger] said there was a book deposited written upon gold plates, giving an account of the former inhabitants of this continent and the source from whence they sprang. He also said that the fullness of the everlasting Gospel was contained in it as delivered by the Saviour to the ancient inhabitants. Also that there were two stones in silver bows and these put into a breast plate which constituted what is called the Urim & Thummin deposited with the plates, and that was what constituted seers in ancient or former times and that God <had> prepared them for the purpose of translating the book.

https://www.josephsmithpapers.org/paper-summary/history-circa-june-1839-circa-1841-draft-2/5

16. Joseph Smith

1841. I wish also to mention here, that the title page of the Book of Mormon is a literal translation, taken from the very last leaf, on the left hand side of the collection or book of plates, which contained the record which has been translated; the language of the whole running the same as all Hebrew writing in general; and that, said title page is not by any means a modern composition either of mine or of any other man's who has lived or does live in this generation. Therefore, in order to correct an error which generally exists concerning it, I give below that part of the title page of the English version of the Book of Mormon, which is a genuine and literal translation of the title page of the Original Book of Mormon, as recorded on the plates. (*Times and Seasons* III.24:943 ¶4)

https://www.josephsmithpapers.org/paper-summary/history-circa-1841-fair-copy/60

17. Joseph Smith

1842. These records were engraven on plates which had the appearance of gold, each plate was six inches wide and eight inches long, and not quite so thick as common tin. They were filled with engravings, in Egyptian characters and bound together in a volume as the leaves of a book, with three rings running through the whole. The volume was something near six inches in thickness, a part of which was sealed. The characters on the unsealed part were small, and beautifully engraved. The whole book exhibited many marks of antiquity in its construction, and much skill in the art of engraving. With the records was found a curious instrument, which the ancients called "Urim and Thummim," which consisted of two transparent stones set in the rim of a bow fastened to a breast plate. Through the medium of the Urim and

Thummim I translated the record by the gift and power of God. ("Church History," [aka the Wentworth Letter], *Times and Seasons*, March 1, 1842)
https://www.josephsmithpapers.org/paper-summary/church-history-1-march-1842/2

18. Joseph Smith
1842. JS-H 1:35. He [Moroni] said there were two stones in silver bows—and these stones, fastened to a breastplate, constituted what is called the Urim and Thummim—deposited with the plates; and the possession and use of these stones were what constituted "seers" in ancient or former times; and that God had prepared them for the purpose of translating the book.

42 Again, he told me, that when I got those plates of which he had spoken—for the time that they should be obtained was not yet fulfilled—I should not show them to any person; neither the breastplate with the Urim and Thummim; only to those to whom I should be commanded to show them; if I did I should be destroyed....

62 By this timely aid was I enabled to reach the place of my destination in Pennsylvania; and immediately after my arrival there I commenced copying the characters off the plates. I copied a considerable number of them, and by means of the Urim and Thummim I translated some of them, which I did between the time I arrived at the house of my wife's father, in the month of December, and the February following.
https://www.lds.org/scriptures/pgp/js-h/1?lang=eng

19. Joseph Smith
1843. SIR:—Through the medium of your paper, I wish to correct an error.... The error I speak of, is the definition of the word "MORMON." It has been stated that this word was derived from the Greek word mormo. This is not the case. There was no Greek or Latin upon the plates from which I, through the grace of God, translated the Book of Mormon.... Here then the subject is put to silence, for "none other people knoweth our language," [Morm. 9:34] therefore the Lord, and not man, had to interpret, after the people were all dead.
https://www.josephsmithpapers.org/paper-summary/letter-to-editor-circa-15-may-1843/1

20. Joseph Smith

1843, Nov. 13. [T]he fact is, that by the power of God I translated the Book of Mormon from hieroglyphics, the knowledge of which was lost to the world, in which wonderful event I stood alone, an unlearned youth, to combat the worldly wisdom and multiplied ignorance of eighteen centuries, with a new revelation, which (if they would receive the everlasting Gospel,) would open the eyes of more than eight hundred millions of people, and make "plain the old paths," wherein if a man walk in all the ordinances of God blameless, he shall inherit eternal life. (letter, Nov. 13, 1843, in *History, 1838-1856, Vol. E-1*)

https://www.josephsmithpapers.org/paper-summary/history-1838-1856-volume-e-1-1-july-1843-30-april-1844/147 and https://www.josephsmithpapers.org/paper-summary/letter-to-james-arlington-bennet-13-november-1843/2

Appendix B

<u>Oliver Cowdery</u> (scribe and witness)

21. Oliver Cowdery
1829, Nov. 9. Now Joseph Smith Jr., certainly was the writer of the work, called the book of Mormon, which was written in ancient Egyptian characters,--which was a dead record to us until translated. **And he, by a gift from God, has translated it into our language**…. This record which gives an account of the first inhabitants of this continent, is engraved on plates, which have the appearance of gold; and they are of very curious workmanship…. And after that which was not sealed, was translated, the book should again be hid-up, unto the Lord, that it might not be destroyed; and come forth again, in the own due time of him, who knows all things unto the children of men.
(Letter Oliver H.P. Cowdery to Cornelius, C. Blatchly, Nov. 9, 1829, Gospel Luminary 2, no. 49 (Dec. 10, 1829): 194, in the Juvenile Instructor (blog), August 21, 2012, https://juvenileinstructor.org/1829-mormon-discovery-brought-to-you-by-guest-erin-jennings/)

22. Oliver Cowdery
1834. On Tuesday the 7th [I] commenced to write the Book of Mormon. These were days never to be forgotten to sit under the sound of a voice dictated by the inspiration of heaven, awakened the utmost gratitude of this bosom! Day after day I continued, uninterrupted, to write from his mouth, as he translated, with the Urim and Thummim, or, as the Nephites would have said, "Interpreters," the history or record called "The book of Mormon." (*Messenger and Advocate*, 1:14)
https://www.josephsmithpapers.org/paper-summary/history-1834-1836/49, also in the Pearl of Great Price, Joseph Smith – History 1:71 footnote at https://www.lds.org/scriptures/pgp/js-h/1?lang=eng

23. The Three Witnesses (*Oliver Cowdery, Martin Harris, & David Whitmer*)
1829. [We], through the grace of God the Father, and our Lord Jesus Christ, have seen the plates which contain this record, which

is a record of the people of Nephi, and also of the Lamanites, their brethren, and also of the people of Jared, who came from the tower of which hath been spoken. And we also know that they have been translated by the gift and power of God, for his voice hath declared it unto us; wherefore we know of a surety that the work is true. ("Testimony of the Three Witnesses")
https://www.lds.org/scriptures/bofm/three?lang=eng

24. Oliver Cowdery *(newspaper report)*
1831 April 9. "During the trial it was shown that the Book of Mormon was brought to light by the same magic power by which he pretended to tell fortunes, discover hidden treasures, &c. Oliver Cowdery, one of the three witnesses to the book, testified under oath, that said Smith found with the plates, from which he translated his book, two transparent stones, resembling glass, set in silver bows. That by looking through these, he was able to read in English, the reformed Egyptian characters, which were engraved on the plates.

So much for the gift and power of God, by which Smith says he translated his book. Two transparent stones, undoubtedly of the same properties, and the gift of the same spirit as the one in which he looked to find his neighbor's goods.

("Mormonites," Evangelical Magazine and Gospel Advocate, Utica, NY, April 9, 1831) at http://www.sidneyrigdon.com/dbroadhu/NY/miscNYSe.htm#040931

25. Evangelical Magazine reporting on Oliver Cowdery *(hostile magazine report)*
1831. Oliver Cowdery, one of the three witnesses to the book, testified under oath [during the June 1830 Colesville trials], that said Smith found with the plates, from which he translated his book, **two** transparent stones, resembling glass, set in silver bows. That by looking through these, he was able to read in English, the reformed Egyptian characters, which were engraved on the plates. (*Evangelical Magazine and Gospel Advocate*, 9 April 1831. Note: that this is quoted by an unbeliever, in an antagonistic magazine, in a spirit of incredulity adds to the force of Oliver's statement)
http://www.olivercowdery.com/smithhome/1877Purp.htm

26. Oliver Cowdery *(Reported by Reuben Miller)*

1848. [Oliver said:] Friends and brethren my name is Cowdrey, Oliver Cowdrey, In the early history of this church I stood Identified with her. And [was] one in her councils.... I wrote with my own pen the intire book of mormon (Save a few pages) as it fell from the Lips of the prophet [Joseph Smith]. As he translated <it> by the gift and power of god, By [the] means of the urum and thummim, or as it is called by that book holy Interpreters. I beheld with my eyes. And handled with my hands the gold plates from which it was translated. I also beheld the Interperters. That book is true. Sidney Rigdon did not write it. Mr [Solomon] Spaulding did not write it. I wrote it myself as it fell from the Lips of the prophet.

Reuben Miller Journal 1848, at https://catalog.churchofjesuschrist.org/assets/22222322-f4fe-41e3-aa86-bfc54b94df92/0/16

Also cited in Richard Lloyd Anderson, "By the Gift and Power of God," *Ensign*, September 1977, online at https://www.churchofjesuschrist.org/study/ensign/1977/09/by-the-gift-and-power-of-god?lang=eng and John W. Welch (ed.), *Opening the Heavens: Accounts of Divine Manifestations 1820-1844* (Provo and Salt Lake City, UT: BYU Press/Deseret Book, 2005), p. 143.

27. Oliver Cowdery *(Reported by Samuel W. Richards)*

1848. (Reported in 1907) "[Oliver] represented Joseph as sitting at a table with the plates before him, translating them by means of the Urim and Thummim, while he (Oliver) sat beside him writing every word as Joseph spoke them to him. This was done by holding the 'translators' over the hieroglyphics, the translation appearing distinctly on the instrument, which had been touched by the finger of God and dedicated and consecrated for the express purpose of translating languages. Every word was distinctly visible even to every letter; and if Oliver omitted a word or failed to spell a word correctly, the translation remained on the 'interpreter' until it was copied correctly."

https://www.lds.org/study/ensign/1977/09/by-the-gift-and-power-of-god?lang=eng

Note: the differences between this typewritten account and the original handwritten account are discussed in chapter 3 of *A Man That Can Translate*.

Lucy Mack Smith (mother of Joseph Smith, Jr.)

28. Lucy Mack Smith
1827 [recorded in 1844-5] Mother said he do not be uneasy all is right see here Said he I have got the key I knew not what he meant but took the article in my hands and upon after examing it <*> <(*with no covering but a silk handkerchief)> <found> that it consisted of 2 smooth <3 cornered diamonds set in glass and the glass was set in silver bows> con[n]ected with each other in the same way that old fashioned spectacles are made…
https://www.josephsmithpapers.org/paper-summary/lucy-mack-smith-history-1844-1845/61

The thing which spoke of it had that Joseph termed a Key was indeed nothing more nor less than a urim and Thummim by which the angel manifested those things to <him> that were shown him in vision by the which also he could at any time ascertain the approach of danger Either to himself or the record and for this cause he kept these things constantly about his person.
https://www.josephsmithpapers.org/paper-summary/lucy-mack-smith-history-1844-1845/69

29. Lucy Mack Smith (*interviewed by Henry Caswall*)
1842 The angel of the Lord appeared to him fifteen years since, and shewed him the cave where the original golden plates of the book of Mormon were deposited. He shewed him also the Urim and Thummim, by which he might understand the meaning of the inscriptions on the plates, and he shewed him the golden breastplate of the high priesthood. My son received these precious gifts, he interpreted the holy record, and now the believers in that revelation are more than a hundred thousand in number.

I have myself seen and handled the golden plates; they are about eight inches long, and six wide; some of them are sealed together and are not to be opened, and some of them are loose. They are all connected by a ring which passes through a hole at the end of each plate, and are covered with letters beautifully engraved. I have seen and felt also the Urim and Thummim. They resemble two large bright diamonds set in a bow like a pair of spectacles. My son puts these over his eyes when he reads unknown languages, and they enable him to interpret them in English. I have likewise carried in my hands the sacred breastplate. It is composed of pure gold, and is made to fit the breast very exactly.

Henry Caswall, *The City of the Mormons; or, Three Days at Nauvoo*, in 1842 (London: J. G. F. and J. Rivington, 1842), 26–27, online at https://archive.org/details/cityofmormonsort00casw/page/26

30. Lucy Mack Smith
1845. [Sept-Nov 1828] For nearly two months after Joseph returned to his family in Pennsylvania we heard nothing from him; and becoming anxious about him, Mr. Smith [Joseph Smith Sr.] and myself set off to make him a visit. When we came withing [sic] three quarters of a mile of his house, Joseph started to meet us; telling his wife as he left, that "Father and mother were coming."

When he met us his countenance wore so pleasant an aspect, that I was convinced he had something agreeable to communicate, in relation to the work in which he was engaged. And when I entered his house the first thing that attracted my attention was a red morocco trunk, that set on Emma's bureau; which trunk Joseph shortly informed me, contained the Urim and Thummim and the plates.

In the evening he gave us the following relation of what had transpired since our separation: "After leaving you' said Joseph, "I returned immediately home; and soon after my travel which, I commenced humbling myself in mighty prayer before the Lord; and, as I was pouring out my soul to God, that, if possible I might obtain mercy at his hands, and be forgiven of all that I had done contrary to his will, an angel stood before me and answered me, saying, that I had sinned in delivering the manuscript into the hands of a wicked man; and, and as I had ventured to become responsible for his faithfulness, I would of necessity have to suffer the consequences of his indiscretion; and must now give up the Urim and Thummim into his (the angels) hands. This I did as I was directed. As I handed them to him, he said, 'If you are very jumble and penitent, it may be you will receive them again; if so, it will be on the 22d. of next September.'"...

"After the angel left me', said he, "I continued my supplications to God without cessation; and, on the 22d of September, I had the joy and satisfaction of again receiving the Urim and Thummim; and have commenced translating again, and Emma writes for me; but the angel said that the Lord would send me a scribe, and <I> trust his promise will be verified. The angel He also seemed pleased with me, when he gave me back the Urim and Thummim; and he told me that the Lord loved me, for my faithfulness and humility...

https://www.josephsmithpapers.org/paper-summary/lucy-mack-smith-history-1845/142

31. Lucy Mack Smith
1844-5. [May 1829] In the meantime Joseph was 150 miles distant and knew naught of the matter except an intimation that was given through the urim and thumim for as he one morning applied them to his eyes to look upon the record instead of the words of the book being given him he was commanded to write a letter to one David Whitmer this man Joseph had never seen but he was instructed to say him that he must come with his team immediately in order to convey Joseph and his family Oliver [Cowdery] back to his house which was 135 miles that they might remain with him there untill the translation should be completed for that an evil designing people were seeking to take away Joseph's life in order to prevent the work of God from going forth among the world.

https://www.josephsmithpapers.org/paper-summary/lucy-mack-smith-history-1844-1845/100

32. Lucy Mack Smith
1845. [May 1829] Not far from this time, as Joseph was translating by means of the Urim and Thummim, he received instead of the words of the Book, a commandment to write a letter to a man by the name of David Whitmer, who lived in Waterloo; requesting him to come immediately with his team, and convey them [3 words illegible] (Joseph & Oliver) to Waterloo; as an evil designing people were seeking to take away his (Joseph's life), in order to prevent the work of God from going forth to the world.

https://www.josephsmithpapers.org/paper-summary/lucy-mack-smith-history-1845/156

Appendix C. Translation and the Critics

Critics have long questioned Joseph's claim that he translated the plates. In this Appendix, we briefly address the most common criticisms from two widely known sources, one old and one recent. The old one is the 1834 book *Mormonism Unvailed* and the modern one is from the online document known as the "CES Letter."

Mormonism Unvailed (https://www.mormonismi.net/pdf/Mormonism_Unvailed_Howe.pdf)

In 1834, Ebert Howe published the book *Mormonism Unvailed* that sought to discredit Joseph Smith and the Book of Mormon. The book supplied many of the basic arguments and evidence against the Mormons that have been used ever since.

Regarding the translation, the book discusses the alternative explanations that prevailed in 1834, including SITH. But ultimately the book explains the Book of Mormon as the creation of Solomon Spalding, claiming that Spalding's novel was edited to add Christian content and then read by Joseph Smith from behind a curtain or "vail."

In response to *Mormonism Unvailed*, Oliver Cowdery wrote the essay, published as Letter I in the LDS newspaper *Messenger and Advocate*, a key excerpt from which is now found in a note to Joseph Smith-History. Oliver Cowdery describes these events thus: "These were days never to be forgotten—to sit under the sound of a voice dictated by the inspiration of heaven, awakened the utmost gratitude of this bosom! Day after day I continued, uninterrupted, to write from his mouth, as he translated with the Urim and Thummim, or, as the Nephites would have said, 'Interpreters,' the history or record called 'The Book of Mormon.' (Joseph Smith—History, Note 1)

Oliver's explanation not only refutes the claims of *Mormonism Unvailed*, but also contradicts the future claims by the SITH witnesses such as David Whitmer and Emma Smith Bidamon. Our comments follow the quotations.

p. 17. The plates in the mean time were concealed from human view, the prophet declaring that no man could look upon them and live. They at the same time gave out that, along with the plates, was found a huge pair of silver spectacles, altogether too large for the present race of men, but which were to be used, nevertheless, in translating the plates.

>Comment: The source for the comment about the size of the spectacles is not specified here, but may be the 1829 articles such as the one in the Rochester Advertiser and Daily Telegraph which reported that "the Bible was found, together with a huge pair of spectacles." Joseph's brother William said Joseph "could only see through one at a time using sometimes one and sometimes the other." Of course, William was not present for any of the translation, so his statement is necessarily hearsay.

p. 18. The translation finally commenced. They were found to contain a language not now known upon the earth which they termed "reformed Egyptian characters." The plates, therefore, which had been so much talked of, were found to be of no manner of use. After all, the Lord showed and communicated to him every word and letter of the Book. Instead of looking at the characters inscribed upon the plates, the prophet was obliged to resort to the old "peep stone," which he formerly used in money-digging. This he placed in a hat, or box, into which he also thrust his face. Through the stone he could then discover a single word at a time, which he repeated aloud to his amanuensis, who committed it to paper, when another word would immediately appear, and thus the performance continued to the end of the book.

>Comment. This statement of the SITH process is essentially what critics and many LDS historians today claim is the reality of the translation. As we saw above, Oliver Cowdery explicitly rejected this

explanation by declaring that Joseph used the Nephite interpreters, which he called the Urim and Thummim.

Another account they give of the translation, is, that it was performed with the big spectacles before mentioned, and which were in fact, the identical Urim and Thumim mentioned in Exodus 28 - 30, and were brought away from Jerusalem by the heroes of the book, handed down from one generation to another, and finally buried up in Ontario county, some fifteen centuries since, to enable Smith to translate the plates without looking at them!

> Comment. Here, *Mormonism Unvailed* makes a clear distinction between the "peep stone" and the Urim and Thummim. Neither Joseph nor any of his associates claimed the Urim and Thummim he used to translate the plates was the same object mentioned in Exodus; that was a misunderstanding on the part of *Mormonism Unvailed*. But the distinction made here is a distinction without a difference in the sense that *Mormonism Unvailed* claimed that even if Joseph used the Urim and Thummim, he still translated the plates without looking at them.

p. 20. It is necessary that the reader should constantly bear in mind, that the impostor is held out to be a very ignorant person, so much so, that he can write nothing except it be dictated to him, word by word, by the mouth of the Lord.

> Comment. This is the common apologetic argument that sought to promote the inspired origin of the Book of Mormon by diminishing the abilities of Joseph Smith. The more ignorant Joseph was, the more impressive the Book of Mormon seemed. The "word by word" concept reflects the transcription argument. As we've discussed in this book, Joseph's freedom to make subsequent changes to the text, as well as errors in the original manuscript, contradict the theory of a "word by word" dictation.

p. 77. We are presented with another method of translating the plates -- possibly the spectacles may get lost, or they may not suit the eyes of all. "And the Lord said, I will prepare unto my servant Gazelam, a stone, which shall shine forth in darkness unto light, that I may discover unto my people which serve me, that I may discover unto them the works of their brethren; yea, their secret works, their works of darkness and abominations."

Now, whether the two methods for translating, one by a pair of stone spectacles "set in the rims of a bow," and the other by one stone, were provided against accident, we cannot determine ... at all events the plan meets our approbation.

We are informed that Smith used a stone in a hat, for the purpose of translating the plates. The spectacles and plates were found together, but were taken from him and hid up again before he had translated one word, and he has never seen them since -- this is Smith's own story.

> Comment. This points out the contradiction between what David Whitmer claimed—that Joseph didn't have the Urim and Thummim after the 116 pages were lost—and the statements by Oliver, Joseph, and Lucy Mack Smith that Joseph did use the Urim and Thummim to translate the Book of Mormon we have today. *Mormonism Unvailed* claims "this is Smith's own story" but there is no record that Joseph ever said or implied that he lost the Urim and Thummim, except temporarily.

Let us ask, what use have the plates been or the spectacles, so long as they have in no sense been used? or what does the testimony of Martin Harris, Oliver Cowdery and David Whitmer amount to? They solemnly swear that they saw the plates, and that an angel showed them, and the engravings which were upon them. But if the plates were hid by the angel so that they have not been seen since, how do these witnesses know that when Smith translated out of a hat, with a peep-stone, that the contents of the plates were repeated and written down? Neither of the witnesses pretend that they could read the hieroglyphics

Appendix C

with or without the stone; and, therefore, are not competent testimony – nor can we see any use, either in finding the plates or the spectacles, nor of the exhibition of them.

> Comment. If Joseph didn't actually translate the engravings on the plates, but instead used the plates as a sort of talisman, then any testimony by witnesses of the existence of the plates would not be a witness of the validity of the translation. While it's also true that if the witnesses could not read the engravings, they wouldn't know whether the translation was accurate, their testimony would at least corroborate Joseph's claim that he translated from engraved plates.

p. 278. We proposed in the commencement of this work, to give to the world all the light, of which we were in possession, as to the real and original author or authors of the Book of Mormon. That there has been, from the beginning of the imposture, a more talented knave behind the curtain, is evident to our mind, at least; but whether he will ever be clearly, fully and positively unvailed and brought into open daylight, may of course be doubted. For no person of common prudence and understanding, it may well be presumed, would ever undertake such a speculation upon human credulity, without closing and well securing every door and avenue to a discovery, step by step, as he proceeded. Hence, our investigations upon the subject have necessarily been more limited than was desirable. At the same time, we think that facts and data have been elicited, sufficient at least to raise a strong presumption that the leading features of the "Gold Bible" were first conceived and concocted by one SOLOMON SPALDING, while a resident of Conneaut, Ashtabula county, Ohio.

> Comment. The Spalding theory was only viable to the extent that Joseph translated from behind a curtain or screen. If, as the SITH witnesses claimed, Joseph produced the entire Book of Mormon by dictating with his face in a hat, then there would be no basis for the Spalding theory. In our view, the principal motivation for the SITH witnesses was to refute the Spalding theory.

The CES Letter https://read.cesletter.org/bom-translation/

The CES Letter book and web page was written by Jeremy Runnels. It started out with questions Runnels asked his Institute teacher. When he didn't get a response, he expanded his original letter into a comprehensive compilation of skeptical and critical challenges to the claims of the Restoration.

Below is the section of the CES Letter that focuses on the translation of the Book of Mormon, again with our commentary indented.

"BOOK OF MORMON TRANSLATION
Concerns & Questions

Runnels begins with an excerpt purportedly from a podcast in 2010.

"I will begin by saying that we still have pictures on our Ward bulletin boards of Joseph Smith with the Gold Plates in front of him. That has become an irksome point and I think it is something the church should pay attention to. Because anyone who studies the history knows that is not what happened. There is no church historian who says that is what happened and yet it is being propagated by the church and it feeds into the notion that the church is trying to cover up embarrassing episodes and is sort of prettifying its own history.

"So, I think we ought to just stop that immediately. I am not sure we need a lot of pictures in our chapels of Joseph looking into his hat, but we certainly should tell our children that is how it worked... It's weird. It's a weird picture. It implies it's like darkening a room when we show slides. It implies that there is an image appearing in that stone and the light would make it more difficult to see that image. So, that implies a translation that's a reading and so gives us a little clue about the whole translation process. It also raises the strange question, 'What in the world are the plates for? Why do we need them on the table if they are just wrapped up into a cloth while he looks into a seer stone?'"

Appendix C

— Richard Bushman, LDS Scholar, Historian, Patriarch, Fairmormon Podcast, Episode 3: Richard L. Bushman P.1, 47:25

Comment. These informal observations from many years ago by Richard Bushman reflect his assumption that the SITH accounts were accurate not only because of what the witnesses observed, but also because of what they assumed or inferred. However, people who study the history look at the identical evidence and reach different conclusions, as we have in this book.

If it is true that no church historian today says Joseph translated the plates, that's not a function of the historical evidence but instead is a product of a consensus interpretation of the evidence. As we've shown in this book, the historical evidence also supports the thesis that whatever Joseph did with the stone in the hat, it was not the translation. There is no specific evidence that whatever words Joseph dictated while looking into the hat are found in the published Book of Mormon. Even if the words he dictated using SITH are in the text, they could have come from Joseph reciting biblical passages from memory, such as the Isaiah chapters in Second Nephi.

Professor Bushman's concluding questions about the plates illustrate the speculative nature of the SITH theory. If Joseph didn't use the plates to translate, as he and Oliver said he did, then the narrative about the plates is difficult to explain or justify. But that narrative is rational and supported by the historical evidence if we accept what Joseph and Oliver said.

"Unlike the story I've been taught in Sunday School, Priesthood, General Conferences, Seminary, EFY, Ensigns, Church history tour, Missionary Training Center, and BYU... Joseph Smith used a rock in a hat for translating the Book of Mormon."

Comment. Here, Runnels relates SITH as a fact, instead of the mere interpretation that it is.

"In other words, Joseph used the same magic device or "Ouija Board" that he used during his treasure hunting days. He put a rock – called a "peep stone" – in his hat and put his face in the hat to tell his customers the location of buried treasure on their property. He also used this same method for translating the Book of Mormon, while the gold plates were covered, placed in another room, or even buried in the woods. The gold plates were not used for the Book of Mormon we have today."

> Comment. Again, Runnels relates SITH as a fact, instead of the mere interpretation that it is.

"UPDATE: These facts are now officially confirmed in the Church's December 2013 Book of Mormon Translation essay. The Church later admitted these facts in its October 2015 Ensign, where they include a photograph of the actual rock that Joseph Smith used to place in his hat for the Book of Mormon translation. Additional photos of the rock can be viewed on lds.org. In June 2016, President Dieter F. Uchtdorf posted on his Facebook page comparing the seer stone in the hat Book of Mormon translation to his iPhone. FairMormon posted new Book of Mormon translation artwork showing Joseph Smith's face in a hat."

> Comment. Runnels makes a good point that the Gospel Topics Essay on Book of Mormon Translation does portray SITH as a fact. Of course, the essay was written by the same historians to whom Richard Bushman referred, reflecting a consensus interpretation among this group of historians about the historical evidence. However, the Gospel Topics essay never even quotes fully what Joseph and Oliver taught, let along explains their accounts. As we have shown in this book, the historical record, taken as a whole, does corroborate what Joseph and Oliver taught.
>
> Runnels' next point looks at how the translation is portrayed in art.

Appendix C

"BOOK OF MORMON TRANSLATION THAT THE CHURCH PORTRAYED AND STILL PORTRAYS TO ITS MEMBERS:

Comment. Here, Runnels shows artwork depicting Joseph using the plates, including the cover of an *Ensign* magazine. This artwork is based on scriptural passages as well as statements by Joseph and Oliver. For example, JS-H 1:62 explains, "I commence copying the characters off the plates, and by means of the Urim and Thummim I translated some of them." The Lord instructed Joseph: "you shall translate the engravings which are on the plates of Nephi" (D&C 10:41), which he could not do if the plates were covered. Oliver was authorized to translate as well: "25 And, behold, I grant unto you a gift, if you desire of me, to translate, even as my servant Joseph."

(D&C 6:25) Only one of these illustrations shows Joseph using the Urim and Thummim, possibly because artists were hesitant to speculate about what it looked like and how it worked.

"BOOK OF MORMON TRANSLATION AS IT ACTUALLY HAPPENED

Comment. Here, Runnels shows artwork depicting Joseph using SITH, based on the SITH accounts. Although these accounts contradict the scriptural explanations and the statements of Joseph and Oliver, Runnels claims the SITH accounts relate what "actually" happened. Based on that assumption, it is understandable "he would reach the conclusions he does.

Since learning this disturbing new information and feeling betrayed, I have been attacked and gaslighted by revisionist Mormon apologists claiming that it's my fault and the fault of anyone else for not knowing this. "The information was there all along," they say. "You should've known this," they claim."

> Comment. Runnels makes a valid point. The typical apologetic response by LDS scholars who promote SITH is to say that SITH was taught all along. While the SITH accounts were in the historical record if you knew to look for them, they were not easily available. The SITH apologists' response is uncharitable and counterproductive to the majority of believers who would not have known to look for, or where to find, these obscure sources.

"Respected LDS historian and scholar Richard Bushman, as quoted above, understands the problem. Unlike these gaslighting revisionist apologists, he has compassion, understanding, and empathy for those who are shocked to learn this faith challenging information."

> Comment. Again, as we have argued, SITH is shocking to the extent it contradicts what Joseph and Oliver taught, but it is not shocking when understood in context as just a scholarly theory with questionable support if one takes account of the full historical record as we have tried to do in this book.

"In 2000, two BYU religion professors, Joseph Fielding McConkie (son of Elder Bruce R. McConkie) and Craig J. Ostler, wrote an essay titled, "The Process of Translating the Book of Mormon." They wrote:

"Thus, everything we have in the Book of Mormon, according to Mr. Whitmer, was translated by placing the chocolate-colored stone in a hat into which Joseph would bury his head so as to close out the light. While doing so he could see 'an oblong piece of parchment, on which the hieroglyphics would appear,' and below the ancient writing, the translation would be given in English. Joseph would then read this to Oliver Cowdery, who in turn would write it. If he did so correctly, the characters and the interpretation would disappear and be replaced by other characters with their interpretation."

> Comment. Runnels is quoting Professors McConkie and Ostler out of context. Here they are only describing David Whitmer's accounts. However, their article goes on to question the accuracy of these accounts, as David himself admitted he was not present for most of the translation. The authors' actual views can be seen in the next section, which points out the problems with SITH.

"After laying the groundwork, the professors continue:
"Finally, the testimony of David Whitmer simply does not accord with the divine pattern. If Joseph Smith translated everything that is now in the Book of Mormon without using the gold plates, we are left to wonder why the plates were necessary in the first place. It will be remembered that possession of the plates placed the Smith family in considerable danger, causing them a host of difficulties. If the plates were not part of the translation process, this would not have been the case. It also leaves us wondering why the Lord directed the writers of the Book of Mormon to take a duplicate record of the plates of Lehi. This provision which compensated for the loss of the 116 pages would have served no purpose either.

Further, we would be left to wonder why it was necessary for Moroni to instruct Joseph each year for four years before he was entrusted with the plates. We would also wonder why it was so important for Moroni to show the plates to the three witnesses, including David Whitmer. And why did the Lord have the Prophet show the plates to the eight witnesses? Why all this flap and fuss if the Prophet didn't really have the plates and if they were not used in the process of translation?

"What David Whitmer is asking us to believe is that the Lord had Moroni seal up the plates and the means by which they were to be translated hundreds of years before they would come into Joseph Smith's possession and then decided to have the Prophet use a seer stone found while digging a well so that none of these things would be necessary after all. Is this, we would ask, really a credible explanation of the way the heavens operate?"

"How could it have been expected of me and any other member to know about and to embrace the rock in the hat translation when even these two faithful full-time professors of religion at BYU rejected it as a fictitious lie meant to undermine Joseph Smith and the truth claims of the Restoration?"

> Comment. Again, Runnels assumes SITH is the correct description of the translation, and he would be reasonable to object to the professors' rhetorical objections if that assumption were correct. However, as we have tried to show in this book (and as Professors McConkie and Ostler argue in the rest of their article, which Runnels does not quote) SITH is not the only available explanation. A close examination of the historical record, distinguishing between direct observations and witnesses' inferences and assumptions, combined with assessment of the context and motivations of the SITH witnesses, provides an alternative working hypothesis consistent with the canonical narrative of translation from the plates using the Jaredite/Nephite interpreters, which we believe offers a credible response to Runnels' SITH-based objections.

INDEX

Anderson, Ricard Lloyd, 17, 70, 76-77, 84, 87, 90, 101, 126, 160, 165, 176, 209-210, 215-216, 226, 255

Augustine of Hipppo, 132, 134, 210

Ballard, M. Russell, 139, 210

Blair, William W., 4, 49-51, 71-72, 211-212

Briggs, E. C., 193, 211

Brodie, Fawn M., 11, 131, 212

Bushman, Richard Lyman, vii, 2, 4, 16, 20, 33, 64, 83, 85, 101, 105, 134, 140, 160, 162, 199, 212, 265-266, 269

Campbell, Alexander, 130-131, 150, 172-173, 213, 215, 233

CES Letter, 259, 264-271

Clarke, Arthur C., 155-156, 213

Church of Jesus Christ of Latter-day Saints (LDS), ii, v, vii, 1-2, 14-16, 18, 20-21, 41, 48-49, 52, 54, 57, 66, 68, 99, 101, 114, 152, 172, 181, 206-207, 209, 225, 231, 234

Coe, Truman, 183, 213

Community of Christ, vii, 4, 38-39, 41, 44, 46, 49, 51-53, 55, 68, 81, 161, 215, 218, 221, 228

composition narrative, v, 4, 6, 10-12, 22-23, 25, 32, 109, 111-142, 162, 195-197, 235, 250

Cowdery, Oliver, i- iii, 1, 3, 5-6, 8-10, 13-15, 18-19, 28-30, 32, 35-36, 40-41, 44-47, 50, 58-59, 62-63, 68, 70-72, 74, 77-80, 82, 84-87, 91, 96-97, 99-104, 143, 152, 155-157, 160-162, 176-177, 179, 181-184, 193, 197, 200, 209, 213-215, 227, 237, 240-241, 243, 247, 253-255, 258-260, 262, 265-269

Cumorah, 3, 18, 66, 74, 127, 129, 177, 188, 201, 203, 222-223

Demonstration hypothesis, 80-86

Edwards, Jonathan, 26, 92, 109, 111, 121-124, 133, 137-139, 149-150, 169-170, 174, 208, 213, 215, 220, 222-223, 230

epic (Boof of Mormon as), 112, 126, 203

Fayette (New York), 28-29, 44, 69, 74, 84, 107, 122, 124, 193, 247

folk magic, 16-20, 83, 155-157, 199

formal equivalence, 191, 196

functional equivalence, 145, 191-192, 196

Godfrey, Kenneth, 69-73, 159, 216, 219

Götterdämmerung, 133

Gurley, Zenas H., Jr., 32, 51, 81-82, 86, 88, 179, 217, 232

Hamilton, Alexander, 132

Harmony (Pennsylvania), 28-29, 33, 44, 46, 62, 69, 74-75, 97-98, 124, 193, 232, 240-241

Harris, Martin, iii, 5, 13, 15, 20, 35, 37-38, 42, 48-49, 56-69, 76, 79, 83, 86-87, 90, 97-98, 103, 114, 117, 155, 177, 179-180, 182-184, 188, 211, 220, 230-231, 237-239, 247-248, 253, 262

Hebraisms, Hebrew, 36, 127, 134, 145-146, 148, 151, 159, 190-191, 223, 229, 232, 250

Hinckley, Gordon B., 157, 199, 218

Hofmann, Mark, 16-18, 155, 157, 231

Interpreter(s), see Urim and Thummim

Jewish, Jews, 78, 107, 124, 134, 136, 145-146, 148, 151, 159, 192, 197, 216, 238, 248

King James Bible (KJV), vi, 5, 24-26, 85, 88, 98, 109, 112, 114, 117, 121, 127, 143, 145, 148, 150-151, 171, 177, 192, 196, 226

"Last Testimony of Sister Emma," 38-39, 41-42, 45, 47-56, 77, 82, 98-99, 161, 228

LDS Church, see Church of Jesus Christ of Latter-day Saints

MacKay, Michael Hubbard, iv, 6, 15, 23, 34, 93, 101, 105, 155, 180, 186, 212, 214, 220

Masonry, freemasonry, 112, 130-131, 132-133, 172, 222

McLellin, William E., 44, 52-53, 56, 81, 99, 159-160, 214, 221

Mormon (person), iii, 29, 105, 107, 110, 131-137, 147, 187, 189

Mormonism Unvailed, 2, 10, 13, 35-37, 44, 79, 87, 162-163, 218, 259, 261-262

Moroni, i, 1, 6-7, 9, 11, 16, 67, 75, 77, 82, 87, 104, 107, 132-135, 166, 171, 177-178, 187, 189, 192, 202-203, 206-207, 214, 249, 251, 270

natural man, 137

Nelson, Russell M., 93, 222

New York Times, 206

Nibley, Hugh, 100, 127-128, 188, 222, 232

NID (non-biblical intertextuality database), 26-27, 91-92, 114, 122, 124, 142, 163-164, 169, 187

Nida, Eugene A., vi, 37-38, 144-146, 150, 173-174, 176, 189-191, 196, 222-223, 230

Oaks, Dallin H., 205, 223

Ostler, Blake, 94, 95, 134, 147, 149-150, 223

Ostler, Craig, 3, 13, 69, 79, 176, 220, 223, 269-271

Palmyra (New York), iii, 3, 11, 13, 26, 35, 63, 66, 91-92, 117, 138, 162-163, 168, 170-171, 216, 230
peep stone, see seer stone
perusal, peruse, 166-167, 171, 221
Pop-Out hypothesis, 80, 86-88
Potter, Harry, 14
Pratt, Orson, 52, 68, 72, 74, 78, 83, 154, 182, 224, 233
Quinn, D. Michael, 11, 17-18, 25, 155, 224
Quran, 94, 106-107, 204
Ragnarok, 133
Reorganized Chruch of Jesus Christ of Latter-Day Saints (RLDS), see Community of Christ
Richards, Samuel W., 165, 181, 184, 203, 233, 255
Riess, Jana, 194-195, 207, 225
Rigdon, Sidney, 2, 10, 36, 47, 100, 160, 172, 184, 236, 255
Rosetta Stone, 187-188, 215
Runnels, Jeremy, see CES Letter
Rust, Richard Dilworth, vii, 23, 126-127, 143, 225-226
Sallust, 131-133, 226
Second Great Awakening, 149, 160, 169-170
secret combinations, 131, 133
seer stone, 2, 6, 12-13, 15, 18-20, 22, 32-35, 43, 46, 49, 51, 57-60, 64-67, 69-70, 76-80, 82-83, 93-100, 103, 143, 152, 154-157, 183-185, 200, 236, 260-261, 264, 266, 271
shamanist explanations, 94, 110, 185, 192, 195, 204
SITH (stone-in-the-hat) narrative, (also see transcription), v-vii, 7, 12-22, 32-37, 41, 44-46, 48, 50-53, 56, 59, 61, 67-70, 72-73, 77-82, 84, 86-88, 93, 96, 98-105, 110, 112, 148, 155, 176-177, 184-185, 192, 199-200, 202-203, 208, 259-260, 263, 265-266, 268-271
Skousen, Royal, 24, 33, 88-92, 108, 143, 226, 227
Smith, Emma Hale (also see Last Testimony of Sister Emma), 2, 7, 13, 20, 37-48, 51-56, 61-63, 79-80, 82, 84, 86, 98, 103-104, 155, 161, 177, 224, 228, 257, 260
Smith, Jesse, 164, 232
Smith, Joseph, Jr., i-vi, 1-30, 32-36, 38-56, 58-120, 122, 124-125, 128-134, 137-143, 146-187, 189-201, 203-206, 208-214, 217, 219-222, 225, 227-228, 230-233, 236-241, 243-244, 247-253, 255- 271
Smith, Joseph III, 38-47, 50-56, 61, 69, 71-73, 81, 98-99, 103, 161-162, 219, 221, 228
Smith, Joseph, Sr., 152, 165-166, 228, 257
Smith, Lucy Mack, 26, 30, 43, 91-92, 96, 161-167, 171, 176, 228-229, 237, 256-258, 262

Spalding theory, vi, 2, 10-11, 20, 36, 41, 44-47, 51-53, 55-56, 98-100, 162, 184, 200, 214, 236, 259, 263

Sperry, Sidney, 100, 127, 143, 188, 229

Stevenson, Edward, 48-49, 52, 56-63, 65-69, 72, 74, 79, 97-98, 103, 179, 183, 229-230

Stoddard, Hannah and James L., 19-20, 70, 230

Talmage, James E., 138-139, 230

targum, 148-150

The Late War, 11, 26, 115-121, 124, 218-219

Three Witnesses, 29, 35, 60, 63, 65, 69-70, 75-76, 80, 87, 179, 183, 230, 253-254

Tolkien, J.R.R., 126

Tolstoy, Leo, 1, 34, 203-204, 233

transcription narrative (also see SITH), v-vii, 2, 4, 6, 12, 19, 24-25, 32, 34, 91, 93, 105-106, 109-110, 176, 184, 187, 194-196, 235, 261

translation narrative (also see Urim and Thummim), i-ii, iv-vii, 1-6, 8-10, 12-16, 18-19, 21-26, 32-33, 36-37, 40-41, 44, 46-47, 49, 51, 56-72, 74-77, 80-88, 94-105, 107-110, 112-116, 121, 124-125, 128, 130, 134-137, 140-152, 154-156, 158, 162, 174, 176, 179-193, 195-196, 198, 200, 202, 204-205, 211, 213-214, 216-217, 222- 224, 229, 235, 240, 244, 247, 250, 255, 258-261, 263-266, 269- 271

Turner, Pomeroy, 171, 231

Turner, Orsamus, 170, 231

Urim and Thummim, interpreter(s), iii-iv, vi, 1, 6-13, 21, 32, 36, 42-45, 50-51, 58-62, 65, 67-70, 73, 77-83, 87- 88, 94, 100-105, 115, 152-155, 157, 178-184, 187, 193, 198, 229, 233, 237, 240-241, 244, 247, 249-253, 255-262, 267

Wagner, Richard, 134

Welch, John W., 33, 100, 127-128, 164, 181, 193, 203, 232-233, 255

Wentworth letter, 44, 50, 79, 227, 251

Widtsoe, John A., 153-154, 157, 233

Whitmer, John, 81, 86

Whitmer, David, 2, 7, 13-15, 20, 28-30, 33-35, 37, 49-56, 61-63, 66, 68-77, 79, 81-82, 84-87, 96-100, 102-103, 107, 155, 160, 176, 179, 183-184, 192-193, 209, 216, 220, 223, 228, 231, 233, 247, 253, 258, 260, 262, 270

Young, Brigham, 14, 38, 49, 53-54, 68, 72-73, 80, 142-145, 152-153, 164, 204, 234

www.ingramcontent.com/pod-product-compliance
Lightning Source LLC
Chambersburg PA
CBHW070941170426
43199CB00030B/2588